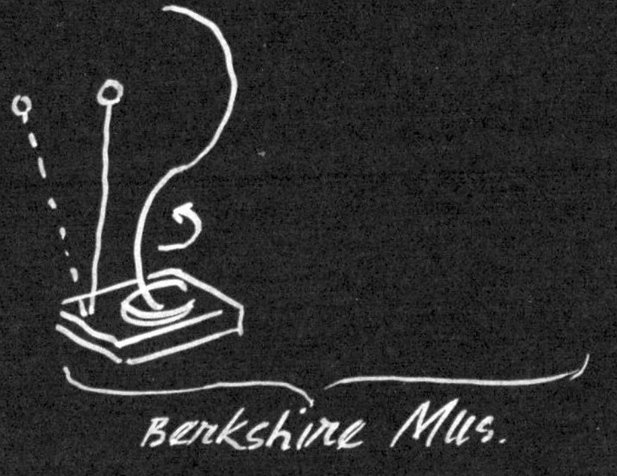

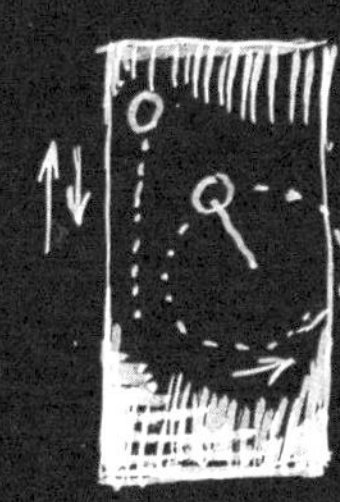

at Harrison's

Wood
Martha Graham

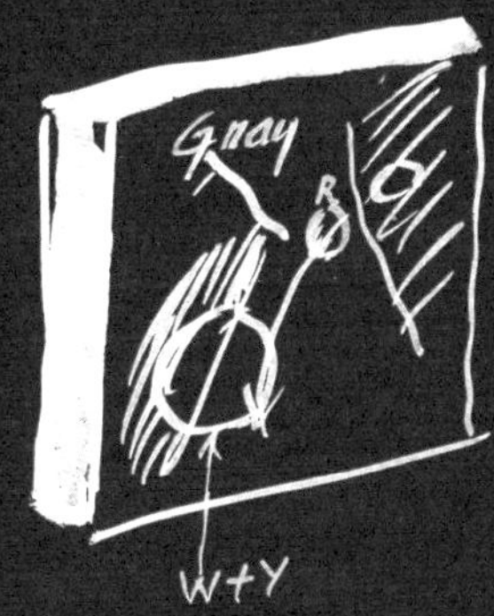

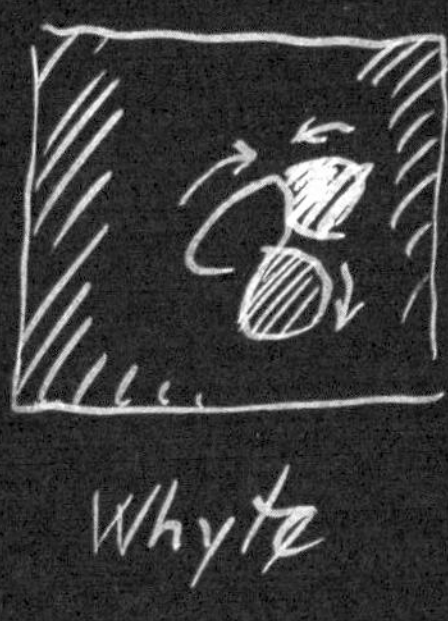

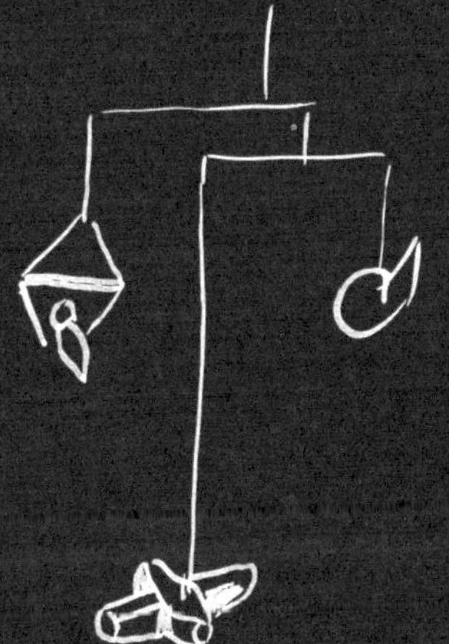

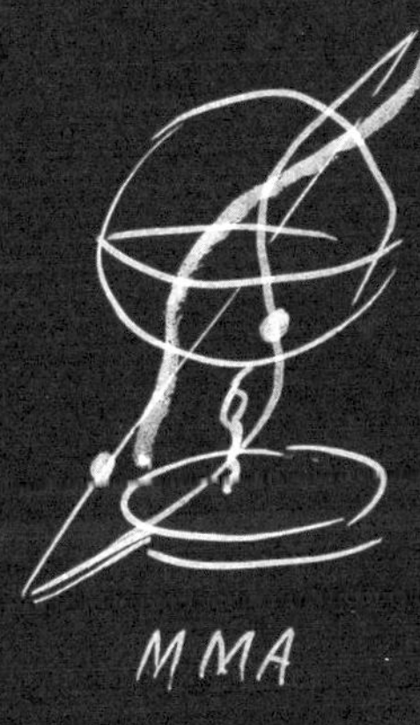

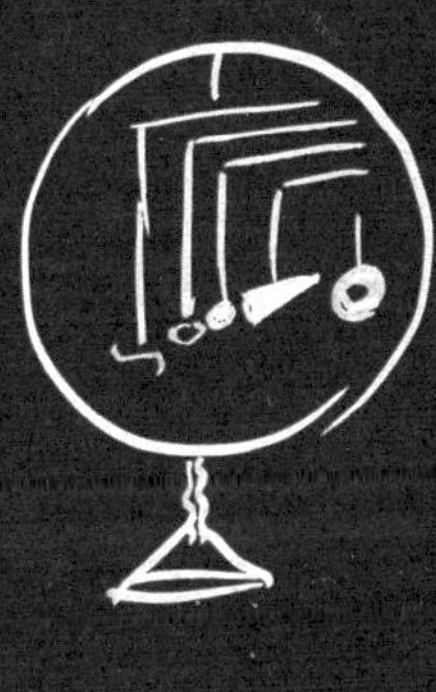

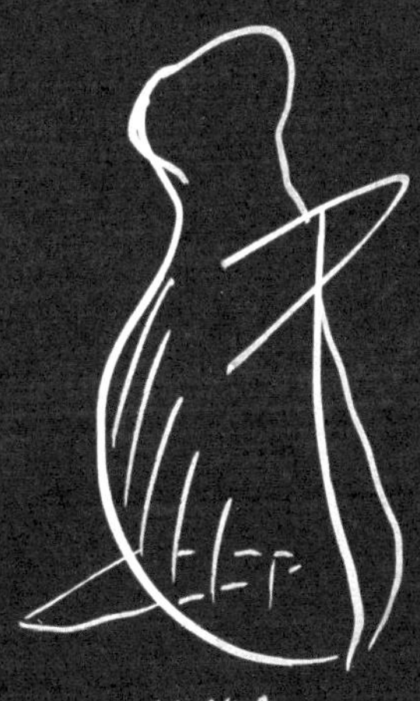

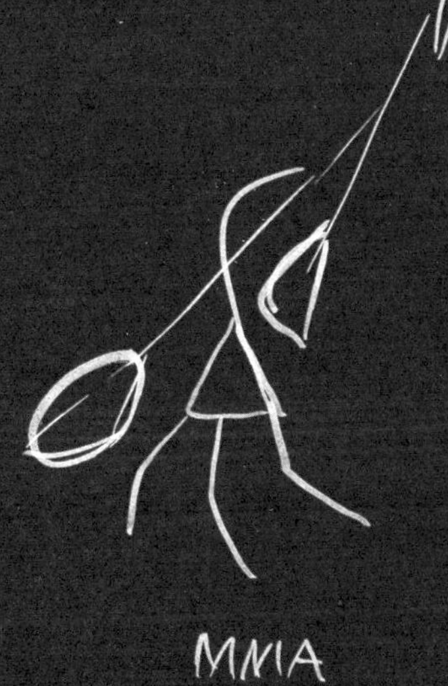

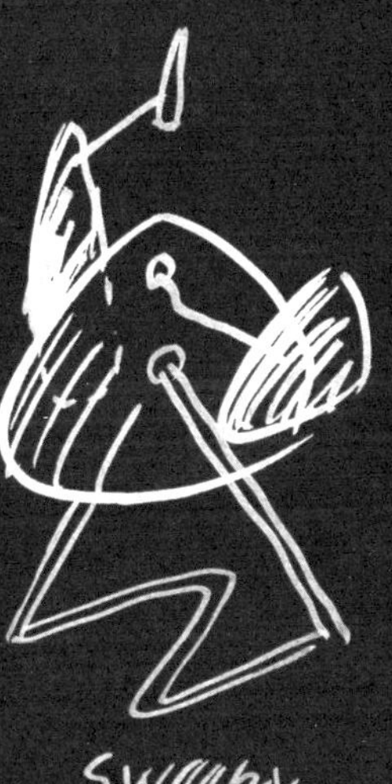

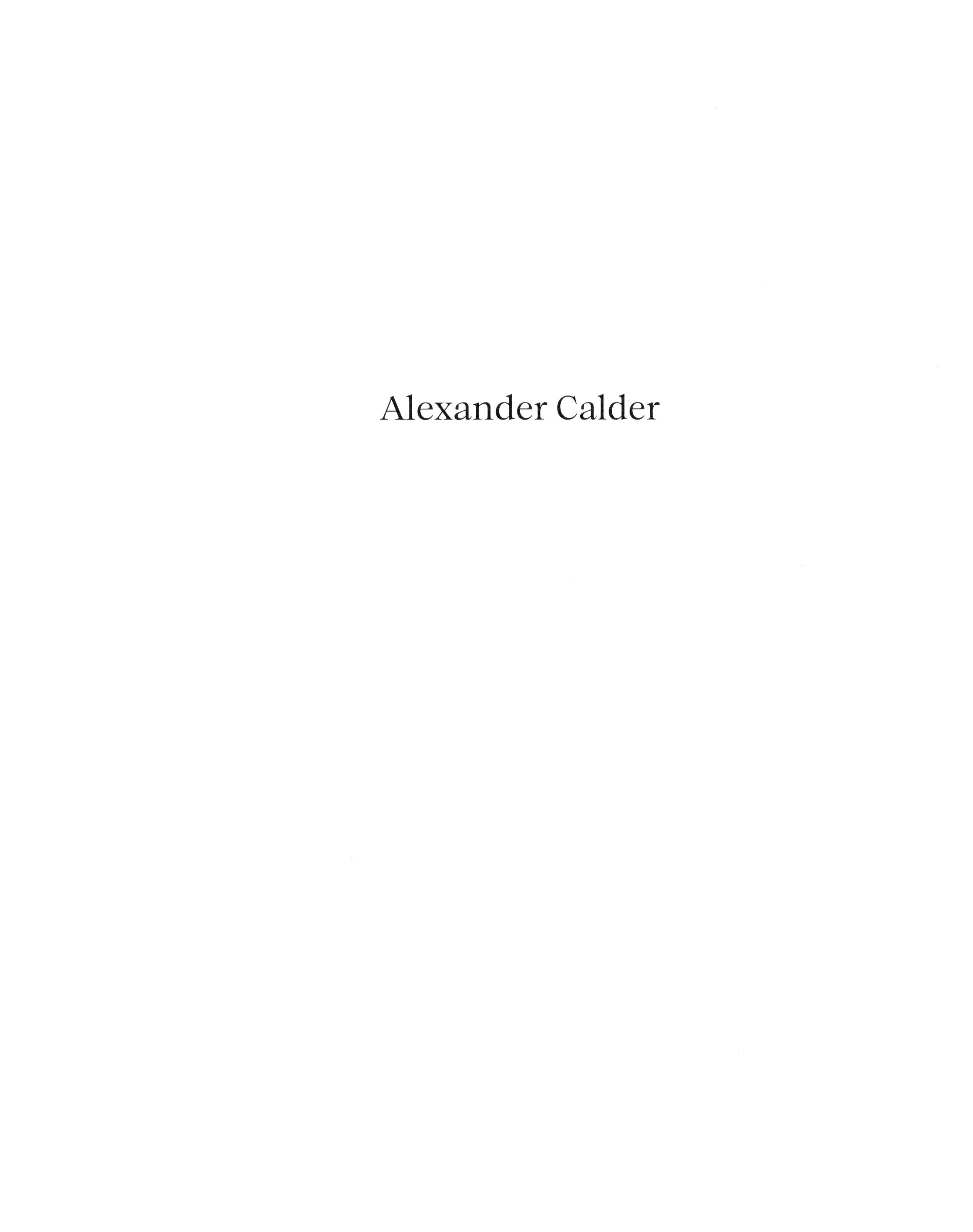

Alexander Calder

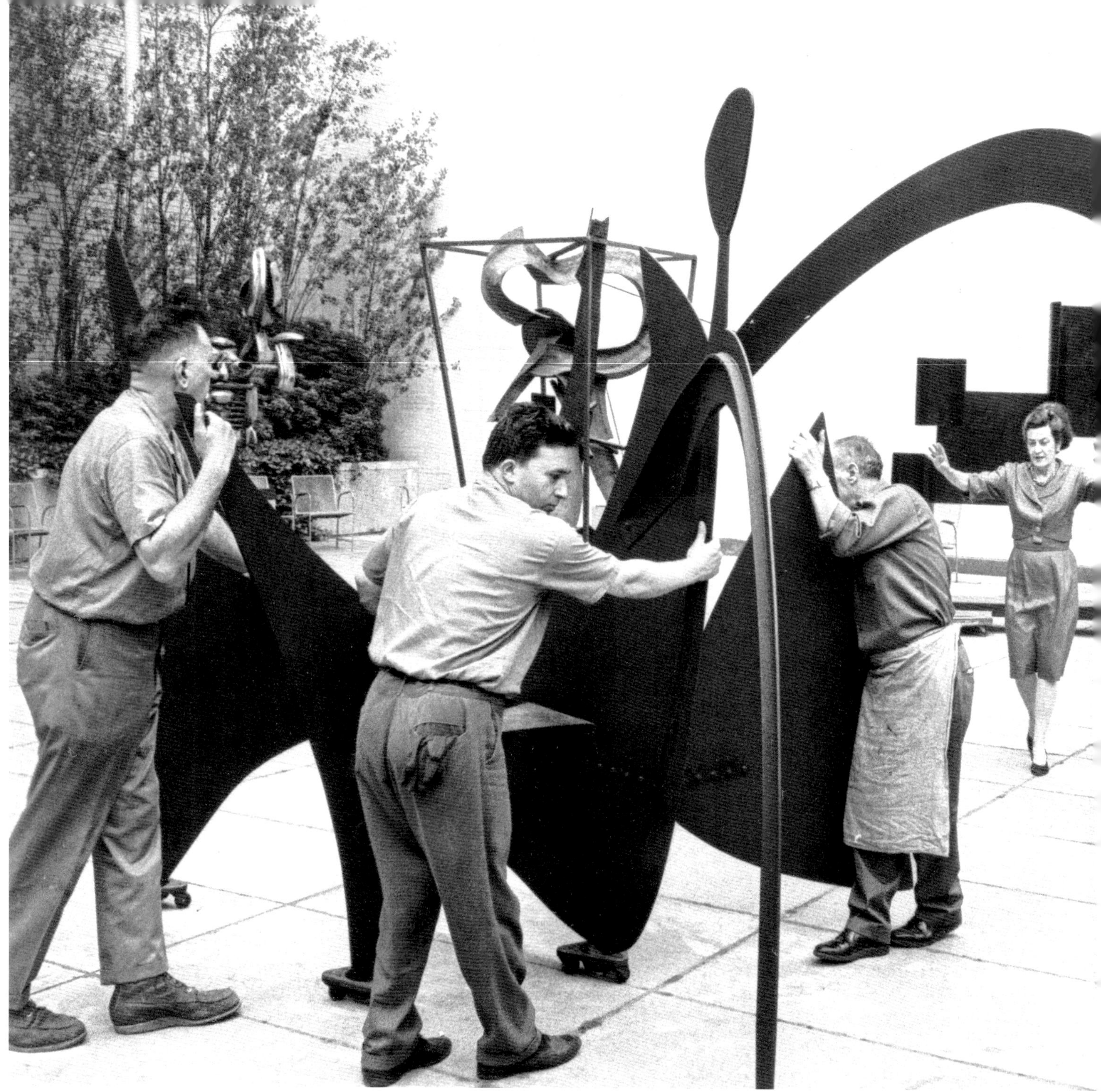

The Museum of Modern Art
New York

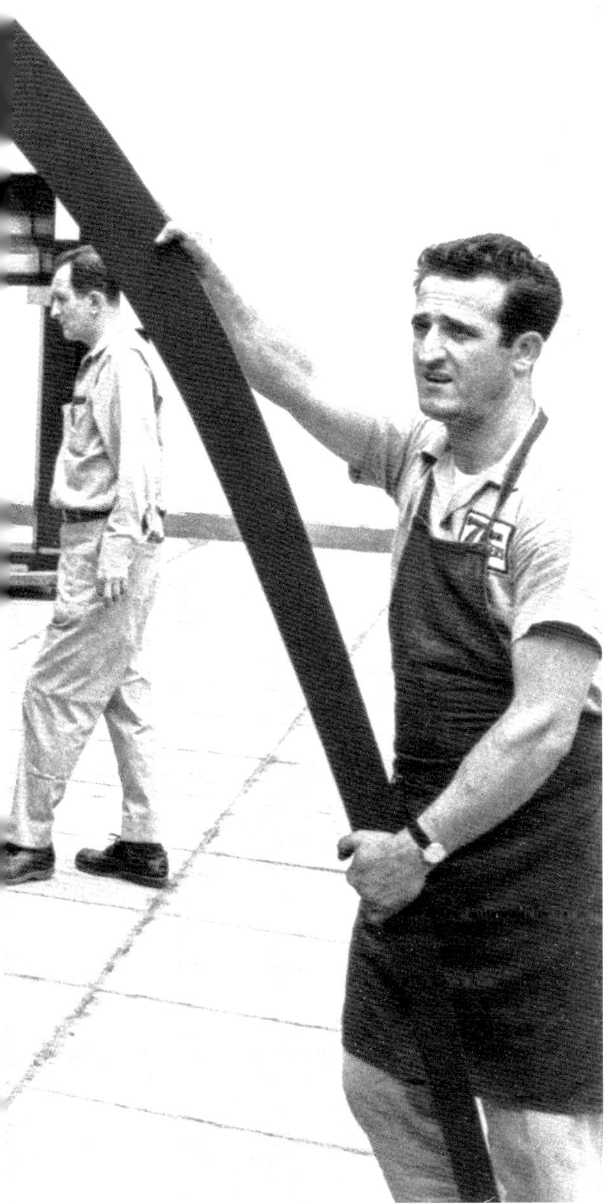

Cara Manes

Alexander Calder
Modern from the Start

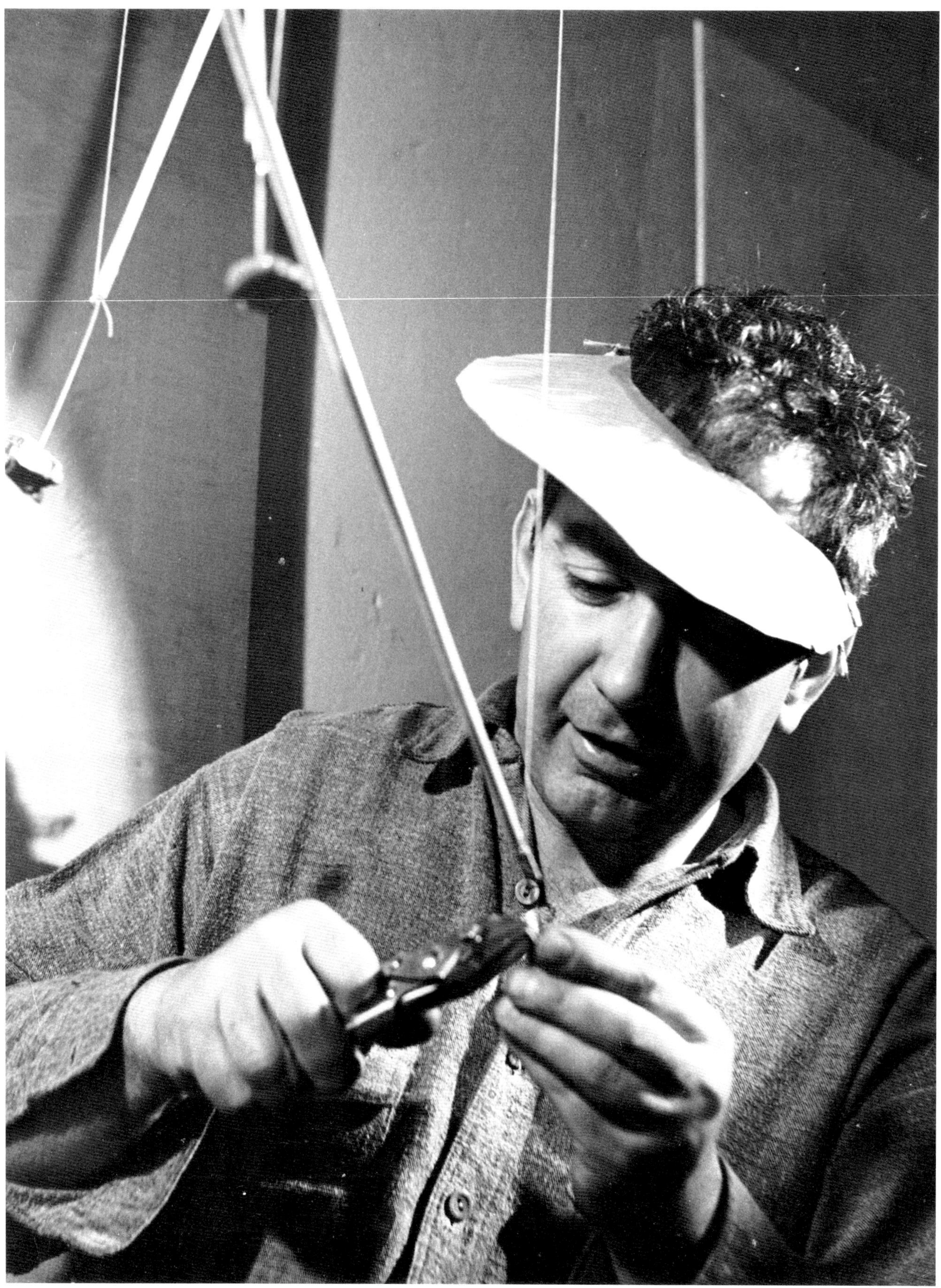

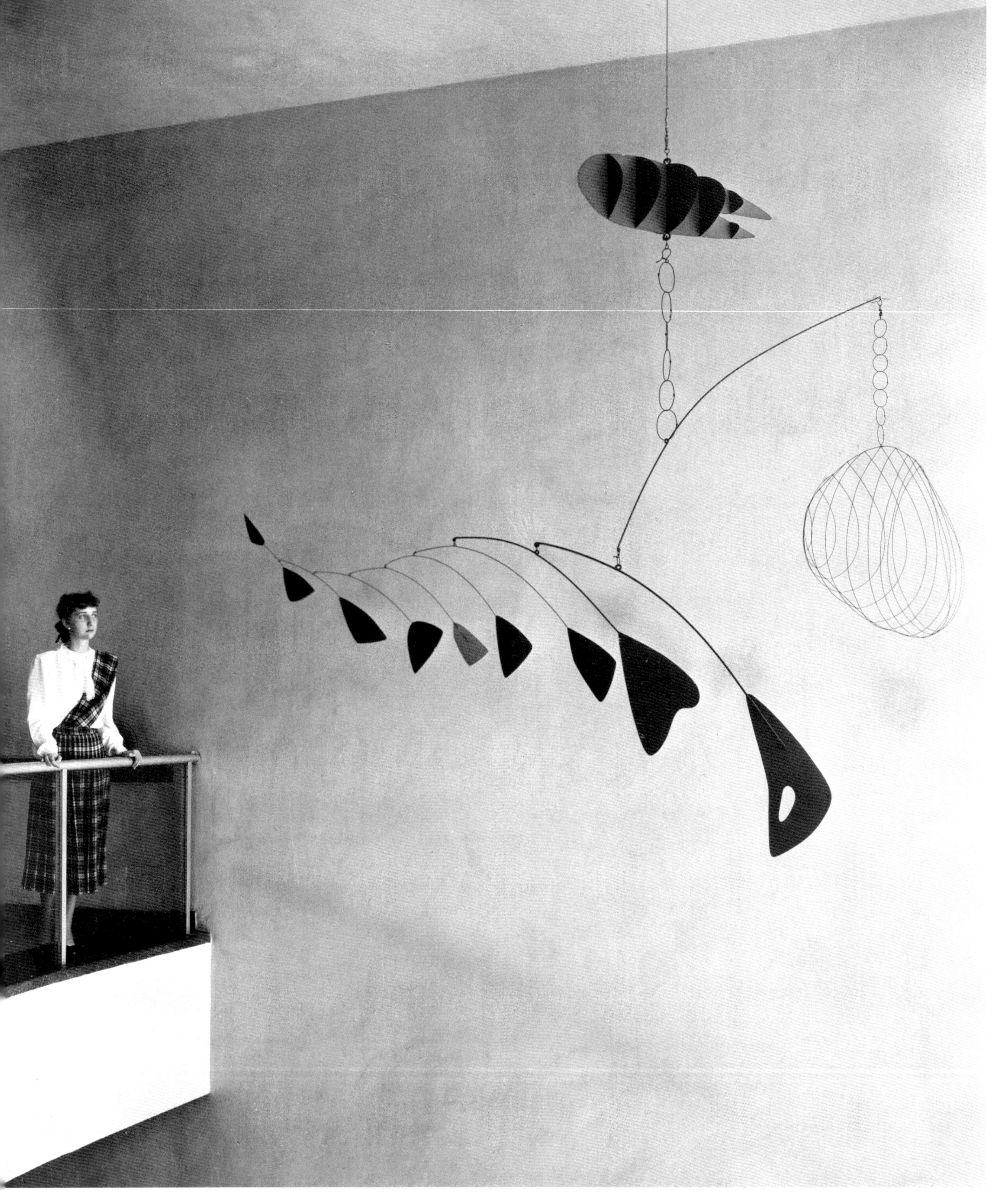

Foreword

It is a pleasure to celebrate, with this publication and the exhibition it accompanies, the unique relationship between Alexander Calder and The Museum of Modern Art. Few artists have played so integral a role in the life of the Museum over a sustained period: enjoying deep (if occasionally bumpy) friendships with curators; collaborating on exhibitions and commissions; and making gifts of his own works to the Museum's collection in an example of exceptional generosity.

We extend our sincere gratitude to Alexander S. C. Rower, President of the Calder Foundation, for his immediate enthusiasm and steadfast support for this project. Rower was a true partner "from the start," and we have benefited enormously from his knowledge and his passion. He and his colleagues at the Calder Foundation made invaluable archival material available, and they were always ready with good advice and ideas.

Cara Manes, Associate Curator in the Department of Painting and Sculpture, has investigated the subject of Calder and MoMA with great dedication and ingenuity. *Alexander Calder: Modern from the Start* reflects her sensitivity to Calder's artworks and her insight into how his creative path and our own institutional history have been entwined. She was superbly assisted by Curatorial Fellows Zuna Maza and Makayla Bailey, who participated in all aspects of the research and preparation for the exhibition and publication.

Essential funding for this exhibition was kindly provided by the Kate W. Cassidy Foundation. Ms. Cassidy's ongoing commitment to our exhibition program is profoundly gratifying. The International Council of The Museum of Modern Art and the Jon and Mary Shirley Foundation were also extremely generous in their support, as was The Lipman Family Foundation. The Jo Carole Lauder Publications Fund of The International Council of The Museum of Modern Art and the Dale S. and Norman Mills Leff Publication Fund made this catalogue possible. In addition, we sincerely thank the many individual donors whose gifts sustain the Annual Exhibition Fund.

In 1939 Calder was invited to create a sculpture to hang above the winding staircase of our new International Style building. The spectacular mobile *Lobster Trap and Fish Tail* was the product of that commission, and for more than eighty years it has been an indispensable presence here at MoMA. Our recent renovation has returned that staircase to its original glory—and *Lobster Trap and Fish Tail* continues to reign over it with elegance and exuberance.

—Glenn D. Lowry
The David Rockefeller Director
The Museum of Modern Art

Introduction

John Russell, in *The Meanings of Modern Art*, a treasure of a book written for this museum nearly fifty years ago, declared that "it would almost be true to say that sculpture in our century has been the secret weapon of art."[1] By this Russell meant that sculpture represented the modern era's surest means of escape from the orthodoxy of Western European tradition. Whereas in the early decades of the twentieth century, the fact of a painting was clear—a flat canvas on which oil paint was applied with a brush—the assumptions about avant-garde sculpture were far less obvious. Yes, you could make the sort of carved or modeled figurative works that often were called "statues." But you did not have to. Unlike a painter, who used centuries-old means to craft new pictorial language, the maverick sculptor faced an open field of possible materials, tools, and techniques. Explorations were inspired by cultures beyond those of Europe, and by fields of endeavor, such as industry, outside the parameters of art.

Alexander Calder exemplifies the free spirit of early modern sculpture. And in Calder's case, the move beyond nineteenth-century sculptural ideals was personal as well as aesthetic. He was the son of a sculptor, Alexander Stirling Calder, and the grandson of a sculptor, Alexander Milne Calder. Both of these earlier Alexander Calders were prominent creators of heroic public monuments, the steady recipients of distinguished commissions that shaped the urban landscape. His grandfather was responsible for the statuary of Philadelphia's City Hall, most notably the grand figure of William Penn at its summit. Calder's father continued the public adornment of Philadelphia—with, among other works, the Swann Memorial Fountain on Benjamin Franklin Parkway—and also that of New York, in, for example, the marble figure of President George Washington on the Washington Square Arch. Both of these artists excelled at precisely the sort of work that their descendant and his fellow modernists would render obsolete.

Alexander "Sandy" Calder cheerfully wielded the "secret weapon" of sculpture for half a century: in the 1920s as a quintessential American in Paris; and from 1933 in New York City, Roxbury, Connecticut, and (from 1953) the French village of Saché, until his death in 1976. Like many sculptors, he had set out to become a painter, following the example of his mother, Nanette, despite having earned a college degree in mechanical engineering. Calder studied painting at the Art Students League in New York, but soon after moving to Paris, in 1926, he became fascinated with making small characters of wire, wood, cloth, and other materials, which he then developed into *Cirque Calder* (*Calder's Circus*). This work, along with a group of related and various objects, sealed his commitment to three-dimensional activity and endeared him to a broad avant-garde milieu. Calder's inventions resisted categorization but acquired names, thanks to his friends Marcel Duchamp and Jean Arp (mobiles and stabiles, respectively), and effectively defined their own artistic territory. Over the course of five decades Calder's objects underwent a complex evolution from the utterly intimate arena of the circus to the monumental works of the 1960s, which return full circle to the civic achievements of his Calder forefathers.

The subject of this catalogue and the exhibition it accompanies is the vital role that Calder's art played in the early history of The Museum of Modern Art. That Calder would have found himself closely entwined with this fledgling institution makes sense on several levels. He was never interested in the idea of art as an obscure language of the few, so the new museum's missionary purpose of introducing a wide public to the art of its own time was one he would have found sympathetic. Calder's connection to an audience differed fundamentally from that of most other artists. *Cirque Calder* came to life only in the presence of spectators, and his early kinetic sculptures relied on the participation of viewers to activate motors or cranks or to galvanize air currents. Before visitor guidelines became as strict as they are today, a museum's usual "do not touch" mandate would be temporarily retired during a Calder exhibition.

Calder's performative mentality underlies even his largest and most immovable sculptures, whose animated forms thrive in human company.

Like many of his peers—Henry Moore in Much Hadham, England, for example, or David Smith in Bolton Landing, New York—Calder retreated to the countryside to secure the space he needed for his work. The landscape provided both the inspiration of nature and the opportunity to site outdoor sculptures. His homes—filled with implements and objects that he had designed, adjacent to the spacious studios where he worked—seamlessly merged art and life. Yet Calder's remove, in northwestern Connecticut and later in the Loire Valley, did not isolate him from the art world. Along with family members, friends, and neighbors, he was provided with essential fuel for his imagination by workmen, fellow artists, art critics, collectors, and curators. Sculpture commissions, exhibitions, and publication projects figured prominently in the general swirl of activity upon which Calder thrived.

MoMA's extensive holdings of Calder's work reflect the long and multifaceted exchange between the artist and our curators and trustees. The collection includes sculptures, jewelry, gouaches, prints, and illustrated books spanning five decades, from the first purchase, in 1934, through a steady number of acquisitions at key moments in Calder's career and then a bounteous gift of nineteen works from the artist himself, in 1966. Today's MoMA is inseparable from Calder's presence. *Lobster Trap and Fish Tail* feels as much a part of the 1939 building by Philip L. Goodwin and Edward Durell Stone as its roof and walls. Over the years, our large-scale sculptures have become beloved inhabitants of The Abby Aldrich Rockefeller Sculpture Garden. Although this upstart institution has its centenary in sight, and these works are universally regarded as modern classics, the experimental spirit in which they were made continues to define the present-day mission of this museum.

—Ann Temkin
The Marie-Josée and Henry Kravis
Chief Curator of Painting and Sculpture
The Museum of Modern Art

1. John Russell, *The Meanings of Modern Art*, rev. ed. (1974; New York: The Museum of Modern Art/Harper & Row, 1981), 384.

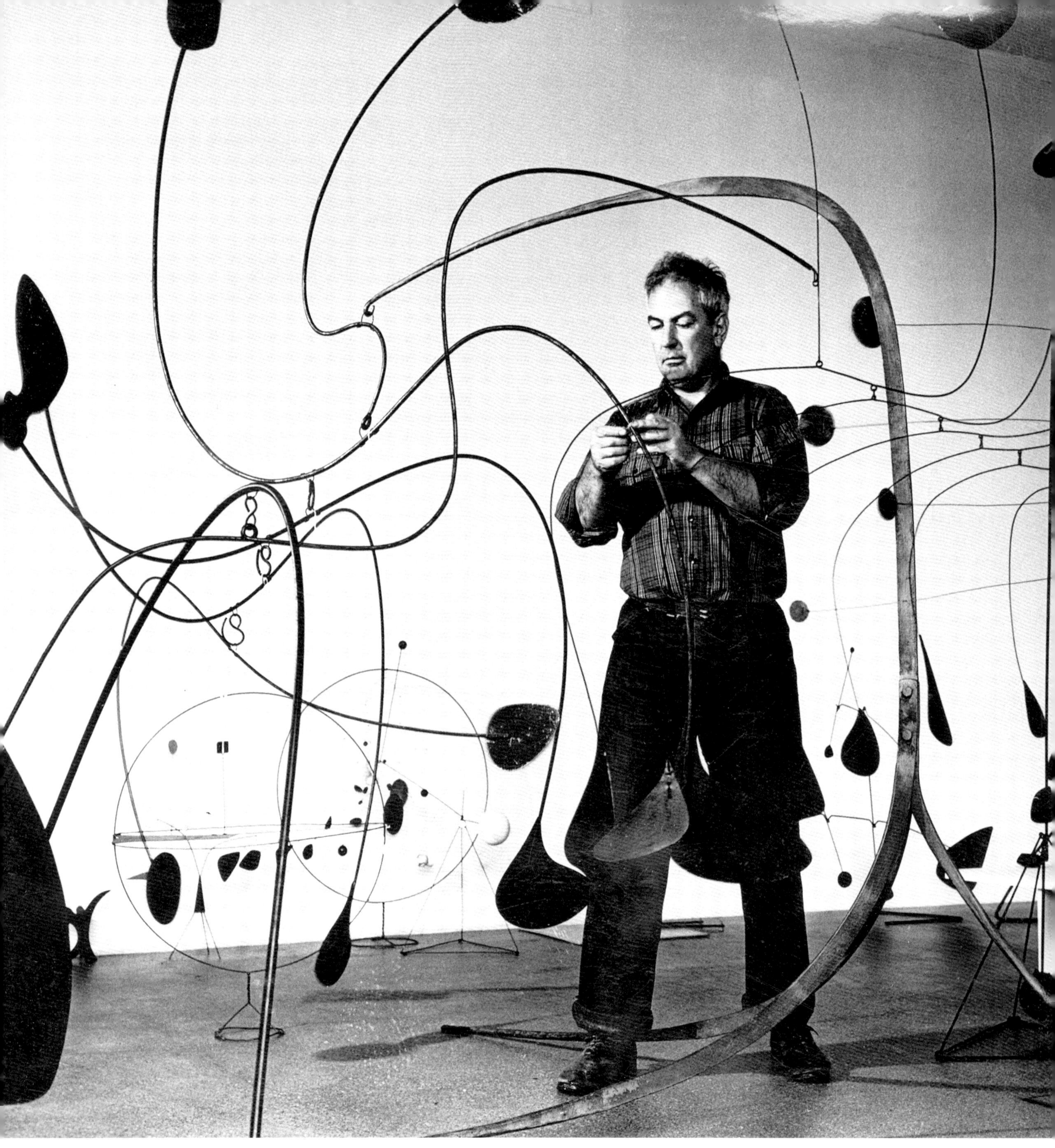

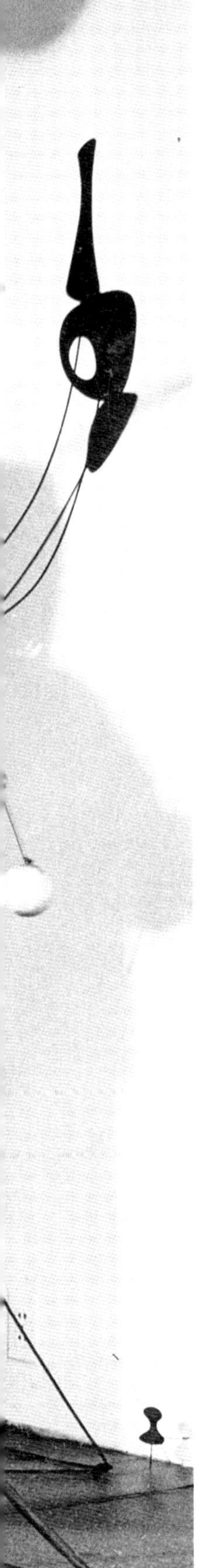

Cara Manes

Alexander Calder Modern from the Start

On December 3, 1930, The Museum of Modern Art, just over a year old, opened its ninth exhibition, *Painting and Sculpture by Living Americans.* Organized by MoMA's founding director, Alfred H. Barr Jr., the exhibition debuted the work of thirty painters and seven sculptors, several of whom had "hitherto been practically unrecognized in New York."[1] Selected by Barr; Jere Abbott, the Museum's associate director; and a jury of four Museum trustees, the works in the show ranged stylistically from Ashcan realism to European-inflected modernism, but they were all largely figurative—painted landscapes, figures, and still lifes, and sculptures carved in wood or cast in bronze.[2] Although by this point Alexander Calder was well known for his groundbreaking bent-wire portraits, Barr chose to represent his recent work with four wood sculptures of animals and people, all made after 1928: *Man, Acrobats, Stooping Girl*, and *Cow* (fig. 1); the latter work, he later reported in a letter to the artist, was "one of the most popular pieces in the exhibition."[3] Carved from a single piece of wood, the cow's sweet, docile face is obviously naturalistic, but its body is less so, intertwined as it is with its source material so as to appear not to have fully emerged from it. Barr had seen Calder's figurative wood and wire works at New York's Weyhe Gallery the previous winter, where critics had deemed them "amusing" and full of "pathos," among other favorable—if somewhat trite—characterizations.[4] Writing to *Cow*'s owner to secure it for loan, Barr urged, "I feel that Calder has been underestimated and frequently dismissed as merely clever. I think such works as the 'Cow' if seriously exhibited would do much to revise popular opinion of his work which has, I think, considerable quality."[5]

At the time of the show's opening, Calder, at thirty-two-years old, was one of the youngest "Living Americans" included, but his life and work experience ran deep and wide. He had grown up in various cities throughout the United States with his parents, both artists, who often relocated the family in order to take various public commissions. He had studied engineering, following the example of a schoolmate, and planned to become a mechanical engineer; worked a number of jobs; taken courses at the Art Students League in New York; and, after a stint as an illustrator for the *National Police Gazette*, taken off for Paris. By the time of the MoMA show, in late 1930, Calder had been living and working in France for the better part of four years.[6] He had become a part of the city's cultural avant-garde, befriending artists, periodically exhibiting his sculptures on both sides of the Atlantic, and performing his *Cirque Calder*, a complex multiact artwork in which he manipulated dozens of handmade sculptures of the actors and architecture of a miniature

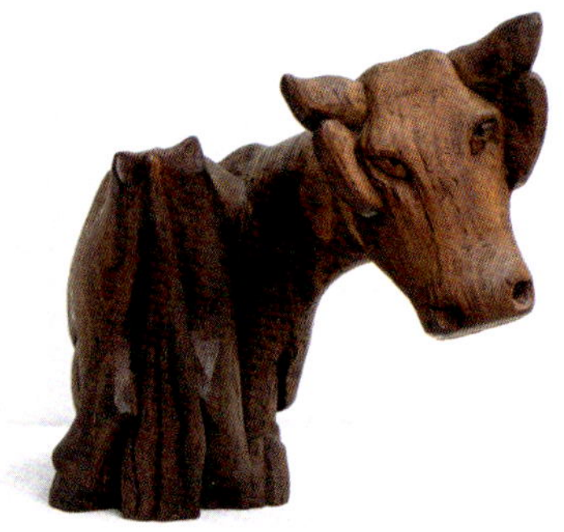

Fig. 1. **Cow**. *1928. Wood, 12⅝ × 15 × 8⅞ in. (32.1 × 38.1 × 22.5 cm). Calder Foundation, New York. Purchase*

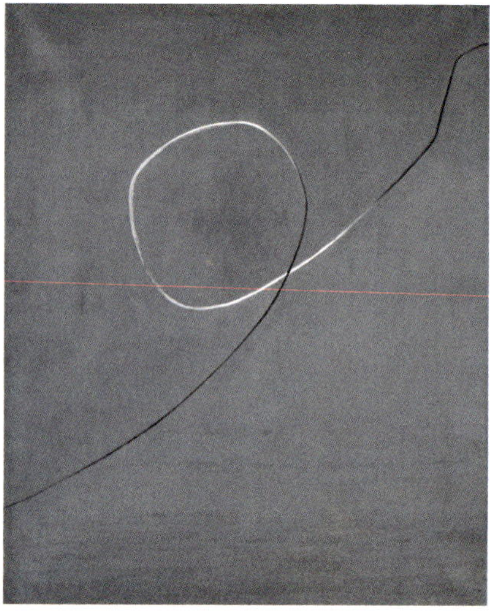

Fig. 2. Untitled. 1930. Oil on canvas, 28¾ × 23¾ in. (73 × 60.3 cm). Calder Foundation, New York

circus. The first performances were given for friends and took place in his Paris studio; eventually those friends brought their friends, until the audience grew so large that Calder had to rent out a space and charge a fee for entrance. In October, a few weeks before the opening of the MoMA show, Calder visited the studio of Piet Mondrian, who had recently come to one of the performances. Mondrian had arranged his workspace as an abstract environment, with the main wall covered in cardboard rectangles in primary colors and shades of white, which he could reconfigure into different compositions. "This one visit," Calder recalled in his 1966 autobiography, "gave me a shock that started things. Though I had heard the word 'modern' before, I did not consciously know or feel the term 'abstract.' So now, at thirty-two, I wanted to paint and work in the abstract. And for two weeks or so, I painted very modest abstractions. At the end of this, I reverted to plastic work which was still abstract" (fig. 2).[7] As Calder's figurative carved-wood sculptures were making their debut on MoMA's stage in front of a broad American audience, he was also in the midst of a radical shift in his art, from figuration toward abstraction—from an art of observing things in the world toward an art that asks to be seen as a world unto itself.

Calder was able to see *Living Americans* during a short stay in New York that December. Three days before Christmas, he had returned to the United States in order to marry Louisa James, whom he had met on a trans-Atlantic ship the summer before. A few weeks after the ceremony (on January 17, 1931, at James's home in Concord, Massachusetts), the newlyweds were back in Paris, and a few months later, in late April 1931, Calder's abstract works were exhibited for the first time, in *Alexandre Calder: Volumes—Vecteurs—Densités / Dessins—Portraits* at Galerie Percier (fig. 3). In introductory remarks for the exhibition's catalogue, Calder's friend Fernand Léger wrote, "Looking at these new works—transparent, objective, exact—I think of [Eric] Satie, Mondrian, Marcel Duchamp, [Constantin] Brancusi, [Jean] Arp—those unchallenged masters of unexpressed and silent beauty. Calder is of the same line. He is 100% American. Satie and Duchamp are 100% French. And yet, we meet?"[8]

The distinction between American and European art that so interested Léger became an ongoing investigation for Barr. Léger was drawn to Calder's European sensibility—the "unexpressed and silent beauty" of his abstractions. At the time of *Living Americans*, American, for Barr, meant figurative. But within a year of that show, Calder had changed course. Barr came to view the artist as Léger had, and in him may have recognized a key to

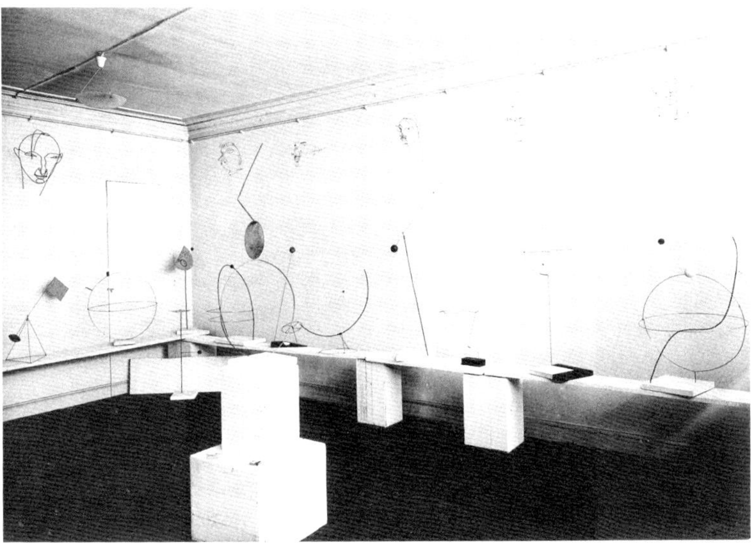

Fig. 3. **Alexandre Calder: Volumes—Vecteurs—Densités / Dessins—Portraits,** *Galerie Percier, Paris, 1931. Installation view. Photograph by Marc Vaux*

institutional success for a fledgling museum trying to find its footing and its audience: an artist as thoroughly modern as he was utterly American.

In a span of less than six months, Calder had his epiphany in Mondrian's studio, exhibited his figurative sculptures at MoMA, abandoned figuration, unleashed a prolific outpouring of entirely abstract work, crossed the Atlantic twice, got married, and exhibited new abstract works in Paris, two of which were kinetic. For a critical period during their respective trajectories, Calder and MoMA enjoyed a generative partnership that was forged early and developed steadily, reaching an apex in 1943 with a major midcareer survey. It was a relationship of ongoing reciprocity: MoMA served as a stage on which Calder could play out his many and varied activities, and in turn Calder's art—vivid, dynamic, and ever ready to be engaged—played a central role in the Museum's championing of a new public modernism.

This essay chronicles significant points of exchange between artist and institution along this productive arc. For clarity's sake, each point is introduced by a specific date. This chronological structure differs from that of *Alexander Calder: Modern from the Start*—the exhibition this catalogue accompanies—which celebrates the objects in the Museum's collection in a nonlinear and heterogeneous spirit. This history of Calder's specific engagements with MoMA provides a scaffold for examining the ambition of his multivalent work: to describe the world in an object and to make work that is unbounded, like nature, always in flux.

On December 19, 1934, The Museum of Modern Art acquired *A Universe* (1934, pages 62, 63). Calder made the work during his productive first months in his home and studio in Roxbury, Connecticut, which he had purchased the previous September after the threat of war in Europe had led him and Louisa to leave Paris. It is an early example of Calder's extraordinary contribution to the history of art in the twentieth century: the "mobile," a sculpture that moves. *A Universe* is powered by a motor, a technique he had devised three years prior in Paris. It was these early motorized works that had prompted Calder's friend Marcel Duchamp, during a studio visit in fall 1931, to describe them as *mobiles*, which in French means both "motion" and "motive," a fitting and satisfying double entendre from an artist famously invested in wordplay.[9]

By 1934, Calder had perfected a means for precipitating movement in his sculptures by air or by a viewer's intervention, and in the early days in Roxbury he was making works of this nature. Yet he chose to use a motor for *A Universe*, which, along with the work's open form, marked a return to some of his earlier concerns. Two intersecting circles of wire describe a sphere that is supported with a length of bent iron pipe anchored to a round base.[10] Running through the vertical center of the sphere is an *s*-shaped piece of wire holding a small white wood sphere; slicing through the wire sphere diagonally is a straight piece of wire attached to an outrigger extending from the base and holding a red wood sphere. A hidden motor moves the

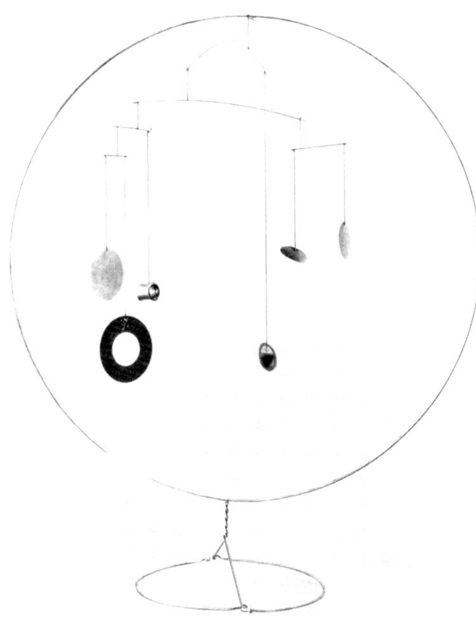

Fig. 4. Untitled. 1934. Wire, sheet metal, and string. Calder Foundation, New York

wood spheres along their wires at different speeds in a cycle that takes approximately forty minutes to complete. The work seems at once to defy and depict gravity: its delicate, open wire form hovers as if floating, yet the lines that demarcate it also trace the forces of energy at work upon the object, holding it in space. The comparatively heavy iron pipe supporting this weightless-seeming structure is itself twisted into a loose *s*-shape, as if torqued by external pressure. As the wood spheres follow distinct but interrelated circuits of motorized motion, they variously work with and against gravity, setting the entire shape of the object into flux.

This sculpture was included in Calder's first exhibition at Pierre Matisse Gallery, in April 1934, where it was shown with its motorized mechanism concealed behind a wall. Barr was so impressed by it that he reconsidered the gift of an untitled (non-motorized) mobile that Abby Aldrich Rockefeller, one of the Museum's cofounders, had purchased for the collection a few weeks earlier (fig. 4).[11] "I would much prefer to have this second mobile for the museum," Barr wrote to Rockefeller, "and Calder feels the same way about it."[12] An official exchange was arranged, in which the original work was deaccessioned and *A Universe* was acquired.

Of objects such as this one, with what seems to be its science-minded approach, Calder wrote that—paradoxically—their "aesthetic value . . . cannot be arrived at by reasoning. Familiarization is necessary."[13] And what could be more familiar, and more strange, to a human observer of this artwork than the universe itself? In fact, the work's title suggests an answer, specifying the object as *a* universe rather than *the* universe, with all its attendant forces. This act of relativization may not have been lost on Albert Einstein, who familiarized himself with *A Universe* years later, at Calder's 1943 retrospective.[14] After staring at it for its entire forty-minute cycle, the man who revolutionized our understanding of space and time is said to have remarked, "I wish I'd thought of that."[15]

On March 2, 1936, Barr opened *Cubism and Abstract Art*, the first of a pair of exhibitions meant to address in "an objective and historical manner the principal movements of modern art."[16] *Cubism and Abstract Art*, with *Fantastic Art, Dada, Surrealism* later that year, provided a framework for what he saw as the essential strains of modern art, and together they played a critical role in introducing European modernism to an American audience. Through these shows, Barr attempted to probe the paradox at the heart of MoMA's project: providing a context for difficult art while at the same time making that art accessible to a potentially doubting public.

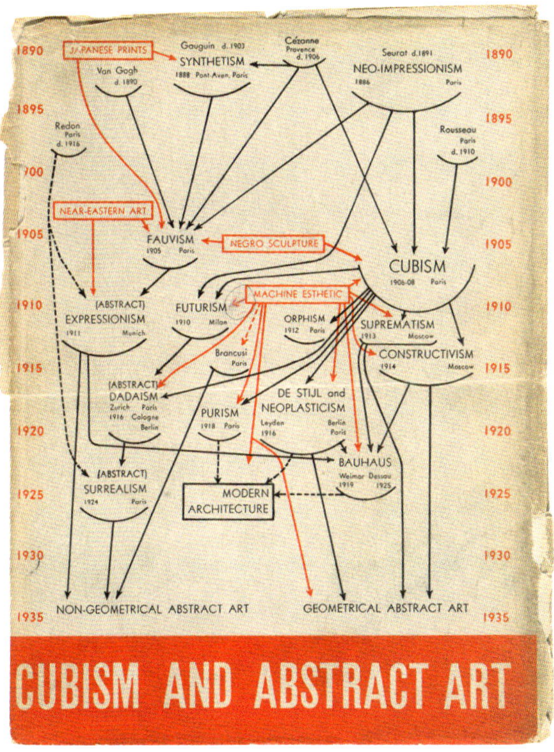

Fig. 5. Cover of the catalogue for the exhibition **Cubism and Abstract Art**, *by Alfred H. Barr Jr., with Barr's diagram of the origins and influences of modern art, 1936. MoMA Archives, New York*

Cubism and Abstract Art featured nearly four hundred works in various mediums, installed in rough chronological order across all four floors of gallery space in the Museum's townhouse building at 11 West Fifty-Third Street. The exhibition gave material form to what Barr referred to, in the accompanying catalogue, as "the impulse towards abstract art during the past fifty years."[17] To illustrate his claim, he created a chart showing how different movements and aesthetics flowed into and out of each other (fig. 5). The chart, which was printed on the catalogue's cover and has since become a famous (and famously controversial) document, proposed a linear history of modern European art. In his essay Barr employed a metaphor from nature to describe this history's two main trajectories, as currents springing from Impressionism. "The first and more important current," Barr wrote, "finds its sources in the art and theories of [Paul] Cézanne and [Georges-Pierre] Seurat, passes through the widening stream of Cubism and finds its delta in the various geometrical and Constructivist movements which developed in Russia and Holland during the War and have since spread through the World." Barr called this current "geometrical abstract art" and characterized it as intellectual, structural, and rectilinear. The "secondary" current developed from Paul Gauguin and then coursed through Henri Matisse's Fauvism and Wassily Kandinsky's Abstract Expressionism to "abstract Dada," and finally into "abstract Surrealism." He defined this current, which he called "non-geometrical abstract art," as emotional, organic, biomorphic, curvilinear, romantic, and decorative. "Often, of course," Barr went on, "these two currents intermingle, and they may both appear in one man. . . . The shape of the square confronts the silhouette of the amoeba."

Barr seems to have considered Calder to be one such artist. A mere six years after he had claimed Calder as archetypically American (and therefore, by and large, figurative), Barr placed the artist squarely in an international realm. This time it was Calder's abstract work that was deployed to bring a boldly international modernism into a local context. In a section of the catalogue on younger artists who had inherited and were reimagining the lessons of their forebears, Barr, invoking the "influence of Mondrian and [Naum] Gabo," credited Calder with turning his back on "the popular success of his wire portraits to experiment with mobile constructions built of wire, iron pipe and metal. . . . They display an ingenuity and visual humor quite different from the kinetic constructions which Gabo designed as early as 1922 or [Aleksandr] Rodchenko's hanging constructions of 1920."[18] In Barr's estimation, Calder's antecedents were clearly practitioners of geometrical abstract art. And yet, he continued, "recently Calder has deserted geometrical shapes for irregular quasi-organic forms."[19]

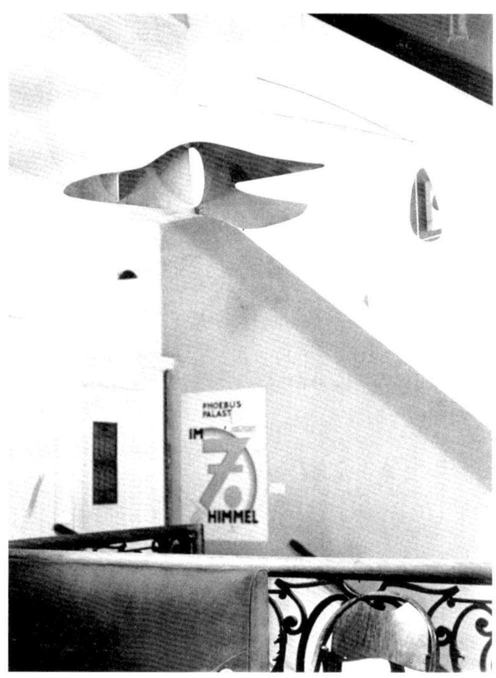

Fig. 6. **Cubism and Abstract Art**, *March 2–April 19, 1936. Installation view, with* **Mobile** *(1936) hanging in a stairwell between galleries. Photograph by Beaumont Newhall. MoMA Archives, New York*

Where, then, to fit him? Despite devising a highly detailed installation plan for the galleries, Barr chose to display Calder's work in an interstitial space (fig. 6).[20] A mobile from 1936, powered by air, was installed in a stairwell between galleries, hanging above a poster for the German release of the 1927 film *7th Heaven*, designed by C. O. Muller, with no other artwork nearby.[21] In this sculpture, which was lent by the artist, four metal elements hang from three rods. The elements vary in color and size; in each of the four unique shapes, which are suggestive of natural forms yet entirely nonobjective, flat sheets of metal intersect at right angles—Barr's two currents intermingling in one artwork. According to the installation plan, Barr had intended to include the mobile in the Surrealism section of the show, alongside work by Arp, Brancusi, Alberto Giacometti, Joan Miró, Henry Moore, and others, but in the end he changed course, settling instead on a transitional location.[22]

Calder's participation in the exhibition went beyond displaying this mobile.[23] He also lent a work from his personal collection, Red Blue Chair (1918–23), by the Dutch designer Gerrit Rietveld, to the design section of the show, and he appears to have assisted in assembling the exhibition, though the details of his involvement are not well documented. His most prominent contribution, however, was an artwork he produced for the building's exterior, a commission from the Museum that functioned as a large and visible banner for the exhibition. Calder made a mobile out of cloth—for him, an early and rare engagement with the material—to hang from a flagpole at the center of the building's uppermost register (pages 70, 71); although the work was not reproduced in the catalogue, Calder called it *Objet volant* (Flying object) in a letter to Barr.[24] In it, two asymmetrical fabric pieces—one red, one blue—intersected one another at their centers, creating four unique lobes, each pierced by a hole. Below, three fabric shapes hung from a horizontal crossbar: a red circle flanked by a slightly larger off-white circle and a much larger yellow teardrop shape. The work—whose shape vaguely resembled a reduplicated butterfly, at once friendly and strange—elicited a variety of responses: in the very early days of the exhibition, a midtown neighborhood association petitioned the Museum to remove the work from the building's facade, complaining, at least according to Calder, that "everyone was going to the museum, and no one to the [speakeasies nearby]."[25] This uncommon flying object, hovering over the sidewalk below, turned out to be a formidable advertisement for the show—not unlike the many examples of the New Typography graphics included in the galleries inside, it reconciled the letter and the spirit of its message.

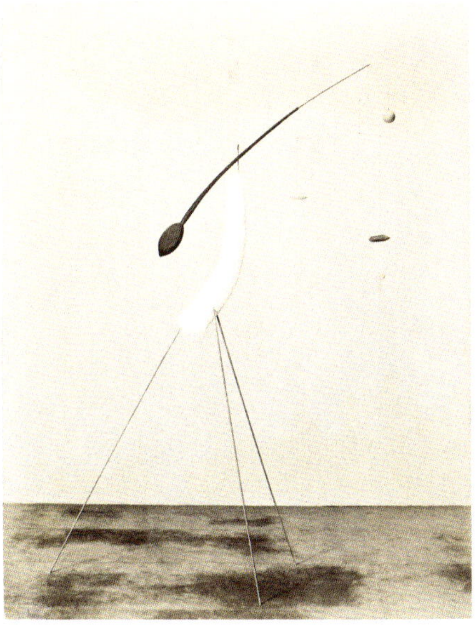

Fig. 7. **Praying Mantis** *(1936), in the exhibition album for* **Fantastic Art, Dada, Surrealism**, *c. 1936. MoMA Archives, New York*

On December 9, 1936, *Fantastic Art, Dada, Surrealism* opened at MoMA. The exhibition was a deeper exploration of Barr's "secondary" current of modernism, in particular the two means by which the Surrealists conveyed spontaneity, according to Barr: through content, as in the fantastical but meticulously rendered images of Salvador Dalí, Yves Tanguy, and others, and through technique, as in the free-form automatic, or chance-based compositional methods employed by artists such as André Masson and Miró, following experiments "previously carried on by Kandinsky, [Paul] Klee, and Arp."[26]

As he had for *Cubism and Abstract Art*, Barr submitted the art to a linear order. The organization of the catalogue's plates made this clear. After three sections tracing Fantastic art from the fifteenth century through the Great War came sections on twentieth-century pioneers: Dada and Surrealism and "Artists Independent of the Dada and Surrealist movements."[27] Calder was grouped in the latter, which was largely made up of American artists, including Peter Blume, Walt Disney, Arthur Dove, and Georgia O'Keeffe. He was represented in the exhibition by two new sculptures. One, *Object with Yellow Background* (1936), is a painted yellow panel with three floating metal objects suspended in front of it. It is a work that reads in both two and three dimensions: the objects are tethered to the plane—and seen from the front, the work resembles a painting—but they exist beyond it as well. The other, *Praying Mantis*, is a standing mobile consisting of a curved piece of carved and painted wood with three metal rods extending out of its center and a four-part mobile at its top (fig. 7).[28] The work is doubly suspended: the central white form above the three supporting rods, and the mobile above the central white form. Rising as it does upon leglike elements, *Praying Mantis* seems to invite the projection of naturalistic qualities such as stance and disposition. But this does not necessarily hold: the work's distinct shapes form no whole, but remain staunchly apart. Despite the weightiness of Barr's doctrine, the work conveys a definite lightness.

On May 8, 1939, at ten o'clock in the evening, trustees and special guests sat down to dinner to celebrate The Museum of Modern Art's tenth anniversary. The table was set with an elaborate multisection candelabra designed by Calder for the occasion; it held 120 candles in cups welded to a wire form, and could be arranged as a whole or in parts (pages 82–83; fig. 8). The grandeur of the decor befitted the occasion: MoMA had just spent $2 million on a new building, designed by the architects Philip L. Goodwin and Edward Durell Stone, to replace its original townhouse. The new six-story structure, made of reinforced concrete with a glass facade, featured state-of-the-art design details, including track lighting, moveable walls, and engineered ventilation. *Art in Our Time*, the inaugural installation, populated the entire building with works from the collection plus many loans, in an effort to present the "achievements of living artists together with the work of certain important masters of yesterday" through "painting, sculpture and graphic arts but also . . . architecture, furniture, photography and moving pictures."[29]

Visitors entering the new building immediately encountered Calder's *Lobster Trap and Fish Tail* (page 85), a work commissioned by the Museum's Advisory Committee for the main entrance's grand

The Bulletin of
The Museum of Modern Art

3-4 Volume 6 May-June 1939

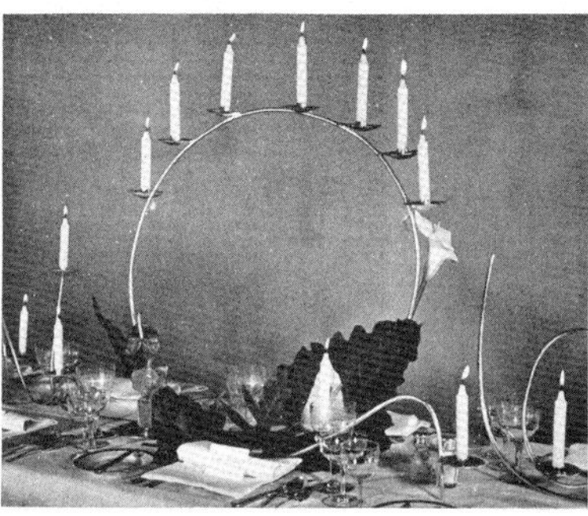

A corner of the table set for the Trustees' dinner on May 8, 1939, in the new Museum building. The candelabra were made for the occasion by Alexander Calder, American sculptor.

10th Anniversary

Opening of the new Museum building

Fig. 8. Cover of The Bulletin of The Museum of Modern Art, *with Calder's candelabra for MoMA's tenth-anniversary Trustees' dinner and celebration of the new building, May–June 1939. MoMA Archives, New York*

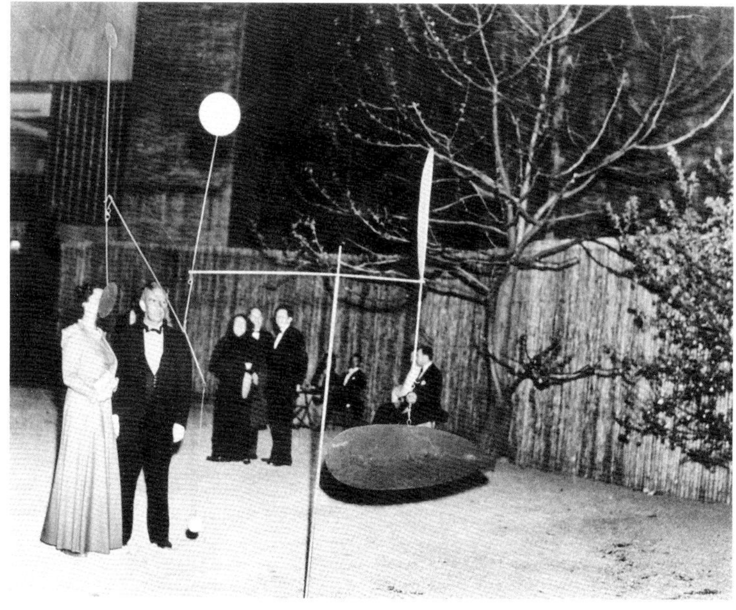

Fig. 9. Calder and Ivy Troutman at a reception, with Steel Fish *(1934), May 1939. Calder Foundation, New York*

staircase, which had been modeled after the one in Walter Gropius's Bauhaus building in Dessau, Germany.[30] In this mobile three main components are counterpoised in delicate balance with one another: above, an abstract form made of intersecting metal sheets painted red and black; below, extending from two arms, a ribbed wire quasi-ovoid structure on one side and a multipart black-painted sheet-metal mobile-within-a-mobile on the other. Its shapes evoke those in its title, yet it remains an example of striking "rhythmical freedom," as the curator James Johnson Sweeney later wrote.[31] The work—one of the few Museum commissions to be subsequently acquired—has, for the most part, hung in that same location since then. "I don't mind planning a work for a given space," Calder said decades later, in an interview in the mid-1960s. "I find that everything I do, if it is made for a particular spot, is more successful. A little thing, like this one on the table, is made for a spot on a table."[32] He was keenly aware of how artworks were informed by context, whether on a friend's lawn, in a corporate park, or on a dinner table. By the time he made *Lobster Trap and Fish Tail*, Calder had already been thinking a lot about "given spaces." Two years earlier he had completed a commission to be shown in the Spanish Pavilion in the 1937 Paris Exposition with Pablo Picasso's *Guernica* and other works: a fountain with flowing silvery rivulets of mercury.[33]

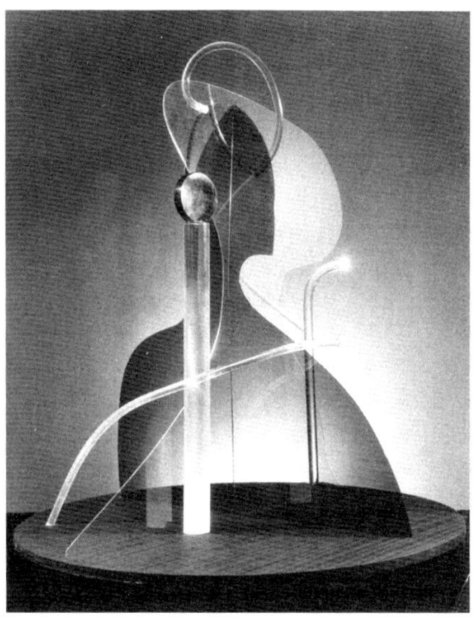

Fig. 10. Calder's winning entry for the "Competition for Sculpture in Plexiglas," May 1939. MoMA Archives, New York

Outside the Museum's new building, abutting Fifty-Fourth Street, was a garden slated for the display, according to a press release, of "a great variety of sculpture ranging in style from realistic to purely abstract."[34] In its architectural plan of loose gravel arranged in biomorphic patches (which would be replaced in 1953 with sleek marble), an abstract Calder work stood in stark contrast to more traditional sculptures by Aristide Maillol, Charles Despiau, Gaston Lachaise, and others. Calder lent one of his first outdoor sculptures, a work now referred to as *Steel Fish*, with six painted metal elements on rods set in suspended equilibrium from a central vertical rod (fig. 9).[35] This sculpture, produced during Calder's first summer in Roxbury, was one of the largest works he had made to date, and it plainly evidences the technical and intuitive experimentation he had undertaken to find its form. Close inspection reveals that he adjusted various components of the work to achieve its final shape and balance, such as a lead ball with S-hooks added to the lowest black element, itself thickened with thin layers of sheet metal. As an open record of the decisions and labors that yielded it, the work contrasts with the flawlessly executed monumental outdoor work of Calder's later career, which often appears to have been realized with ease.

The opening of MoMA's new building was timed to coincide with that of the 1939 World's Fair in New York, when the number of international tourists in the city was sure to swell. Anyone taking in the city's cultural life in spring and summer 1939 would have encountered Calder's work both in midtown Manhattan and at the fair, in Queens. Calder had been commissioned by Wallace Harrison and J. André Fouilhoux, the architects of the Consolidated Edison pavilion, to create a water ballet, "whose acting elements," Calder explained, "are jets of water from 14 nozzles which are designed to spurt, oscillate or rotate in fixed manners and at times as carefully predetermined as the movements of living dancers."[36] The project was never fully realized, but a row of jets was installed around the pavilion and activated.[37]

Despite the politically fraught backdrop against which the exposition was staged, its tenor was upbeat—a celebration of industrial progress and its effect on contemporary civilization. The chemical company Röhm and Haas sponsored the "Competition for Sculpture in Plexiglas," to bring attention to its newly developed material.[38] Calder won first prize, and the winning entry was displayed in the fair's Hall of Industrial Sciences: a work in multicolored Plexiglas illuminated by a concealed light source (fig. 10). The jury, selected by MoMA, described it as "equally interesting and strong when seen from any side," and noted that "the use of Plexiglas [rods gave] motion and sweep to the whole design."[39]

On January 28, 1943, Monroe Wheeler, the director of Exhibitions and Publications at MoMA, wrote to Calder, "I hope we shall be able to arrange a comprehensive show of your work in the not too distant future."[40] Wheeler's dual role—unusual by today's standards—came about during a period of flux at the Museum, one that included Barr being dismissed from his directorial post on account of increasing difficulties with the Museum's trustees.[41] Afterward, James Thrall Soby, a trustee, took over as the director of the Department of Painting and Sculpture and the assistant director of the Museum.

Soby was Calder's dear friend and a crucial early supporter, with some important sculptures by Calder in his personal collection. He had commissioned what was Calder's largest outdoor work at the time, *Well Sweep* (1935, page 67), for the grounds of his house in Farmington, Connecticut, about forty miles from Roxbury: a standing mobile that made use of an old wellhead in front of Soby's modernist house; its funnel bucket was designed to pull water out of the well, an action that changed the sculpture's balance dynamics as the weight of each element shifted. When Soby died, in 1979, he made a bequest of this sculpture and several others by Calder to MoMA: the wall panel *Swizzle Sticks* (1936, pages 68, 69) and other more personal works—including a pair of cuff links bearing his initials (c. 1935, page 86) and three wire sculptures in the shape of a fork, knife, and spoon that Calder gave to Soby after he lost many of his possessions in a divorce (1936, page 65). Soby was an avid photographer and often captured Calder at work and at play (fig. 11).

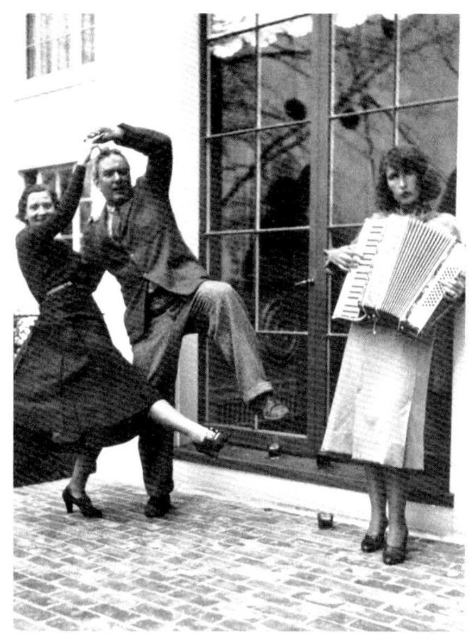

Fig. 11. Calder dancing with Margaret French, with Louisa Calder on the accordion, at James Thrall Soby's house, Farmington, Connecticut, 1936. Photograph by James Thrall Soby

Despite this strong relationship, Calder was experiencing a mounting frustration with the Museum, and it may have been that Wheeler was proposing an exhibition in order to quell it. Calder had been in touch with Soby the previous summer, detailing all that had "passed between them"—all the work he had made for or shown at the Museum thus far—and cordially but sternly asking for more support, morally and financially.[42] In his proposal letter Wheeler asked Calder to compile a list of his activities to that point, which included "book jackets, theater posters, newspaper drawings, paintings, wood sculptures of animals and acrobats, 'wire sculptures,' circus, wire toys—stuffed toys, what can be done with a tin can, what can be done with one piece of wire, mobiles, sonorous mobiles, stabiles, jewelry, book illustrations, grills for broiling meat, clothing: sweaters, gloves, galoshes, ties."[43] Through Wheeler an exhibition was planned; by early May, it was determined, at Soby's suggestion, that the curator James Johnson Sweeney would organize it.[44]

Among Calder's many MoMA relationships, the most significant was with Sweeney. By the time of the exhibition, Calder and Sweeney had been friends for more than a decade. Sweeney was born in Brooklyn in 1900, to well-to-do Irish immigrants who owned Sweeney and Johnson, a successful lace and textile import company, with headquarters in New York and outposts in Cincinnati and Chicago. After studying literature at Georgetown and then at Cambridge, Sweeney spent time in Paris, where he became acquainted with many of the city's artistic avant-garde, was the editor of the literary magazine *Transition*, and assisted James Joyce on the texts that eventually became *Finnegans Wake*. Calder first approached Sweeney when Sweeney had returned to New York, in a letter dated May 9, 1932, in which Calder explained that he was writing at the suggestion of Léger, and asked him to go see his mobiles on view at Julien Levy Gallery in midtown Manhattan. Their early correspondence found Calder extending invitation after invitation—to come see a performance of his circus, to visit him in Roxbury, to produce a catalogue—which Sweeney often had to decline because of other writing, travel, and curatorial commitments.[45] Calder earnestly persevered with his appeals. From 1932 to about 1935, as the men got to know one another, Calder made his appreciation

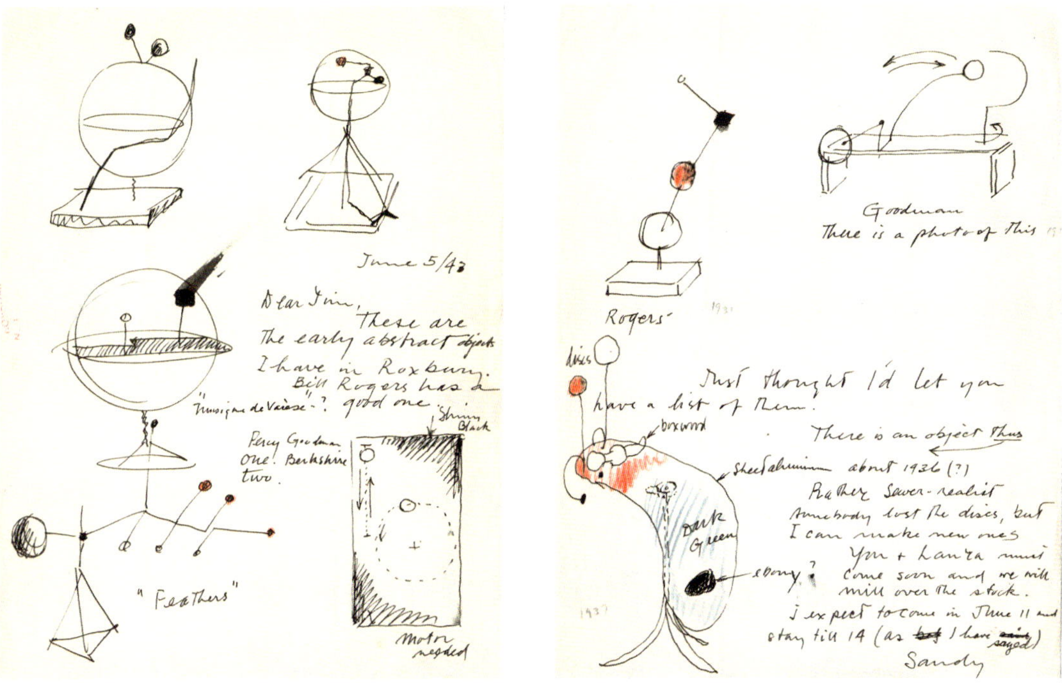

June 5/43

Dear Jim,
These are
The early abstract objects
I have in Roxbury.
Bill Rogers has a
good one.

Percy Goodman
One. Berkshire
two.

Shiny
Black

"Feathers"

Motor
needed

Goodman
There is a photo of this

Rogers'

discs

Just thought I'd let you
have a list of them.

boxwood

There is an object thus

sheet aluminum about 1936 (?)
Rather Sewer-realist
Somebody lost the discs, but
I can make new ones

Dark
Green

ebony?

You + Laura must
Come soon and we will
mill over the stock.
I expect to come in June 11 and
stay till 14 (as I have sayed)
Sandy

Fig 12. Letter from Calder to James Johnson Sweeney, June 5, 1943. Calder Foundation, New York

for Sweeney well known through a variety of persistent overtures, such as sending hand-drawn daily timetables for buses running between New York and the Connecticut towns convenient to Roxbury, and invitations for their families to vacation together. Sweeney began most of his responses with some form of regret, whether for his delay in writing or for disappointing news. In a letter of August 11, 1934, Calder jokingly suggested that Sweeney "have the apology made up in the form of a rubber stamp . . . like my letterhead," which became a running joke in future correspondences.[46] By 1935, when Sweeney was hired as a curator in MoMA's Department of Painting and Sculpture, they and their families had become close. Apart from a handful of artists who had written about Calder's work, by the time of the MoMA exhibition Sweeney had effectively become the artist's author of record.[47] He had contributed essays for Calder's first show at Pierre Matisse Gallery, in 1934; for an exhibition of mobiles that he organized at the Renaissance Society in Chicago the following year; and for other various publications including the arts journals *Axis* and *Plus*. He was therefore Calder's natural choice for an essay in the MoMA catalogue.

By mid-May 1943, Sweeney and Calder were in the throes of exhibition planning, exchanging letters on a near-daily basis. The subjects of their correspondence ranged from practical administrative matters to more conceptual questions. Their creative scheming is evident in a letter from Calder to Sweeney, from June 7, 1943, about the budget for the publication, which they had hoped to increase. Sweeney had already offered his $300 honorarium in an effort to fund an increase in page count, from thirty-two to forty-eight. Calder had heard from Sweeney that "Barr displayed a lively interest in the 'Horse' for the Museum [1928, page 51]. Do you think we could bait that catalogue trap with horse-meat, and offer them this in exchange for further expanding the catalogue. Perhaps you could suggest it to Barr better than I. Would you like to try?"[48] *Horse* did enter the collection that year, but as a purchase with funds from the Lillie P. Bliss Bequest rather than as a gift from the artist. Bliss, one of MoMA's three cofounders, had bequeathed her collection of works by late-nineteenth- and early-twentieth-century French artists to the Museum, with the idea that they could be sold as needed to create funds for new acquisitions.

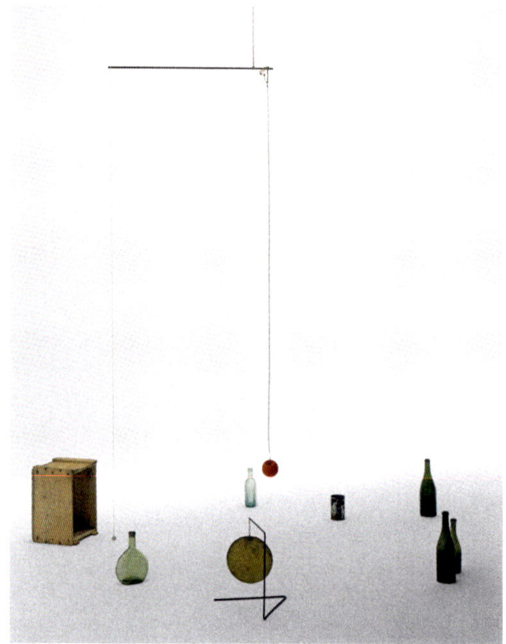

Fig. 13. **Small Sphere and Heavy Sphere**. *1932/1933. Cast iron, rod, wire, wood, cord, thread, paint, and impedimenta, 10 ft. 5 in. (317.5 cm) high; installation dimensions variable. Calder Foundation, New York. Mary Calder Rower Bequest*

Calder and Sweeney conceptualized and executed the show in tandem, although Sweeney maintained his autonomy over the catalogue text, in which he reiterated Barr's positioning of Calder as a truly American artist, "an American speaking an international language, not a regional expression."[49] From the tenor of their exchange, it is clear that Calder was both guiding voice and willing administrator in the show's organization. Over the course of the summer, he took on a variety of clerical tasks, such as collecting information about his works' insurance values and hunting down their current whereabouts, which would have been at least partially handled by a gallerist, had Calder not also been in the process of dissolving his ten-year relationship with Pierre Matisse. He frequently illustrated his letters to Sweeney with sketches of particular objects for the exhibition (fig. 12), and the show's final checklist suggests that Sweeney often took Calder's suggestions.

In one case, he did not. In a late-August letter, a month before the show opened, while Sweeney was on vacation, Calder suggested a work for inclusion, accompanied by an illustration: *Small Sphere and Heavy Sphere*, begun in Paris in 1932 and shown there, at Galerie Pierre Colle, in 1933 (fig. 13). The work's elements—five glass bottles, a tin can, a wood box, and a brass gong hanging from an iron rod—can be freely arranged by viewers in the area underneath two suspended spheres: a small white wood sphere and a larger (heavy) red cast-iron one, each hanging from the end of a rod affixed with cable to a single point in the ceiling. In his letter, Calder described this work, his first hanging mobile: "One swings the red (iron) ball in a small circle—this movement + the inertia of the rod and the length of thread develop a very complicated pattern of movement. The impedimenta—boxes, cymbal, bottles, cans, etc. add to the complication, and also add sounds of thuds, crashes, etc."[50] With these words, he described a new system of interlocking features synthesized in a single artwork: ready-made objects, viewer participation and intervention, sound, and indeterminacy. Although it was an aesthetic outlier in Calder's oeuvre, this wonderfully strange set of objects nevertheless marked a shift in Calder's practice—toward a new attention to hanging mobiles, and toward vivid engagement with sound and chance as well.[51] Perhaps this was why Sweeney chose not to include it in the exhibition.

In August, Calder convinced a good friend, the Swiss photographer Herbert Matter, to collaborate with him and Sweeney on the exhibition's installation, saying, "Our three minds travel in the same direction."[52] Matter had left Switzerland in the mid-1930s and come to New York, where he established himself as a graphic designer and photographer for *Harper's Bazaar* and *Vogue*.[53] He eventually became the artist's premier documentarian, capturing his work in photography and film over many decades. In 1950 Matter would make *Works of Calder*, with a score by John Cage and narration by Burgess Meredith, in which a young boy (played by Matter's son) finds himself in Calder's Connecticut studio and watches the artist at work on his sculptures.

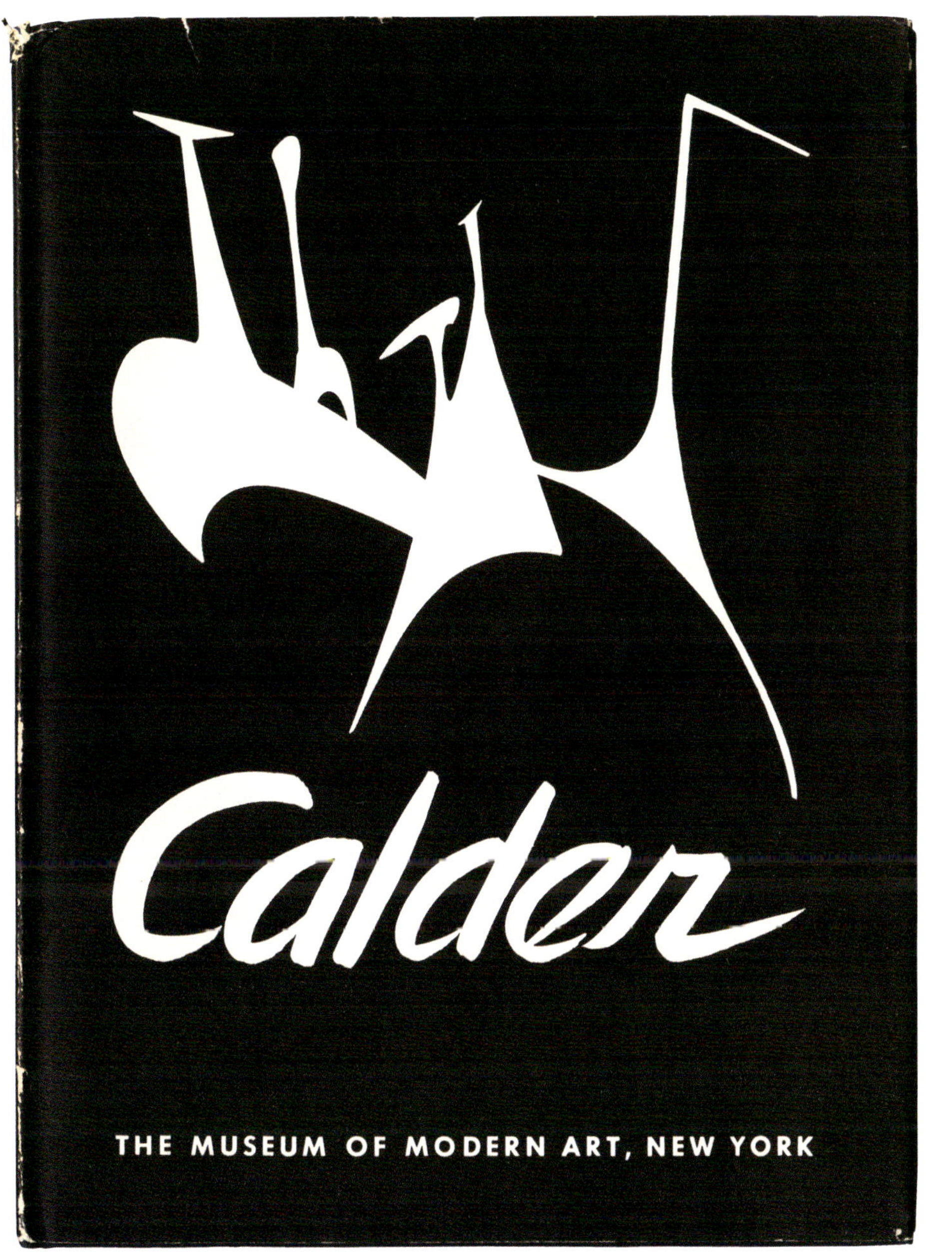

Fig. 14. Cover of the catalogue for the exhibition Alexander Calder: Sculptures and Constructions, *by James Johnson Sweeney, designed by Herbert Matter, 1943. Calder Foundation, New York*

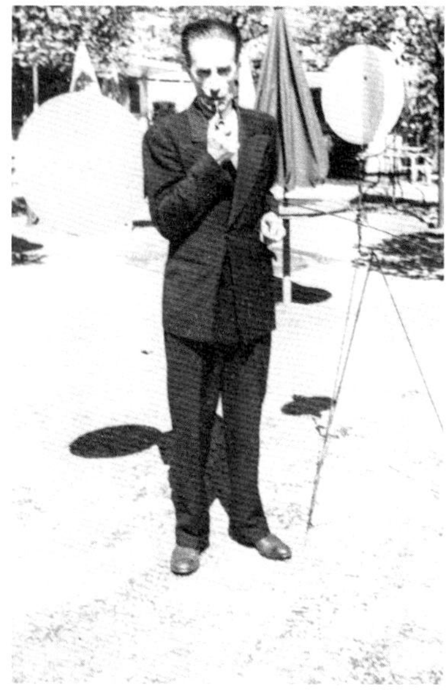

Fig. 15. Marcel Duchamp at MoMA, with **Red and Yellow Vane** *(1934), 1943*

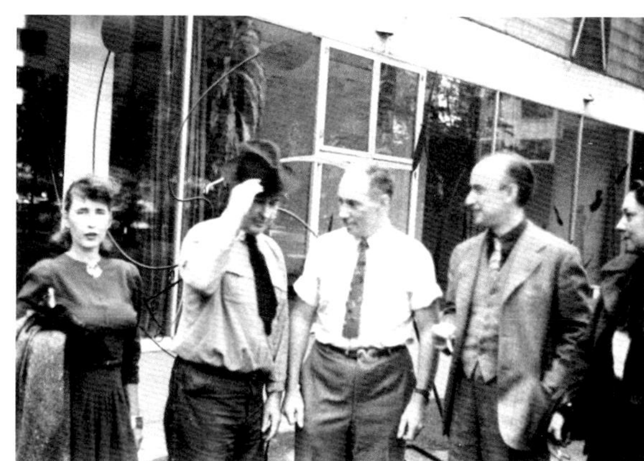

Fig. 16. Louisa Calder, Alexander Calder, James Johnson Sweeney, Yves Tanguy, and Kay Sage at **Alexander Calder: Sculptures and Constructions**, *September 1943*

For the MoMA exhibition, a $150 consultation fee was agreed upon. Matter was sent a plan of the exhibition space on the Museum's first floor and informed that there was no budget for elaborate construction or painting because of wartime financial constraints. Matter also designed the exhibition catalogue (fig. 14) and, with the art historian Agnes Rindge Claflin, made a public relations–style film of the show.[54]

A photograph of Duchamp taken during installation places him, too, at the scene, although the precise nature of his involvement remains unclear (fig. 15).[55] Sweeney and Duchamp had known each other since the early 1930s. They had served together on the jury for a salon at Peggy Guggenheim's Art of This Century gallery, and for a time Sweeney had done weekly interviews with Duchamp for a book-length monograph that never came to pass.[56] Duchamp and Calder had first met in Paris in 1931, introduced by Duchamp's partner, the artist Mary Reynolds, who was a friend of the Calders, and the two became friends. Duchamp had nursed an interest in curatorial matters long before Calder's MoMA exhibition—and in fact had arranged for the first exhibition of Calder's mobiles, at Galerie Vignon in Paris in 1932. In *First Papers of Surrealism*, which he had organized with André Breton, at Whitelaw Reid House in midtown Manhattan the previous autumn, he had laid out the exhibition's objects, including Calder's *The Spider* (1940), within a tangled mile-long web of string.[57]

There is also a photograph of Tanguy during the exhibition's installation (fig. 16). Calder and Tanguy had been friends since Tanguy and his wife, the Surrealist Kay Sage, moved to Woodbury, Connecticut, in the 1940s and joined the Calders' Connecticut circle of artists, curators and collectors.[58] Upon his death, Tanguy left a bequest to MoMA, through Sage, of a small but fundamental group of Calder's works from the couple's personal collection, including an early motorized panel (c. 1934, page 78), a standing tabletop mobile (1939, page 77), and a rare Plexiglas mobile inscribed "Pour 3 ans d'assez bonne conduite" (For 3 years of fairly good behavior)—a jab at Tanguy's attempt to quit drinking (1941–43, page 76).

On September 29, 1943, Calder's monographic exhibition opened at The Museum of Modern Art. It was a memorable art-world event, with celebrities turning up for the opening party (fig. 17), and at least two performances of Calder's circus for an elite group of patrons scheduled during the run of the show (fig. 18). Among the celebrants were some of the European émigrés Calder had known in Paris, such as Léger and Tanguy.

The show, which opened at a point when the United States' extensive engagement in World War II

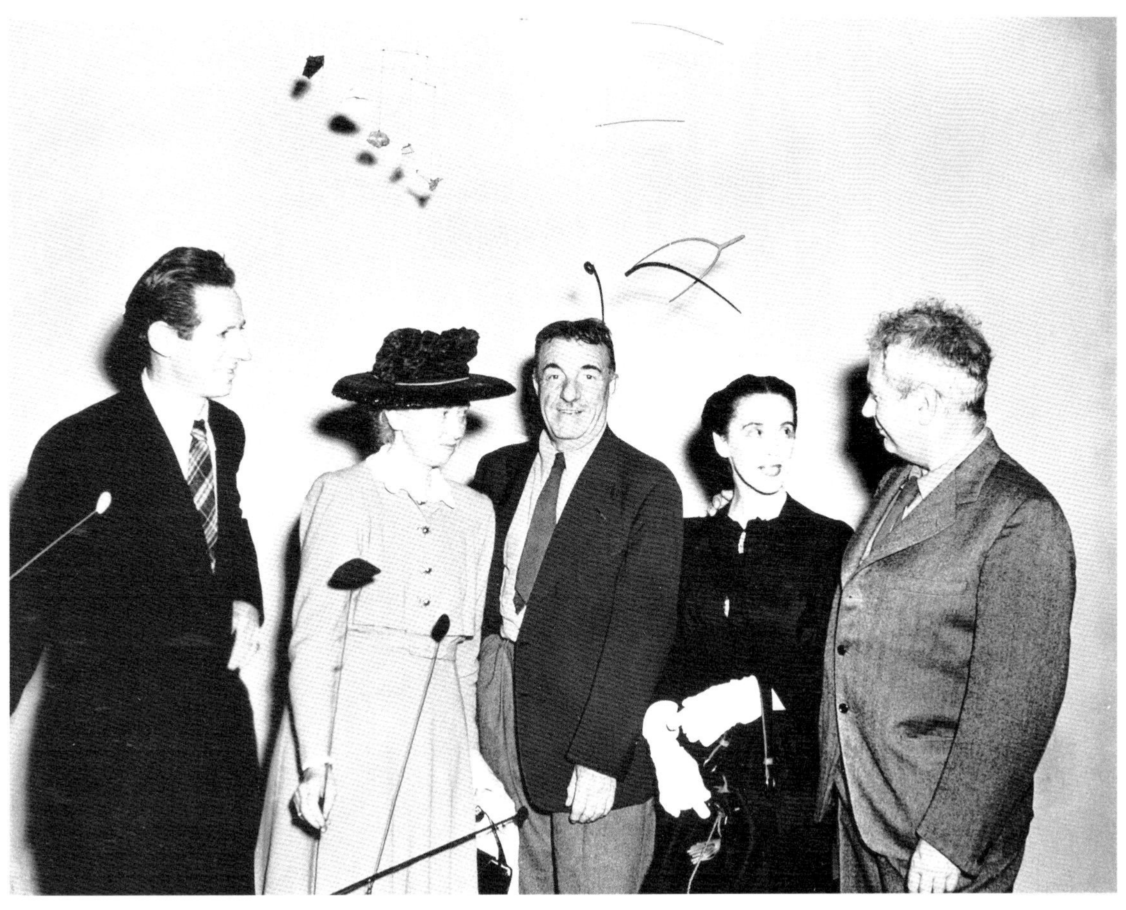

Fig. 17. Herbert Matter, Marianne Moore, Fernand Léger, Martha Graham, and Calder, at the opening reception for **Alexander Calder: Sculptures and Constructions**, *September 28, 1943. MoMA Archives, New York*

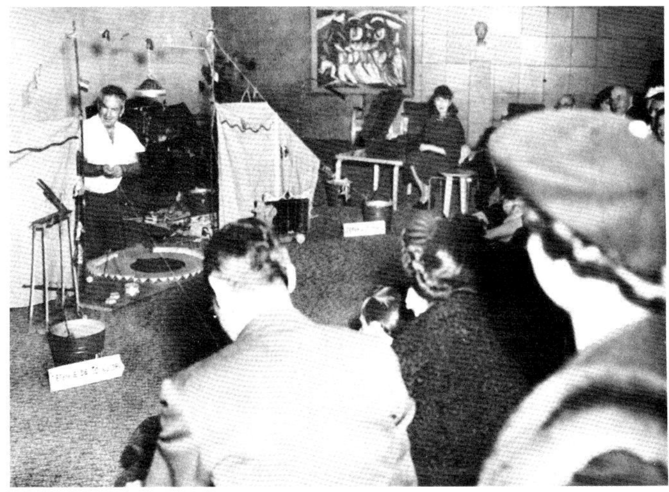

Fig. 18. Calder performing **Cirque Calder** *in the Members' Room, October 20 or 21, 1943. MoMA Archives, New York*

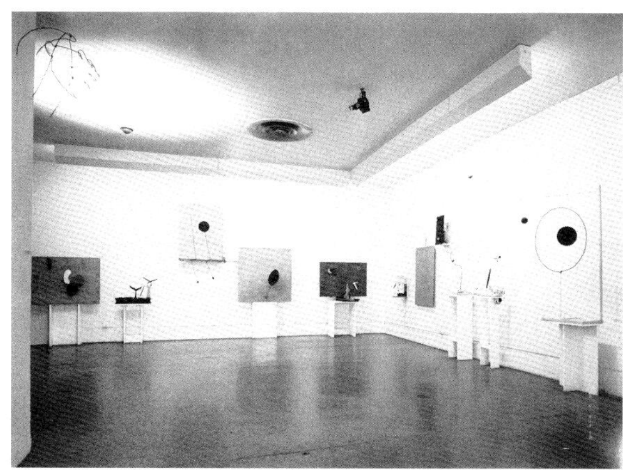

Fig. 20. **Alexander Calder: Sculptures and Constructions**, *September 29, 1943–January 16, 1944. Installation view of the second gallery, with* **Object with Red Ball** *(1931) at far right. MoMA Archives, New York*

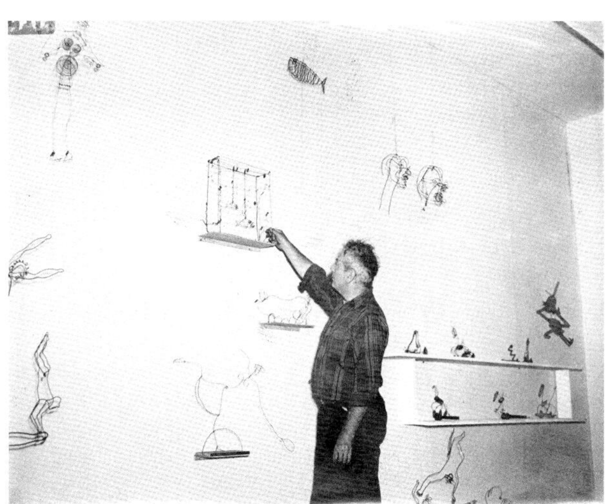

Fig. 19. Calder installing **Alexander Calder: Sculptures and Constructions**, *September 29, 1943–January 16, 1944. Installation view of the early works in the first gallery. MoMA Archives, New York*

had produced an atmosphere of high tension and low spirits, met a level of critical acclaim that understood a new set of stakes for art: its ability to not only transcend political turmoil but perhaps even heal it. The *New York Sun* critic Henry McBride welcomed the exhibition as "an astonishing number of proofs that nature never can be entirely thwarted, and that even when at the last gasp, as I presume nature is at the moment, she can still supply to poets and to genuine artists the manna which the soul craves and upon which alone the soul thrives."[59] This timely midcareer retrospective and its enthusiastic reception would set the course for Calder's subsequent success.

The exhibition contained some eighty sculptures, plus jewelry, and occupied the ground floor of the Museum and part of the sculpture garden. The layout was relatively open, allowing for broad vistas and multiple sightlines. Works overlapped one another, partially obscuring some views and framing others. The lobby was outfitted with large-scale works in painted black steel, including *Black Beast* (1940, page 110).[60] An enlarged version of a tabletop sculpture, it is at once elegant and imposing, its form both abstract and beastlike. Scaling up was an approach that Calder had begun to seriously embrace, so that viewers entering the exhibition were immediately oriented to the artist's more current concerns. From there, the exhibition jumped back in time. The first gallery contained figurative works from the 1920s, the earliest on view, with wood sculptures on one side (each on its own pedestal) and wire sculptures—suspended from the ceiling, mounted on walls, or affixed to shelves—on the other (fig. 19). It was a closely packed group of at least thirty artworks in very tight dialogue with one another, making it difficult at times to discern where one object ended and another began. The first gallery emptied into the center of a large second room containing a wide variety of works from the 1930s. Half the room was devoted to a selection of motorized sculptures from 1931—the objects that Duchamp had first termed "mobile"—alongside other related freestanding and wall-mounted panel works from the early 1930s. Together these works charted Calder's first experiments with abstraction, in the fruitful period after his revelation in Mondrian's studio. Installed among the motorized works was *Object with Red Ball*, a sculpture that predated them slightly and was intended to be recomposed by hand—that is, to be activated rather than beheld. It is a constellation of three shapes: in descending order of scale, an open wire circle, two intersecting black sheet-metal disks describing the diameter and circumference of a sphere, and a red

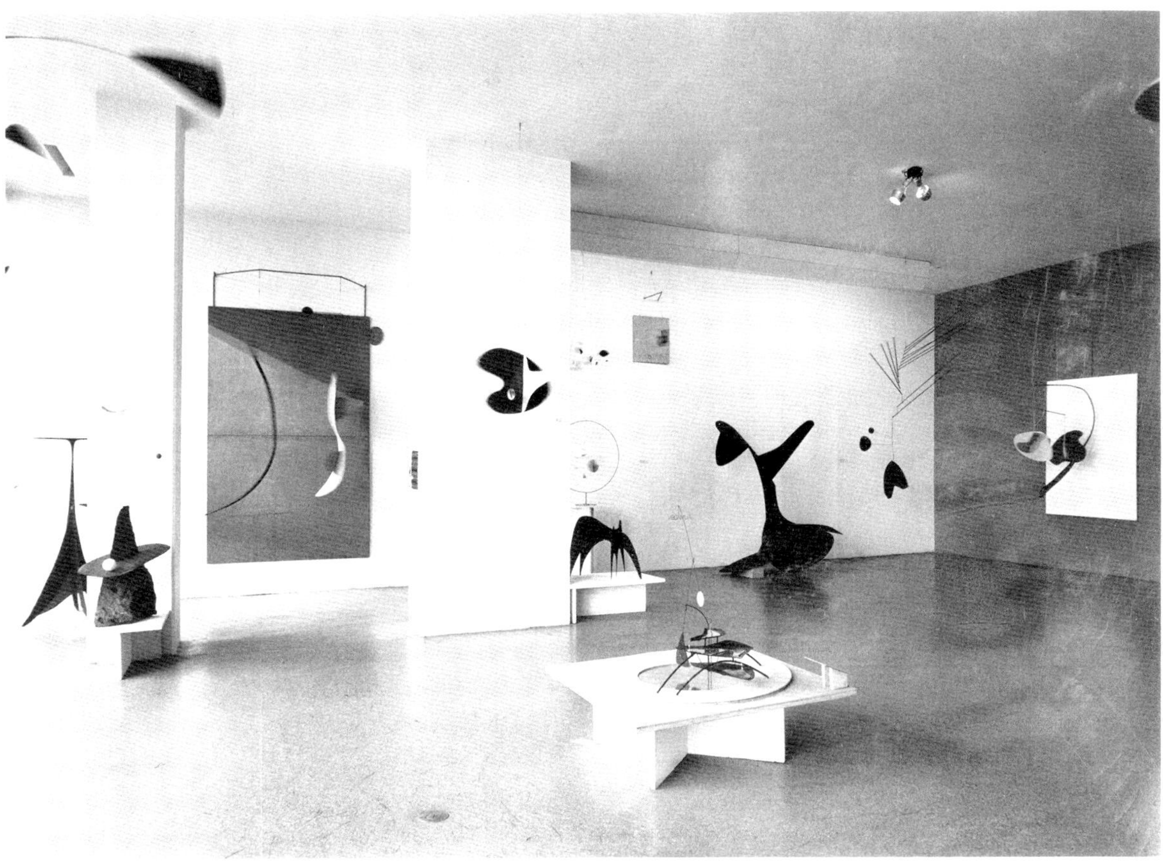

Fig. 21. **Alexander Calder: Sculptures and Constructions,** *September 29, 1943–January 16, 1944. Installation view, with* **Devil Fish** *(1937) in the back, at right. MoMA Archives, New York*

wood sphere (fig. 20). The wire circle, supported by a rod and two wires, remains static; the orientation of the two smaller elements, suspended from a rod above the wire circle, changes as viewers move them along the rod or rotate the rod around its vertical post. Thus the work has no fixed composition, no single vantage point. With every adjustment, the work changes, moving from one unfinished state to another.

The other half of this gallery presented Calder's varied work from the second half of the 1930s. Anchoring this wide space was the 6½-foot-tall *Devil Fish* (reproduced in the catalogue as *Whale* [1937, page 74]), which Calder had lent to the Museum in 1941 and had since become a mainstay in the garden.[61] Brought indoors for the exhibition, its imposing matte-black sheet-metal form was a contrast to the buoyant, tensile, spindly wire mobiles around it (fig. 21). The work marked a breakthrough in the artist's process: it was the first that Calder made by bolting together pieces of bent sheet metal, and the first that he had enlarged from a maquette; both maneuvers would become his standard procedure (by the time of *Black Beast* and other works in the Museum's lobby) and for the rest of his career. Stable and grounded, by turns transparent and opaque, *Devil Fish* prefigures Calder's later and larger outdoor work in both technique and form.

A long gallery with glass walls overlooking the sculpture garden presented a sprawling mix of objects, with works from the mid-1930s to the artist's most recent. The works ranged in material (wood, wire, steel), palette (painted wood, natural wood, painted metals), type (mobile, stabile, standing

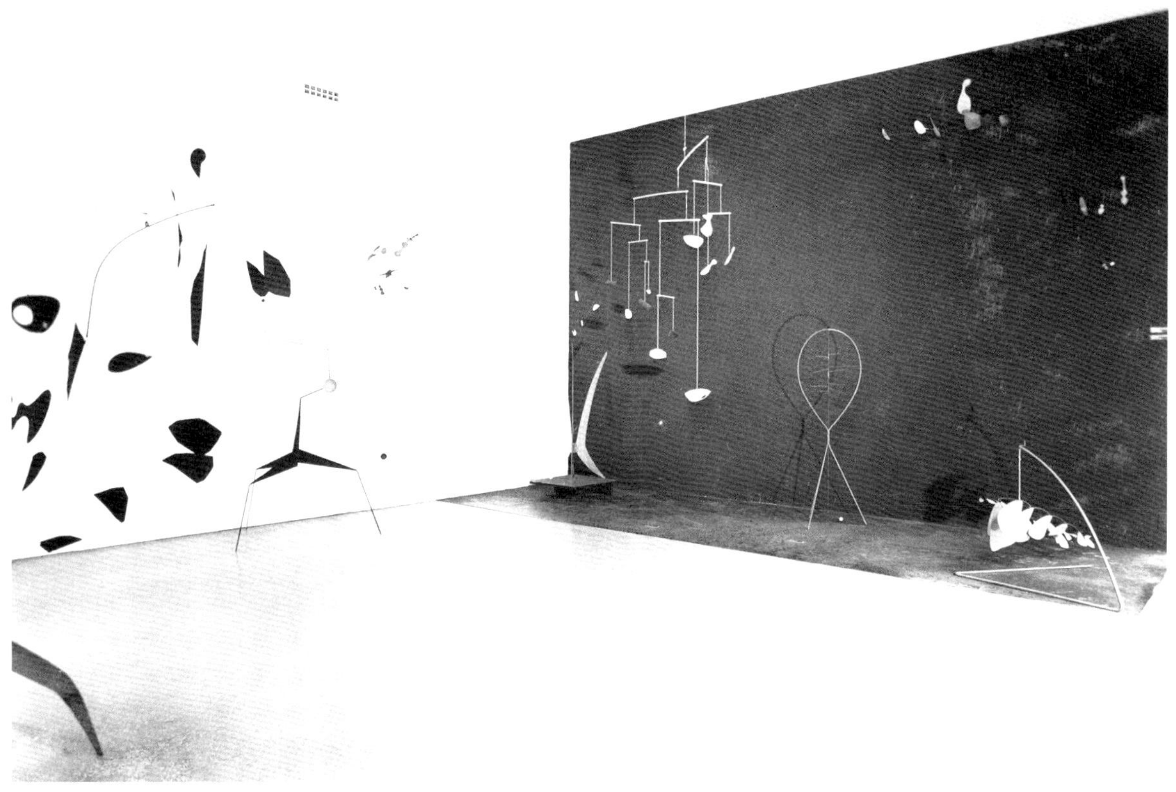

Fig. 22. **Alexander Calder: Sculptures and Constructions**, *September 29, 1943–January 16, 1944. Installation view, with Constellation works (all 1943) hanging at upper right. MoMA Archives, New York*

mobile), and presentation (hanging from the ceiling, standing on the floor, perched on a pedestal or off a wall). Most of them offered Calder's by-then signature abstract vocabulary of line, shape, and volume. Some could seem referential, such as *Gibraltar* (1936, page 73), installed on a pedestal low to the ground, which could be seen to refer to the rock it was named for. A rough-hewn triangular lump of lignum vitae (a tropical hardwood) forms its base; intersecting it partway down is an ovoid plane of highly polished walnut, on which sits a white-painted wood ball and two steel rods topped with a crescent and a sphere, respectively.

Sweeney had originally titled this work *Volcano*, but Calder had renamed it *Gibraltar* by the time the show's catalogue went into production. Calder's position on titles varied. He later recalled that "before the 1943 MoMA show, when Sweeney insisted things should have names, I used to make a little drawing when talking about a thing instead of using a name." At times, however, he seemed invested in the naming of things. *Morning Star* (1943, page 91), for example, was one of several works making their debut in the exhibition—a spiny stabile made of acutely angled steel rods capped with painted wood spheres. Although the work's title seems to invite a reading of the work as a kind of astronomical map, with line segments between each star delineating its shape, Calder cited a different origin of the term: "a Morning Star—it's not a star—is a medieval weapon thrown from a horse—sort of a lance with a round head and little spikes."[62]

The final section of the exhibition featured a selection of jewelry displayed in a case, some works on paper, and some recent Constellation sculptures (fig. 22). Duchamp played a part in naming these works, too, which he and Sweeney had done after viewing them together in Calder's studio. Calder had first presented them four months earlier at Pierre Matisse Gallery, in his eighth and final show there: carved, sometimes painted wood objects connected to one another with wire in webbed compositions. Hung high on the wall—which had been an unexpected style of installation at the time—or set on plinths, "They had a suggestion of some kind of cosmic nuclear gases—which I won't try to explain," Calder later said. "I was interested in the extremely delicate, open composition."[63] As was often the case for Calder, the materials of the Constellation works were determined by the situation. "There wasn't much metal around during the war years," Calder wrote, "so I tried my hand at wood carving."[64] He had worked with wood since the 1920s in Paris, first carving animals and then abstract shapes, but during the 1930s he was also experimenting with wire and sheet metal. The resolutely abstract works depend on the interrelationships of their parts, such as in *Wall Constellation with Red Object* (1943, page 92), in which each of the seven wood elements are connected to at least one other with taut steel wire. Some of the elements are painted, and some reveal the natural hues and surface patterning of their source materials. The work attaches to the wall at its highest point with a single nail, and it makes contact with the wall at several others. The relationships among these elements vary, but the individual members appear to take their respective places in the ensemble only in the real time of perception. And still the whole continues to shift depending on the viewer's vantage point.

The MoMA retrospective was scheduled to run through November 28, but because of the enthusiasm with which it was received it was extended to the following January 16, in order to capture the audience of tourists and students home for the holidays. Its critical success extended to popular lifestyle and news outlets, which tended to highlight Calder's personality—calling him "fanciful"; "for all his social ebullience . . . a serious artist and a persuasive talker"; and "the art world's No. 1 playboy; a kind of robust machine age Peter Pan."[65] Even the staunchly programmatic art critic Clement Greenberg admitted that he found Calder's art "gay and exuberant," although he then went on to lament what he considered the limited reach of Calder's project: "Calder's chief asset is felicity; so few of his objects lack it; but felicity exhausts their content—as is most obvious in the larger pieces."[66] Sweeney had already considered this topic, but had come to a different conclusion in his catalogue essay:

Calder's most original contribution is his unique enlivening of abstract art by humor. Through humor he satisfies the observer's appetite for feeling or emotion without recourse to direct representation. . . . The result in Calder's work is the replacement of representational interests by humor that stirs up no specific associations and no emotional recollections to distract the observer's attention from the work of art itself. Through this conscious infusion of a playful element, Calder has maintained an independence of the doctrine school of abstract art as well as of orthodox surrealism. At the same time the humor in his work is a protest against false seriousness in art and the self-importance of the advance-guard painter, as well as the academician. From this viewpoint it is genial development of certain aspects of the dada movement.[67]

On June 19, 1945, following his solo exhibition's success, another commission made its debut at MoMA, this time in the sculpture garden. Calder's largest sculpture to date, *Man-Eater with Pennants* (page 97) stood 14 feet tall, with a wingspan of 30 feet and fourteen elements of varying shapes affixed to rods hanging vertically from supporting beams that were attached to a central post. Under proper weather conditions, the twelve flat sheet-metal elements—painted in bold matte colors and cut into distinct shapes of varying sizes, some with perforations—were meant to move freely, circling the post, so that the overall shape, like much of Calder's work, was perpetually in flux, determined by either nature (air) or visitor involvement (touch), or both. Calder had intended for Museum visitors to interact with the work, changing its composition as they did so. Like *Small Sphere and Heavy Sphere*, *Man-Eater* was a remarkable, curious object, an exception in Calder's otherwise interconnected oeuvre. He made it in response to Barr's request for a sculpture that could be viewed at ground level, in the garden, but would also be seen from above, through the windows of the interior galleries on the Museum's upper floors.

This commission, like *Lobster Trap and Fish Tail*, was meant to be a permanent installation. From the start, however, it did not quite satisfy. As had been evident in the lobby area of the retrospective, Calder was at that time engrossed with handsome, sleek, abstract, black-painted sheet-metal sculptures enlarged from maquettes, such as *Black Beast*. This may have been the aesthetic that Barr imagined the commission would embody, rather than the outsize interactive standing mobile Calder ultimately produced. A few months after its debut, Philip Goodwin deemed it "clumsy."[68] The longtime curator Dorothy C. Miller, who would develop a very close relationship with Calder over the coming years, suggested it was simply "too heavy to blow around much except in very strong wind."[69] And Barr expressed that it "had not been a really successful piece" because, while "successful when seen from above, . . . unfortunately few people saw it from this angle" (fig. 23).[70] He wrote this in a letter to Calder on June 3, 1949, the day after he made the decision to remove it. *Man-Eater* had been on view for just under four years.

Perhaps Sweeney, Calder's greatest ally at MoMA, would have been able to advocate for *Man-Eater's* viability, had he not recently left for the Guggenheim Museum, under rather acrimonious circumstances.[71] Calder had tried to fight for it. To remedy Miller's lament that it did not move around enough, he had proposed to modify the sculpture by adding a ball bearing at the point of attachment at the top of the central post. He brought up the idea for this

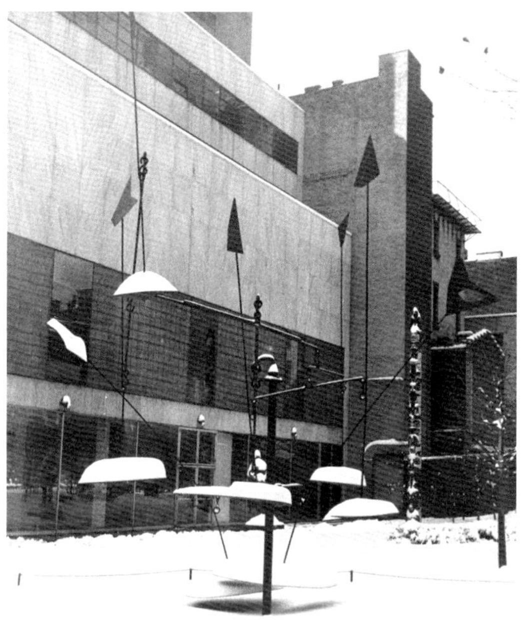

Fig. 23. **Man-Eater with Pennants** *(1945) in the sculpture garden, winter 1946–47. MoMA Archives, New York*

intervention from time to time, but the change was never made.[72] In response to Barr's news, the artist took a cheeky tone: "Cheer up! I am sorry the object is gone, but not angry. What I am most sorry about is that the Man-Eater was never placed on a roller bearing and allowed to revolve freely . . . for all that mass and height moving under influence of the wind would produce a fine movement."[73] The following year, in a letter to René d'Harnoncourt, who had recently been appointed the Museum's director, Calder clarified that he did not share the opinion that the work was unsuccessful and that he would have liked the opportunity to "let her rip!"[74]

To develop the form of *Man-Eater*, Calder made a maquette, which he later donated to MoMA (page 96). He had begun working this way in the mid-1930s, at the time of *Devil Fish*, and was beginning to employ this approach more and more, as he made larger sculptures. Scale was central to Calder's practice, and some of his works exist in multiple sizes. Sometimes, as in the case of *Man-Eater*, the maquette was enlarged right away. *Black Beast* was enlarged in 1940, from a maquette made the previous year; a second version was commissioned in 1957, by Eliot Noyes, a former director of MoMA's

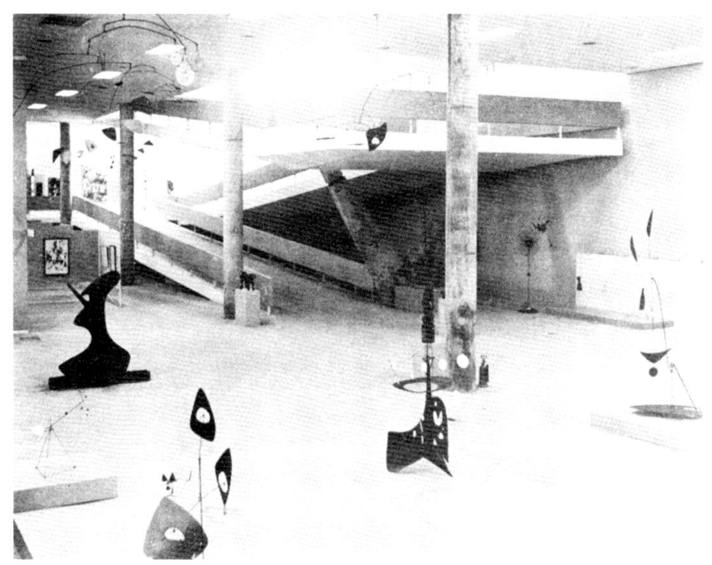

Fig. 24. II Bienal do Museu de Arte Moderna, São Paulo, December 13, 1953–February 28, 1954. Installation view of the U.S. contribution. MoMA Archives, New York

Department of Industrial Design, and it entered the Museum's collection as part of Noyes's bequest, in 1987. Other maquettes existed for some time before being enlarged: *Spiny* (c. 1939, page 79) was included in the MoMA retrospective and was reproduced on the cover of the catalogue, presented in dramatic silhouette by Matter; decades later, in 1966, when Nelson Rockefeller commissioned *Large Spiny* for his house at Kykuit, north of New York City, *Spiny* served as its maquette.

On December 13, 1953, the second Bienal de São Paulo opened to the public. A grand-scale gallery on the ground floor of a new modernist exhibition hall, designed for the occasion by architect Oscar Niemeyer, was devoted to an extensive survey of Calder's work (fig. 24). The other thirty-nine countries in the Bienal all presented selections made and installed by their governments' cultural agencies, but the U.S. contribution was overseen by The Museum of Modern Art, under the auspices of d'Harnoncourt and the curator Margaret Miller. Any hard feelings Calder may have suffered in the *Man-Eater* debacle must have been put aside: the Museum had chosen Calder's work for one of its two large solo presentations.[75] Calder's display featured some forty-five works spanning his career up to that point, including *Shark Sucker* (1930, page 61), *Double Arc and Sphere* (1932), *Gibraltar*, *Devil Fish*, and *Morning Star*, among others.

Calder was already well known in Brazil, thanks in large part to the efforts of the architect Henrique Mindlin and the cultural critic and art historian Mário Pedrosa, both of whom had met Calder in New York around the time of his MoMA exhibition. "Just give me some time and I will have a Calder craze in Rio," Mindlin wrote to Calder in November 1944, and by September 1948, a solo exhibition of Calder's work opened at the Ministério da Educação e Saúde in Rio de Janeiro, followed by another in São Paulo in October.[76]

Pedrosa's goal was to define the modernist project in Brazil—to reveal what made Brazilian modern art Brazilian, much as Barr had done in the United States for American art. Pedrosa was a crucial voice for the Concrete art movement in South America, campaigning for "autonomous" art and championing abstraction as the tool for achieving it. In Calder's work he was able to refine some of his ideas around the potential of art. "If there is indeed an artist who is close to the artistic ideals of the future," he wrote in 1944, in an article for Rio de Janeiro's major daily newspaper, "[to] that ideal society in which art would be confused with day-to-day routine activities and quotidian ways of life, that artist is Alexander Calder."[77]

Calder's Bienal presentation provided an opportunity for a public already acquainted with

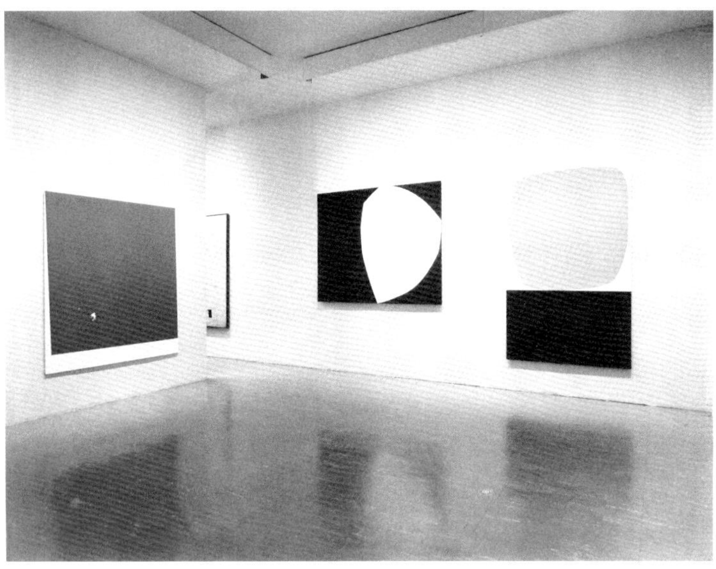

Fig. 25. **16 Americans**, *December 16, 1959–February 17, 1960. Installation view, with works by Ellsworth Kelly. From left to right:* **North River**, **York**, *and* **Charter** *(all 1959). MoMA Archives, New York*

his work to engage with it on a grand scale, and a younger generation of artists (such as Abraham Palatnik and Waldemar Cordeiro) may have found in Calder's fluid forms a way to move forward from the hard-edged geometries of Concretist painting, toward the curved volumes of Niemeyer's pavilion.[78]

At midcentury, against the backdrop of Cold War distress, biennials and other international art expositions provided an important platform for participating countries to speak through the art and artists they officially chose to display—the art that best represented a nation's attitudes and ideals. The Museum of Modern Art's contribution—under the auspices of Nelson Rockefeller, a trustee and the director of the Office of the Coordinator of Inter-American Affairs, the U.S. government agency in charge of propaganda efforts in Latin America—resulted in an ideological convergence, on a world stage, of Barr's modernism with the question of what it meant to be American. In *What Is Modern Painting?*, a book first published in 1943 and then translated into Portuguese as a kind of handbook for the Bienal exhibition, Barr wrote of the "freedom of expression, freedom from want and fear . . . an embodiment of the freedom which we all want but which we can never really find in everyday life with its schedules, regulations, and compromises."[79] For MoMA, Calder's art embodied these fundamental desires.

On December 9, 1954, Calder wrote a letter to Barr. "Dear Alfred," he wrote, "I have just seen the paintings of a young ex-GI painter—recently returned from Paris . . . and said I would write and ask you to visit him. He is Ellsworth Kelly."[80] Kelly lived in Paris in the late 1940s and early 1950s, where he had begun the work he would develop over the course of his long career, of observed scenes transposed into painted abstract forms. Calder had crossed paths with Kelly in Paris during his time there and visited his studio in Lower Manhattan that summer. Impressed, Calder covered his rent and contacted Barr on his behalf. Barr was too busy to make the trip downtown, but in a providential turn of events, he sent Dorothy Miller, his deputy, in his place. Her visit marked the beginning of a lifelong friendship, the first manifestation of which was Kelly's U.S. debut, in Miller's exhibition *16 Americans* in December 1959, which featured nine of his recent paintings (fig. 25). The exhibition extended the tradition, established at the Museum's founding, of periodic surveys of contemporary American art, such as the *Living Americans* show in which Calder's work had first been on view. As the previous exhibitions had done, *16 Americans* brought together "distinct and widely varying personalities," as Miller wrote in the catalogue, "contrasting these personalities sharply rather than attempting to unite them within any given movement or trend. These sixteen are presented simply as individuals and Americans."[81]

The new class of Americans included Alfred Leslie, Louise Nevelson, and Richard Stankiewicz—artists associated with Abstract Expressionism's resolution of Barr's binary of European abstraction versus American figuration—for suddenly to be abstract *was* to be 100% American. But also included were a few young, relatively unknown Americans—Jay DeFeo, Jasper Johns, Kelly, Robert Rauschenberg, and Frank Stella—who, as the focus shifted from Paris to New York, would be at the forefront of a new and truly "American" American art. This new, younger American art reined in abstraction to make room for everyday objects, images, and materials.

By this time Calder's status at the Museum had also shifted: he had gone from being an artist "on call" to an elder statesman. As Kelly was returning from France, Calder was establishing new roots there, in a house and studio in Saché, a few hours southwest of Paris. He continued his friendship with Dorothy Miller throughout the 1950s and '60s, corresponding with her regularly about personal and professional matters. As the curator in charge of the collection, she was responsible for displaying Calder's works in the galleries and garden during these decades.

On October 11, 1966, Calder made an extraordinary gift to The Museum of Modern Art. At that point, he was a widely celebrated artist: among his many recent accomplishments were another career retrospective, this time at the Solomon R. Guggenheim Museum, in New York, and Musée national d'art moderne, in Paris, in 1964–65; induction into the American Academy of Arts and Letters, in 1965; the publication of an autobiography, in 1966; and public sculptural commissions around the world, including *Teodelapio* (1962, page 116), a 59-foot-tall stabile made for the Festival dei Due Mondi in Spoleto, Italy. Before the gift, MoMA had owned twenty-three works across mediums, styles, and dates—starting with *A Universe*, which had entered the collection in 1934, through the large-scale outdoor work *Black Widow* (1959, page 113), purchased in 1963 with the Mrs. Simon Guggenheim Fund, which had been established in 1938 and was responsible for some of the collection's most beloved artworks.[82] The previous May, Calder had written to Barr, who was nearly at the end of his tenure, to say, "I have long felt that whatever my success has been has been greatly as a result of the show I had at the MoMA in 1943." He went on to write that "now, as I seem to have a lot of important objects 'left over,' I would like to make a gift of several of them to the museum—if you'd be interested."[83]

Barr was indeed interested, but he was careful to emphasize the mutual nature of the relationship "What you propose seems to us very handsome indeed," he wrote, "but you should not feel obligated to the Museum. After all, the Museum depends on such an artist as yourself."[84] Nevertheless, he made a trip to Roxbury that summer with his wife and Miller to comb through Calder's storage, and he then drew up a wish list—at the top of which were *Gibraltar* (fig. 27), *Morning Star*, and *Sandy's Butterfly* (1964, pages 120–21), now some of the best known and most popular works in the collection. After their visit, Calder assured Barr that he was welcome to take everything on the list and then some.[85] The final selection comprised nineteen artworks: fourteen works were given to the Museum by the end of 1966, and five officially joined the collection the following January. All of them were exhibited together from February to September that year.[86] With this gift Calder entered into a new collaboration with the institution, this time as a donor.

Alexander Calder's gift to MoMA is significant not only in number but also in the nature of the works themselves and the window they provide onto the artist's vision. One of the exceptional works in the gift is *Snow Flurry I*, a large-scale hanging mobile (1948, page 107).[87] Thirty white-painted metal disks of varying circumference, each attached to the end of a steel rod, are suspended from a single point, grouped roughly by proportions into three clusters. Each element functions a bit like a paddle, with a disk "face" on one end of a bare wire-rod "handle," and each of the rods is connected to the next one in the sequence. The elements at the terminus of each of the three clusters have a disk at both ends. Physics determines the general shape of *Snow Flurry I*: its cascading curvilinear form derives from the moment of force created by gravity. The length of the rods defines the shape of the curves, but the curves' points are delineated by the mass of the attached disks—with less mass a rod floats up, with more, it plunges. Different forces acting upon the work—gravity, air currents, vibration at the hanging point—torque the elements, setting them in motion. In 1946 Jean-Paul Sartre observed that "one of Calder's objects is like the sea and equally spellbinding: always beginning over again, always new. A passing glance is not enough; you must live with it, be bewitched by it. Then the imagination revels in these pure, interchanging forms, at once free and rule-governed."[88] Equally complex and nuanced physical circumstances determine the continuous motion of the sea, which responds to the moon's gravitational pull. In each case, nature is both an armature and an arm, holding bodies in perpetual flux. Yet in neither case is the apparatus evident in the experience of its effects. Calder's "technical, almost mathematical combinations," as Sartre noted, are "the tangible symbol of Nature, of that great, vague Nature that squanders pollen and suddenly causes a thousand butterflies to take wing."[89] His art honors nature both by referring to it and by harnessing it as a means: the question of how to see the fullness of the world in an object engaged him for his entire life.

Like the action of its title, this artwork depicts and encompasses motion—it is and it does. "Flurry" is both noun and verb, each implying motion, describing both a swirling mass of objects and the swirling action itself. Like Sartre's sea, a flurry is a phenomenon of nature. It is a weather event. It requires a witness to experience its effects, indeed to effect its transition from noun to verb. Calder's sculptures likewise depend on a viewer's perception of their many elements to achieve their full expression: they contain infinite forms, none of them final. His is an aesthetic of adjustment, of a body to an object, an object to a body, and an object to itself and to its surroundings. In time, or as Calder wrote, with "familiarization," some of a given work's infinite possible expressions will emerge.[90] The longer we spend with his work, the more we see, as physical interventions and their perceptions occur in their own time, with accumulating impact. In precisely the same manner that the work implies no fixed viewpoint, achieves no final form, the Calder story, even laid out in a chronological series of events, eludes simple telling. Which seems to be how the artist wanted it:

The admission of approximation is necessary, for one cannot hope to be absolute in his precision. He cannot see, or even conceive of a thing from all possible points of view, simultaneously. While he perfects the front, the side, or rear may be weak; then while he strengthens the other facade he may be weakening that originally the best. There is no end to this. To finish the work he must approximate.[91]

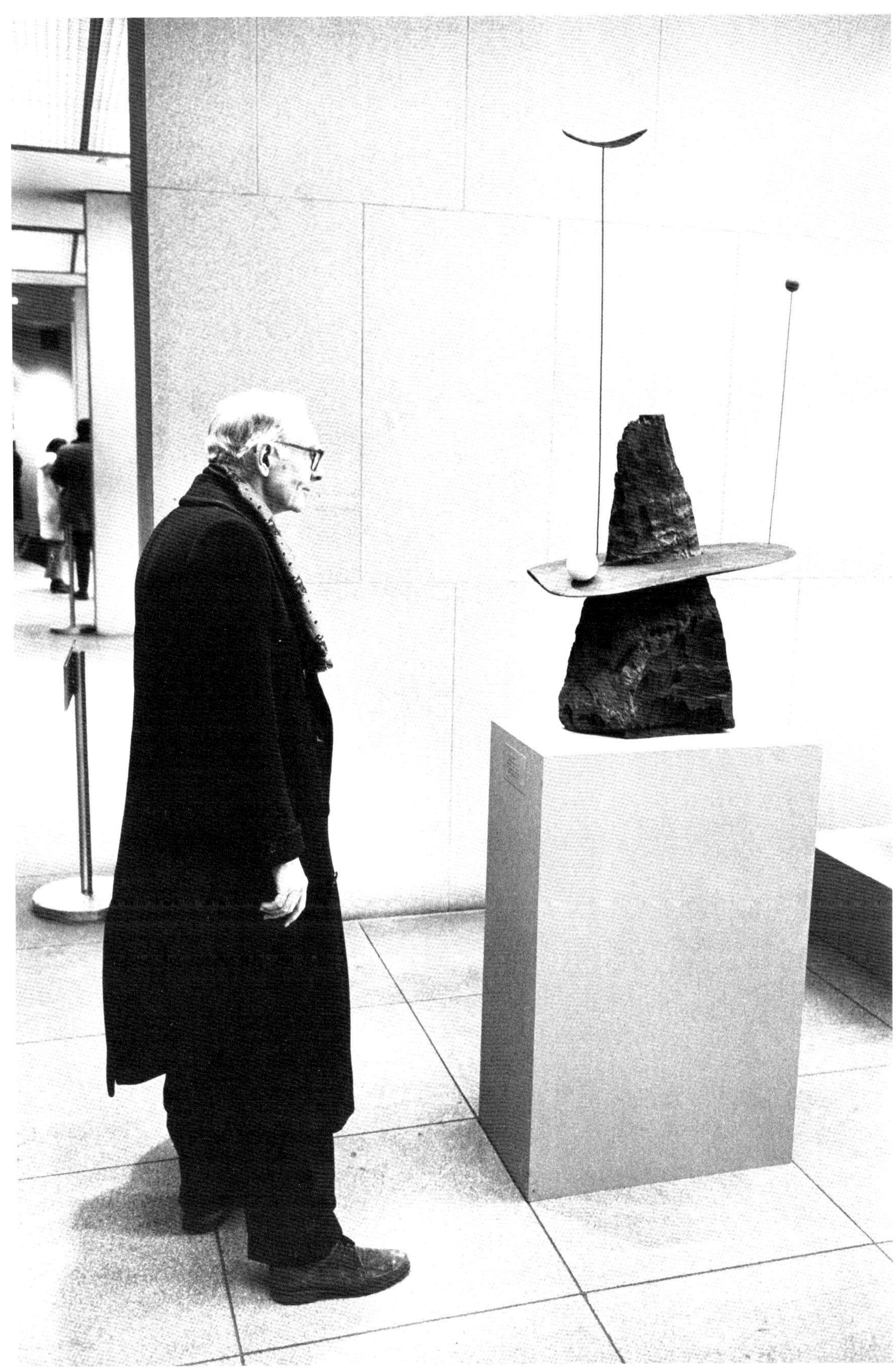

Fig. 27. Alfred H. Barr Jr., with **Gibraltar** *(1936), 1967.*
MoMA Archives, New York

Notes

1 Alfred H. Barr Jr., foreword to *Painting and Sculpture by Living Americans*, exh. cat. (New York: The Museum of Modern Art, 1930), 5.

2 The trustees were A. Conger Goodyear, President; Lillie P. Bliss, Vice President; Samuel A. Lewisohn; and Stephen C. Clark. On Tuesday, October 21, 1930, they met with Barr and Jere Abbott to draw up a preliminary list of twenty-one painters and seven sculptors. In assembling the exhibition, the directors "were to be at liberty to drop one or two names if it seemed advisable and to add several younger painters in order to increase the life and gaiety of the exhibition." MoMA Archives, The Museum of Modern Art Exhibition Records (MoMA Exhs.), 9.2.

3 Barr, letter to Alexander Calder, January 8, 1931. MoMA Exhs., 9.2. *Stooping Girl* had by this time been referred to as *Licorice* and *Liquorice* in two gallery exhibitions in New York in 1929.

4 Murdock Pemberton, "The Art Galleries: Pigment and Tea Leaves," *New Yorker*, February 23, 1929, 76–77; and "Seen in Various Galleries," *New York Times*, February 10, 1929, 125.

5 Barr, letter to George D. Pratt, November 12, 1930. MoMA Exhs. 9.2. *Cow* appeared in a show of Calder's wood carvings at Weyhe Gallery in February 1929 and was also shown at 56th Street Gallery, New York, in December 1929.

6 On Calder's time in Paris, see, for example, Jed Perl, *Calder: The Conquest of Time; The Early Years, 1898–1940* (New York: Knopf, 2017); and Joan Simon, ed., *Alexander Calder: The Paris Years, 1926–1933*, exh. cat. (New York: Whitney Museum of American Art, 2008).

7 Calder, *Calder: An Autobiography with Pictures*, ed. Jean Davidson (New York: Pantheon, 1966), 113.

8 Fernand Léger, introduction to *Alexandre Calder: Volumes—Vecteurs—Densités / Dessins—Portraits* (Paris: Galerie Percier, 1931), n.p.

9 According to Calder, one kinetic work (now lost) made up of an attenuated wood ellipsoid and two wood spheres that each moved along its own wire trajectory when activated by a motor, attracted Duchamp's attention and prompted his suggestion of the term "mobile." Later, another friend, Jean Arp, came up with the term "stabile" to describe a nonmoving work meant to be seen and engaged with in the round. Calder, *An Autobiography with Pictures*, 126–27, 130. Some twenty-five years after Duchamp first used the term, Calder attempted to recreate the original kinetic sculpture, from memory and a photograph, for an exhibition, organized by Pontus Hultén, on the machine in art history. See Hultén, *The Machine as Seen at the End of the Mechanical Age* (New York: The Museum of Modern Art, 1968), 148, in which it appears as "*The motorized mobile that Duchamp liked*." After the exhibition it stayed at MoMA; it is now in the collection under the title *The Bicycle*.

10 See Calder, "What Abstract Art Means to Me," *The Museum of Modern Art Bulletin* 18, no. 3 (Spring 1951): 8–9.

11 Abby Aldrich Rockefeller had purchased the mobile after seeing it in the First Municipal Art Exhibition, at Rockefeller Center, February–March, 1934.

12 Barr, letter to Rockefeller, October 16, 1934. Department of Painting and Sculpture (P&S) Museum Collection (MC) files, "Alexander Calder, A Universe, 1934."

13 Calder, statement in *Alexander Calder: Modern Painting and Sculpture*, exh. cat. (Pittsfield, Mass.: Berkshire Museum, 1933), 2–3.

14 *A Universe* was displayed in the collection galleries during the run of the exhibition—rather than in the special-exhibition space on the first floor—and doesn't appear in any of the exhibition's installation images. Collection Management and Exhibition Registration (CMER) MC files, "Alexander Calder, *A Universe*, 1934."

15 Nicholas Guppy, "Alexander Calder," *Atlantic Monthly*, December 1964, 55. Quoted in Perl, *The Conquest of Time*, 97.

16 Barr, *Fantastic Art, Dada, Surrealism*, exh. cat. (New York: The Museum of Modern Art, 1936), 7. *Cubism and Abstract Art* (MoMA Exhs., 46; March 2–April 19, 1936) and *Fantastic Art, Dada, Surrealism* (MoMA Exhs., 55; December 7, 1936–January 17, 1937) were followed by *Romantic Painting in America* (MoMA Exhs., 246; November 11, 1943–February 6, 1944).

17 All quotations in this paragraph are from Barr, *Cubism and Abstract Art*, (New York: The Museum of Modern Art, 1936), 19. See also Glenn D. Lowry, "Abstraction in 1936: Barr's Diagrams," in Leah Dickerman, ed., *Inventing Abstraction, 1910–1925*, exh. cat. (New York: The Museum of Modern Art, 2011), 359–63.

18 Barr, *Cubism and Abstract Art*, 197.

19 Ibid.

20 Barr planned discrete installations for early, analytical, and synthetic Cubism, and he expanded modern architecture into several categories, and included categories for furniture, posters, typography, and theater. MoMA Exhs., 46.2, "Cubism and Abstract Art Circulating Exhibition, Installation."

21 While in Munich in 1927, Barr acquired this poster, along with many other examples of the New Typography—graphic design rooted in the clean functionalism of the machine age. He periodically showed these in U.S. exhibitions and eventually gave a group of works, including this poster, to the Museum in 1960. I thank Juliet Kinchin for her insights on this topic.

22 MoMA Exhs., 46.2, "Cubism and Abstract Art Circulating Exhibition, Installation."

23 Because *A Universe* was reproduced in the catalogue (as an untitled mobile), it is believed to have been included in the exhibition. It does not, however, appear in any of the installation images, nor is it noted in the Registrar Collection files. So although it is now on record as having been on the exhibition checklist, there is no indication that it was actually on view. CMER MC files, "Alexander Calder, *A Universe*, 1934."

24 From time to time Calder titled his works in French. He proposed *Objet volant* in a letter to Barr: "I don't know whether or not you have made any mention of this in the catalogue, but when the show travels I think it would be very nice to call it a 'flying object' (for a flag flies) and list it somehow." Calder, letter to Barr, March 31, [1936?]. MoMA Archives, Alfred H. Barr, Jr. Papers, I.A.20. The work was no longer in exhibitable condition after its outdoor installation during the show; it was remade in 1969 for an exhibition of Calder's work in MoMA's collection.

25 "I had a note from Goodyear the other day thanking me for making it, and saying that it had been quite a success, until the 5th Ave. Ass. has intervened in behalf of the speakeasies—s—because everybody was going to the museum, and no one to the speaks." Ibid. In 1966 the MoMA curator Dorothy C. Miller wrote to Calder, "Alfred and I can remember that the Fifth Avenue Association wouldn't let us hang it because it stuck out further than the prescribed number of feet." Miller later recalled, in a letter to Dorothy Dudley, the Museum's head registrar, that "the Fifth Avenue Association protested that the Calder banner was visible from Fifth Avenue, violating their rules, and it had to be removed." P&S MC files, "Alexander Calder, Sign for 'Cubism and Abstract Art,' 1936."

26 Barr, "A Brief Guide to the Exhibition *Fantastic Art, Dada, Surrealism*," exh. brochure, 1936. Reprinted as the introduction to the revised second edition of Barr, *Fantastic Art, Dada, Surrealism* (New York: The Museum of Modern Art, 1947), 12.

27 Ibid., 3.

28 *Object with Yellow Background* was lent to the exhibition by the Honolulu Academy of Arts. *Praying Mantis* was lent by Calder; it is now in the collection of the Wadsworth Atheneum, Hartford, Connecticut.

29 Barr, "The Plan of the Exhibition," in *Art in Our Time*, exh. cat. (New York: The Museum of Modern Art, 1939), 13.

30 The Bauhaus had been a touchstone for Barr since his visit in the winter of 1927, while traveling in Europe with Abbott, a Harvard classmate, to collect materials for a course on contemporary art he was teaching at Wellesley College. (Abbott became the museum's first associate director in 1929.) Two years later, Barr modeled MoMA's medium-specific curatorial departments after the Bauhaus workshops.

31 James Johnson Sweeney, *Alexander Calder*, exh. cat. (New York: The Museum of Modern Art, 1943), 54.

32 Calder, in Katharine Kuh, ed., *The Artist's Voice: Talks with Seventeen Artists* (New York: Harper and Row, 1962), 42. Which table sculpture he was referring to is unknown.

33 On this project and all of Calder's commissions in the 1930s, beginning with stage sets for Martha Graham Dance Company in 1935, see Perl, "Mercury Fountain" and "Turning Forty," in *The Conquest of Time*, 513–36, 554–81.

34 "Facts on the Two-Million-Dollar Building and Sculpture Garden of The Museum of Modern Art," MoMA press release May 8, 1939. MoMA Archives.

35 The cloth mobile that hung outdoors for *Cubism and Abstract Art* was also listed in the catalogue but was not illustrated—nor does it appear in any extant installation images from the show. *Steel Fish* was reproduced as *Mobile*, dated 1935, with a height of 6 feet. In fact the correct date is 1934, and the work's overall height is approximately 10 feet. Barr, *Art in Our Time*, 270.

36 Calder, "A Water Ballet," *Theatre Arts Monthly* 23, no. 8 (August 1939). The 1939 World's Fair was held in Flushing Meadows Park, in Queens.

37 Calder, *An Autobiography with Pictures*, 176.

38 In 1933 Röhm and Haas trademarked the name Plexiglas for their recently developed thermal plastic. The jury of three, selected by MoMA, included the artist and collector Katherine Dreier, the artist Robert Laurent, and Sweeney. MoMA Archives, Department of Circulating Exhibitions Records, II.1.47.5.

39 From a pool of 250 sketched submissions, the jury selected five to be produced as full-size sculptures with Plexiglas provided by Röhm and Haas. First prize was $800; the Swiss photographer Herbert Matter, the installation designer for Calder's 1943 exhibition at MoMA, won second prize, which was $300. Ibid.

40 Monroe Wheeler, letter to Calder, January 28, 1943. MoMA Exhs., 242.3.

41 Wheeler became the first director of exhibitions in 1940 and had been the director of publications since the previous year. He held the two titles from 1940 to 1967. Barr was officially fired from his director position on October 15, 1943, but he continued to serve the Museum under various advisory titles until his retirement, in 1967.

42 Calder, letter to James Thrall Soby, June 4, 1942. MoMA Archives, James Thrall Soby Papers, I.57.

43 Wheeler, memo to Goodyear, Barr, and Soby on January 28, 1943. MoMA Exhs., 242.3. On stabiles, see note 9.

44 "I discussed Sandy Calder's exhibition with him last night and he told me quite frankly that he had his heart set on Jim Sweeney doing the text for his catalog. I understand Sandy's reasons perfectly and suggest that Sweeney be made Director of the exhibition since it would be clearer for one person to do the whole show. Sweeney is to have his book on T. S. Eliot finished by May, so could take on the Calder show." Soby, memo to Wheeler, April 10, 1943. MoMA Exhs., 242.3. Wheeler officially invited Sweeney to organize the exhibition in a letter of May 7, 1943, which also served as confirmation of employment for Sweeney to submit to the draft board in case it became necessary for him to do so. MoMA Exhs., 242.3.

45 Among the many projects keeping Sweeney busy were a survey of contemporary art at the Renaissance Society at the University of Chicago in the summer of 1934; the publication *Plastic Redirections in 20th Century Painting* that same year; and the exhibition *African Negro Art* at The Museum of Modern Art in March 1935, his first at the Museum. Sweeney did agree to write a foreword for Calder's first New York solo show, at Pierre Matisse Gallery, in April 1934.

46 Calder, letter to Sweeney, August 11, 1934. Calder Foundation archives.

47 Jules Pascin wrote a short text for a show of Calder's wood and wire works at Galerie Billiet-Pierre Vorms, Paris, in 1929; Léger wrote the foreword to the catalogue of Calder's first show of abstract works, at Galerie Percier, Paris, in 1931; and André Masson handwrote the poem "L'Atelier d'Alexander Calder" in 1942, which was translated and published in a catalogue that accompanied a solo show at Curt Valentin's Buchholz Gallery, New York, in 1949.

48 Calder, letter to Sweeney, June 7, 1943. Calder Foundation archives.

49 In 1951 the catalogue was republished as a monograph, with an extended essay by Sweeney. Sweeney, *Alexander Calder* (New York: The Museum of Modern Art, 1951), 67.

50 Calder, letter to Sweeney, August 28, 1943. Calder Foundation archives.

51 In 2008 *Small Sphere and Heavy Sphere* was shown for the first time since its debut, in Paris in 1933, in the exhibition *Alexander Calder: The Paris Years, 1926–1933*, at the Whitney Museum of American Art, New York. In September 2019, it was shown in an exhibition at Pace Gallery, New York. See *Calder: Small Sphere and Heavy Sphere*, exh. cat. (New York: Pace Gallery, 2019); and Gryphon Rue, "Calder and Sound," in Susanne Meyer-Büser, ed., *Alexander Calder: Avant-Garde in Motion*, exh. cat. (Düsseldorf: Kunstsammlung Nordrhein-Westfalen, 2013).

52 Calder, letter to Sweeney, August 5, 1943. Calder Foundation archives.

53 Perl has noted that Calder and Matter had many mutual friends and acquaintances. Perl, "Spirit Photographs," in Alexander S. C. Rower, ed., *Calder by Matter* (Paris: Cahiers d'art, 2013), 180, 182.

54 Wheeler, letter to Matter, August 6, 1943. MoMA Exhs., 242.2.

55 In the catalogue's acknowledgments Matter is thanked "as consultant in the installation and for his invaluable assistance in making special photographs," but there is no mention of Duchamp. Sweeney, *Alexander Calder*, 1943, 5. See also Marla Prather, *Alexander Calder, 1898–1976* (Washington, D.C.: National Gallery of Art, 1998), 143–44; and Rower's chronology in ibid., 149.

56 Calvin Tomkins, *Duchamp: A Biography* (New York: Henry Holt, 1996), 335, 352–53. On Art of This Century, see ibid., 329–43.

57 *First Papers of Surrealism* was held at Whitelaw Reid House, at 451 Madison Avenue, New York. Duchamp had asked Calder to contribute to the show's overall installation concept; in response, Calder made constructions of bits of twisted newspaper that were to be hung at intervals from the string that filled the gallery. Breton ultimately vetoed their inclusion, "putting an abrupt end," as André Masson said, "to what he characterized as a joke." Masson, in Perl, *Calder: The Conquest of Space; The Later Years, 1940–1976* (New York: Knopf, 2020), 58–59. On the exhibition, see Tomkins, *Duchamp*, 332–34.

58 See Susan Davidson's essay in *Tanguy, Calder: Between Surrealism and Abstraction*, exh. cat. (New York: L&M Arts, 2010).

59 Henry McBride, "The Age of Metal: Sandy Calder's Steel Constructions Tremble Poetically Like Aspens," *New York Sun*, October 29, 1943.

60 When the exhibition was extended to January 1944, *Red Petals* (1942), lent by the Arts Club of Chicago and installed in the lobby alongside *Black Beast*, was unable to remain on view for the additional months. The Arts Club of Chicago's exhibition *Calder Jewelry* was opening in December and had requested that the sculpture be sent in advance for installation. Calder made a work to replace it: *The Big Ear* (or *Elephant Ear*, as it was called in the extended exhibition checklist). MoMA Exhs., 242.2.

61 Calder donated *Devil Fish* to MoMA in 1950, and its replacement was accessioned into the collection in January 1965. When shown outdoors, it has always been accompanied by a log on the ground that supports it from below, although this was not part of the original conception. The original, now in the collection of the Calder Foundation, has had its original support returned (as seen in Matter's 1937 photographs of the work at Pierre Matisse Gallery). See *Calder by Matter*, 35, 44.

62 Calder, in *A Salute to Alexander Calder*, exh. cat. (New York: The Museum of Modern Art, 1969), 14.

63 Calder, in H. H. Arnason and Ugo Mulas, *Calder* (New York: Viking, 1971), 202.

64 Ibid.

65 Robert M. Coates, "The Art Galleries: Alexander Calder and Some Others," *New Yorker*, October 9, 1943, 91; "A Connecticut Constructivist Sets a Challenge," *Interiors*, November 1943; Edward Alden Jewell, "Calder Sculpture on Display Today," *New York Times*, September 29, 1943, 16. Calder had been called a playboy as early as 1923, and it came up in published and casual references to him throughout his career. See also Perl, *The Conquest of Space*, 153–54.

66 Clement Greenberg, "Review of Exhibitions of Alexander Calder and Giorgio de Chirico," *Nation*, October 23, 1943, 480. He went on to say, "It becomes plain, then, that the fundamental aesthetic concept setting Calder in motion is good taste—a good taste already established by others, since his shapes and especially his color stem entirely from the works of Picasso, Miró, and Arp. Good taste has its advantages, and Calder is one of our best artists. I do not think he is in the same class as David Smith, who works in a similar medium and drives from the same ancestry, but he comes next." Ibid.

67 Sweeney, *Alexander Calder*, 1943, 8–9.

68 Goodwin wrote to Sweeney on November 19, 1945, and Sweeney responded the next day, calling the work "one of Calder's most successful ventures in this field." Sweeney, letter to Goodwin, November 20, 1945. P&S MC files, "Alexander Calder, Man-Eater with Pennants, 1945."

69 Dorothy C. Miller, letter to Sweeney, October 3, 1945. P&S MC files, "Alexander Calder, Man-Eater with Pennants, 1945."

70 "All of us felt, in any case, that in spite of the best intentions and efforts on everyone's part, the Man-Eater had not been a really successful piece. As you will remember, we had commissioned you to design a mobile which would be interesting when seen from above as well as from the garden. The Man-Eater was successful when seen from above, but unfortunately few people saw it from

this angle by comparison with those who saw it at eye level." Barr, letter to Calder, June 3, 1949. P&S MC files, "Alexander Calder, Man-Eater with Pennants, 1945."

71 MoMA press release, November 1, 1946.

72 P&S MC files, "Alexander Calder, Man-Eater with Pennants, 1945."

73 Calder, letter to Barr, June 6, 1949. P&S MC files, "Alexander Calder, Man-Eater with Pennants, 1945." See also Ann Temkin and Peter Reed, "A Garden Grows," in Reed and Romy Silver-Kohn, eds., *Oasis in the City: The Abby Aldrich Rockefeller Sculpture Garden at The Museum of Modern Art* (New York: The Museum of Modern Art, 2018), 22, 65.

74 Calder, letter to René d'Harnoncourt, May 31, 1950. P&S MC files, "Alexander Calder, Man-Eater with Pennants, 1945." D'Harnoncourt succeeded Barr as the Museum's director, but he did not officially take the position until 1949, after several interim solutions.

75 The other solo exhibition was devoted to Pablo Picasso. The works of Calder and Picasso had been previously paired in the 1937 Paris Exposition.

76 Henrique Mindlin, letter to Calder, November 8, 1944. Calder Foundation archives. Reproduced in Roberta Saraiva, ed., *Calder in Brazil: The Tale of a Friendship* (São Paulo: Cosac Naify, 2006), 35.

77 Mário Pedrosa, "Calder, Sculptor of Wind Catchers," *Correio da manhã*, December 10 and 17, 1944. Reprinted in Saraiva, ed., *Calder in Brazil*, 51.

78 My thanks to Beverly Adams for her insights on this topic.

79 Barr, *What Is Modern Painting?* (New York: The Museum of Modern Art, 1943), 39. See also Jordana Mendelson's essay "The 'Mild' Manifesting of Pablo Picasso and Alexander Calder in Protest Ephemera and International Art Expositions during the Postwar," in Rower, Claire Garnier, Emilia Philippot, and Bernard Ruiz-Picasso, eds., *Calder–Picasso* exh. cat. (Paris: Musée Picasso/Skira, 2019), 68–83.

80 Calder, letter to Barr, December 9, 1954. P&S MC files, "Kelly, Ellsworth—General."

81 Miller, foreword to *16 Americans*, exh. cat. (New York: The Museum of Modern Art, 1959), 6.

82 Mrs. Simon Guggenheim provided ongoing financial support that enabled the Museum to purchase some seventy works between 1938 and 1968, including Henri Matisse's *The Red Studio* (1911) and Picasso's *Girl before a Mirror* (1932), among many others.

83 Calder, letter to Barr, May 18, 1966. P&S MC Files, "Alexander Calder, Gifts from the Artist."

84 Barr, letter to Calder, May 24, 1966. P&S MC files, "Alexander Calder, Gifts from the Artist."

85 On this handwritten list of works, Barr noted a telephone conversation with Calder on June 5, 1966, in which Calder confirmed that Barr was welcome to all the works listed. P&S MC files, "Alexander Calder, Gifts from the Artist."

86 *Calder: 19 Gifts from the Artist* opened on February 1, 1967. MoMA Exhs., 819. Many of these works were included in *A Salute to Alexander Calder*, an exhibition organized by Bernice Rose in 1969–70.

87 This work is one in a series of four, each of them signed, dated, and numbered. They are the only instance of Calder's working in this manner.

88 Jean-Paul Sartre, "Les Mobiles de Calder," in *Alexander Calder: Mobiles, Stabiles, Constellations*, exh. cat. (Paris: Galerie Louis Carré, 1946). English translation as "Calder's Mobiles," in Sartre, *The Aftermath of War*, trans. Chris Turner (Kolkata: Seagull, 2008).

89 Ibid.

90 Calder, Berkshire Museum statement, 1933.

91 Calder, "A Propos of Measuring a Mobile," unpublished manuscript, October 7, 1943. Calder Foundation archives. Reprinted on page 40 of this volume.

A Propos of Measuring a Mobile

Alexander Calder

It was more or less directly as a result of my visit to Piet Mondrian's studio in 1930, and the sight of all his rectangles of color deployed on the wall, that my first work in the abstract was based on the concept of stellar relationships. Since then there have been variations from this theme, but I always seem to come back to it, in some form or other. For though the lightness of a pierced or serrated solid or surface is extremely interesting the still greater lack of weight of deployed nuclei is much more so.

I say nuclei, for to me whatever sphere, or other form, I use in these constructions does not necessarily mean a body of that size, shape or color, but may mean a more minute system of bodies, an atmospheric condition, or even a void, i.e. the idea that one can compose *any things* of which he can conceive.

To me the most important thing in composition is *disparity*. Thus black and white are the strong colors, with a spot of red to mark the other corner of a triangle which is by no means equilateral, isosceles, or right. To vary this still further use yellow, then, later, blue. Anything suggestive of symmetry is decidedly undesirable, except possibly where an approximate symmetry is used in a detail to enhance the inequality with the general scheme.

The admission of approximation is necessary, for one cannot hope to be absolute in his precision. He cannot see, or even conceive of a thing from all possible points of view, simultaneously. While he perfects the front, the side, or rear may be weak; then while he strengthens the other facade he may be weakening that originally the best. There is no end to this. To finish the work he must approximate.

In a way it is even desirable that one face be of finer quality than the others, for this gives a head and a tail to the object and makes it more alive.

A knowledge of, and sympathy with, the qualities of the materials used are essential to proper treatment.

Stone, the most ancient, should be kept massive, not cut into ribbons. The strength must be retained.

Bronze, cast, serves well for slender, attenuated shapes. It is strong even when very slender.

Wood has a grain which must be reckoned with. It can be slender in one direction only.

Wire, rods, sheet metal have strength, even in very attenuated forms, and respond quickly to whatever sort of work one may subject them to. Contrasts in mass or weight are feasible, too, according to the gauge, or to the kind of metal used, so that physical laws, as well as aesthetic concepts, can be held to. There is of course a close alliance between physics and aesthetics.

Strength and durability in sculpture are highly desirable. However, fineness and delicacy may be even more essential to the general concept, and it will then be necessary to decide which is to control the design.

Also there is the possibility of using motion in an object as part of the design and composition. The sculpture then becomes in one sense a machine, and as such it will be necessary to design it *as* a machine, so that the moving parts shall have a reasonable ruggedness. Even those sculptures designed to be propelled by the wind are still machines, and should be considered thus, as well as aesthetically.

However the mechanical element must never control the aesthetic. Much better a poor machine and a good sculpture.

So-called Industrial Design is not a fine art. Its motive is to instill "style," i.e. a yearly trend, be it up or be it down, in our daily commodities. There are certain makes of automobiles, whose body designs of a few years ago were simpler and much better than those of 1941–42. And after accustoming ourselves to the hardy simplicity of Army trucks and Jeeps for a few years we are threatened with being subjected to cars after the war whose design will be essentially that of the 1941–42 vintage.

As mobiles are so particularly my product I feel a word or two about their measuring and handling to be fitting.

A mobile in motion leaves an invisible wake behind it, or rather, each element leaves an individual wake behind its individual self. Sometimes these wakes are contracted within each other, and sometimes they are deployed. In this latter position the mobile occupies more space, and it is the diameter of this maximum trajectory that should be considered in measuring a mobile.

In their handling, i.e. setting them in motion by a touch of the hand, consideration should be had for the direction in which the object is designed to move, and for the inertia of the mass involved. Perhaps it is necessary to be fairly familiar with at least that *type* of mobile in order to decide upon the direction in which it will best move, but a simple glance should be sufficient to estimate the inertia of the various masses. A slow gentle impulse, as though one were moving a barge is almost infallible. In any case, gentle is the word.

Alexander Calder, "A Propos of Measuring a Mobile," unpublished manuscript, October 7, 1943. Calder Foundation archives

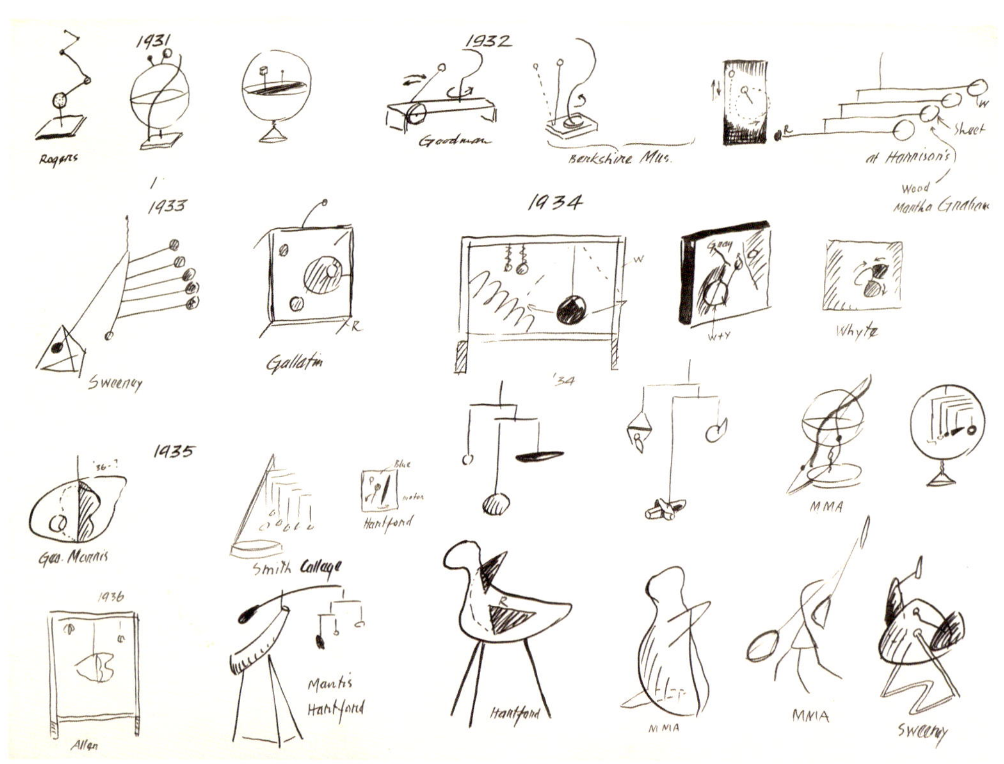

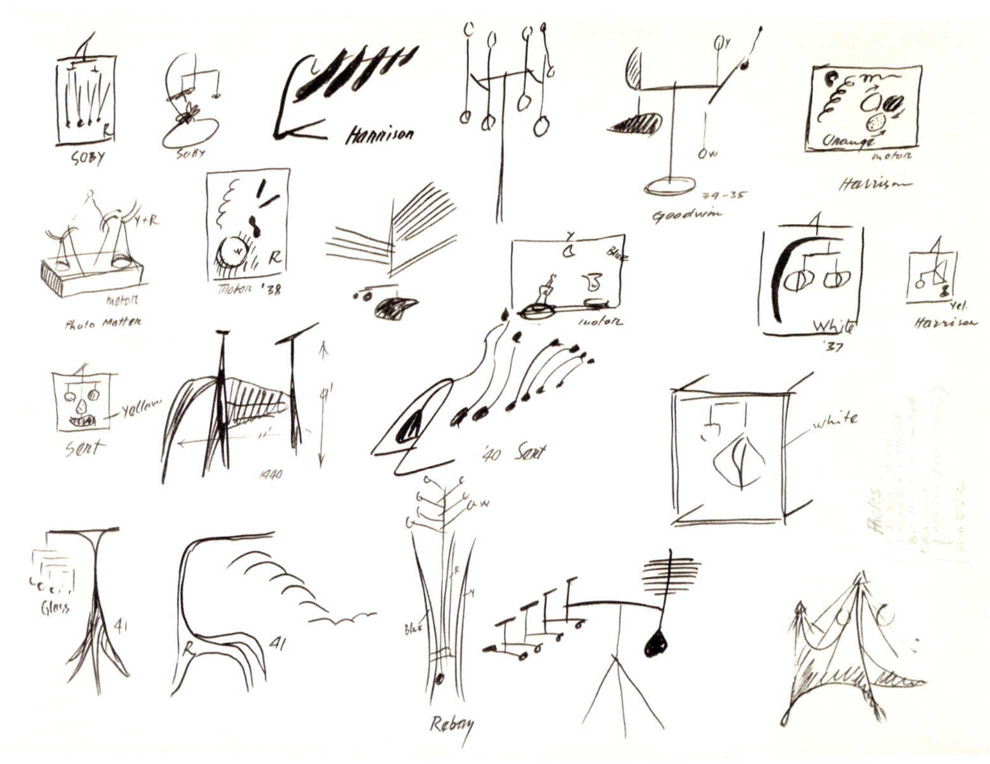

Untitled (recto and verso). 1943. Ink on paper, 21 ¾ × 30 ¼ in. (55.2 × 76.8 cm). Calder Foundation, New York. Anonymous gift

Tracing Lineages

Alexander S. C. Rower

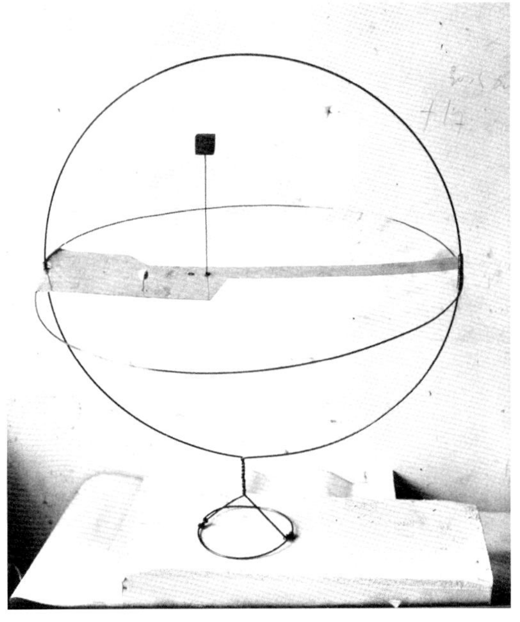

Fig. 1. **Musique de Varèse**. *1931. Wire, sheet metal, wood, and paint, 32 × 27 × 27 in. (81.3 × 68.6 × 68.6 cm). Photograph by Marc Vaux*

My Grandfather's double-sided drawing from 1943 is an extraordinary document that could have been titled *My Development in Abstract Sculpture* (opposite). The drawing, never before published or exhibited until now, attests to Calder's remarkably fertile relationship with The Museum of Modern Art. It was made in the lead-up to his retrospective that year at MoMA, probably after a conversation with James Johnson Sweeney, a longtime supporter and confidant as well as the exhibition's curator. Of the forty-eight critical works defined in the drawing, thirty-two appeared in the retrospective.[1]

The illustrations are arranged in rough chronological order, beginning at the most dramatic shift in Calder's evolution as an artist. In the late 1920s, already well known in Paris as "le roi du fil de fer" (the king of wire), he turned away from the figure and plunged into pure abstraction. "To take [this step] into the abstract field was an extremely serious departure for an artist in Calder's position at the time," Sweeney wrote in the MoMA catalogue. "Now those who had enjoyed what he had previously done so well were left completely at a loss."[2] Like Picasso, Duchamp, and Picabia, Calder bewildered audiences with his lifelong dedication to self-assassinations and reinventions.

Opening the drawing's chronology are three of the nonobjective wire objects that debuted in Calder's 1931 show at Galerie Percier in Paris; he called those first abstractions *volumes*, *vecteurs*, *densités*, and *sphériques*.[3] The third one from the left, *Musique de Varèse* (1931, fig. 1), is a mysterious and extraordinary *sphérique*, with a platform of shiny, oddly shaped sheet metal cutting through the hooped void space with two objects rising out of it. Although Calder was close friends with Edgard Varèse—the vanguard composer was known to pay visits to the artist's studios at villa Brune and rue de la Colonie—the reference to his name in the work's title remains a mystery. Maybe it's the way ephemeral light glances off the shiny metal that was the resonating characteristic; we will probably never know.

It is clear to me that this document was drawn in one sitting, entirely from memory. There are surprisingly few errors in the compositions of the sculptures, which span the period from 1931 to 1942 and cover a range of entirely new and radical objects, often created simultaneously: stabiles, motorized mobiles, standing mobiles, hanging mobiles, wall sculptures, large-scale outdoor works. There are no depictions of works from 1943; I assume that's because everybody involved with the MoMA show was very familiar with Calder's recent work. "Didn't used to name them at all, in the beginning," he once remarked. "When I wanted to talk about one of them, I'd have to draw it."[4] My grandfather drew the objects with a brush, so that they were at once lucid and buoyant. His stroke easily expresses his volumetric concerns.

Although the document delineates forty-eight objects, only forty-six are drawn; the remaining two exist as annotations to specific sketches. In the first row on the front page, next to a sketch of *Double Arc and Sphere* (1932), is an empty space meant to represent *Dancing Torpedo Shape* (1932). The bracket below indicates that both works are in the collection of the "Berkshire Mus."—a highly significant fact, as the Berkshire Museum's purchase of these two motorized mobiles in 1933 was Calder's first sale to a museum. "The two motor driven 'mobiles,'" Calder

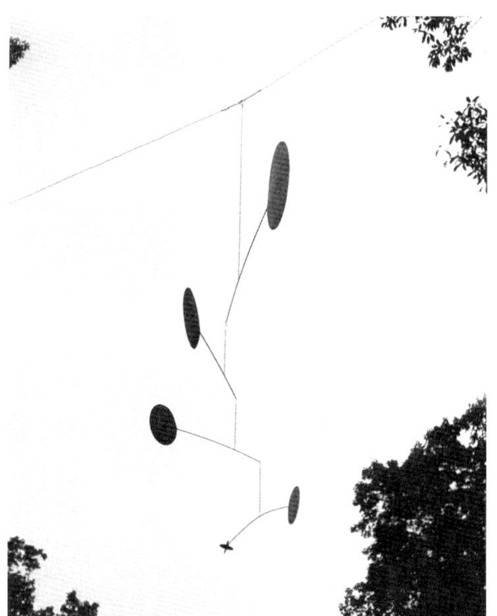

Fig. 2. Untitled. 1934. Sheet metal, rod, wire, and paint. Photograph by Herbert Matter, c. 1940

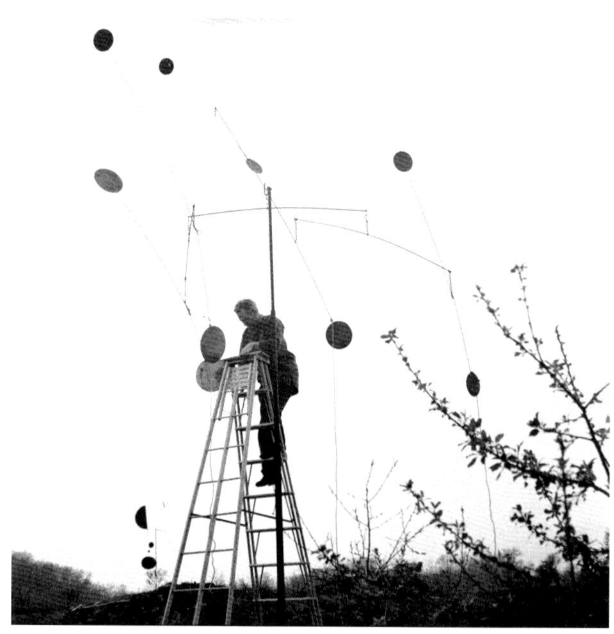

Fig. 3. Calder assembling **Five Rods and Nine Discs** *(1936), Roxbury, Connecticut, summer 1938, with* **Steel Fish** *(1934) in the distance. Photograph by Herbert Matter*

wrote in the catalogue of an exhibition at that museum in 1933, "are from among the more successful of my earliest attempts at plastic objects in motion. The orbits are all circular arcs or circles. The supports have been painted to disappear against a white background to leave nothing but the moving elements, their forms and colors, and their orbits, speeds and accelerations."[5]

At the end of the first row is the other annotated sketch. This mobile's first iteration was made in Paris in 1932, with large white spheres arranged over an impressive span of twelve feet. Another iteration, from 1934, was a sheet-metal mobile hung off the end of a very long diagonal rod "for the open air." Two photographs of this version in the outdoors were published in the English avant-garde magazine *Axis* in 1935, with an article by Sweeney. "This and the seeming care-free spirit of his essays lift his work out of the ruck of still-born, self-conscious, contemporary experimentation," Sweeney wrote. "Calder's expressions seem almost spontaneous growths."[6] On the drawing Calder identified the object as being made of sheet metal, with elements painted in white and red, and noted that it was on loan to the architect Wallace K. Harrison (fig. 2). Below the sketch, Calder wrote "wood / Martha Graham." He had worked with the choreographer on two important dances, *Panorama* (1935) and *Horizons* (1936), and a version of this mobile figured into their first collaboration.[7]

There are some inaccuracies in the drawing's timeline. It's easy to imagine Calder getting caught up drawing an object such as *Cadre rouge* (1932), for example, which appears on the second row (labeled "Gallatin"), and following its lineage through other paintings-in-motion from a few years later—a lineage that functions as a dissertation on the expanded canvas. There are telling juxtapositions, such as the pairing of *Cône d'ébène* (1933), a lumbering hanging mobile created and exhibited in Paris, with *Starfish* (1934), its sister composition, made in Roxbury, Connecticut (the fourth and fifth works in the drawing's third row). The Paris mobile is made of dense ebony; *Starfish* is markedly different in sensibility—made of bright mahogany and more extreme in its tension with gravity—but there are clear affinities. *Steel Fish* (1934) was one of Calder's first works for the outdoors, made that summer in Roxbury; it appears to the right of *Five Rods and Nine Discs* (1936) in a juxtaposition that brings to mind Herbert Matter's photograph of the works installed together on the Roxbury grounds (fig. 3).

What is absent from this timeline is also revealing. In presenting it to Sweeney, Calder left out some of his most radical efforts, which might not have a place in a usual museum setting. They include the objects that remain unfinished until momentarily recomposed and completed by the viewer, such as *Object with Red Ball* (1931; page 26, fig. 20), and the highly experimental series of theatrical ballets-without-dancers, which he worked on at various times from 1934 to 1948 (pages 94, 95). Of these, *Objects Oscillating within a Cube* (1934) is a fascinating cubic volume, with elements performing in a theatrical viewing space. This was a major effort—its model was captured in numerous photographs from the time—yet Calder left it off the list. The most significant omission from the chronology is *Small Sphere and Heavy Sphere* (1932/1933; page 22, fig. 13), a provocative interactive assemblage that included Calder's first mobile suspended from the ceiling—a constantly unfolding composition. My grandfather later regretted the omission of this work, with its sonorous aural elements; he returned to *Small Sphere and Heavy Sphere* in a letter to Sweeney on August 28, 1943, finally proposing it for the show (fig. 4).

Although this drawing represents a procession, it also leaves us with a sensation of nonlinearity; as we look up and down and across the drawing, we can map kinships among works created at different times. It's as though Calder was presenting the impracticalities of tracing a direct lineage. "This has no utility and no meaning," he once said of his work. "It is simply beautiful. It has a great emotional effect if you understand it. Of course if it meant anything it would be easier to understand, but it would not be worthwhile."[8] Even today, after decades of research, we are still only beginning to fully grasp my grandfather's intentions and transformations. This drawing suggests the drama and exhilaration of abstraction as it reaches new heights—what Calder once described as *grandeur-immense*.

object has been at Herberts and the Museum all this time, and though I hate diplomacy in museum exhibitions, I feel quite perturbed about leaving it out, as Drew really is a very good friend (although we have disagreed so much, since a long time)— and he bought it from me, and is very proud of it, etc, etc — so if it isn't too much against the grain I would like you to show it.

I forgot to show you this object

One swings the red (iron) ball in a small circle — This movement + the inertia of the rod and the length of thread develops a very complicated pattern of movement. The impedimenta — boxes, cymbal.

cord
rod
thread
cord
box
cymbal
wood ptd. white
empty
iron (red)
can

Fig. 4. Letter from Calder to James Johnson Sweeney, August 28, 1943, with an illustration of **Small Sphere and Heavy Sphere** *(1932/1933)*

1 At the time of the MoMA retrospective, only one work depicted on this drawing—*A Universe* (1934)—was in the Museum's collection. The drawing also includes the untitled standing mobile from 1934 that MoMA had acquired but exchanged for *A Universe*, and three others that entered the collection at a later date: *Devil Fish* (1937), as a gift from the artist in 1950 (and exchanged in 1964 for *Whale II*, an updated steel-plate version); *Swizzle Sticks* (1936), as part of the James Thrall Soby Bequest, in 1979; and *Spider* (1939), one of nineteen works Calder gave to MoMA in 1966. Calder labeled *Tripod* (1939) "MMA"—it was probably on extended loan to the Museum—although he later gave this work to his friends Rufus and Leslie Stillman.
2 James Johnson Sweeney, *Alexander Calder*, exh. cat. (New York: The Museum of Modern Art, 1943), 30.
3 Calder's solo show at Galerie Percier, in Paris, was titled *Alexandre Calder: Volumes–Vecteurs–Densités / Dessins–Portraits*. He further grouped his new nonobjective sculptures into four categories: *sphériques*, *arcs*, *densités*, and *mouvements arrêtés*. The following year Jean Arp gave these "arrested movements" a new name: "stabiles."
4 Calder, quoted in Phil Casey, "His Art Stumps Man of Motion," *Washington Post*, January 25, 1958.
5 Calder, *Modern Painting and Sculpture*, exh. cat. (Pittsfield, Mass.: Berkshire Museum, 1933), 3.
6 Sweeney, "Alexander Calder," *Axis* 1, no. 3 (July 1935): 19.
7 It's not clear how the mobile was used in Martha Graham's performance. In a letter from Calder to Agnes Rindge Claflin, c. 1936, he described it as being "enlarged for use by M. Graham" and residing in her New York studio.
8 Calder, quoted in "Objects to Art Being Static, so He Keeps It in Motion," *New York World-Telegram*, June 11, 1932.

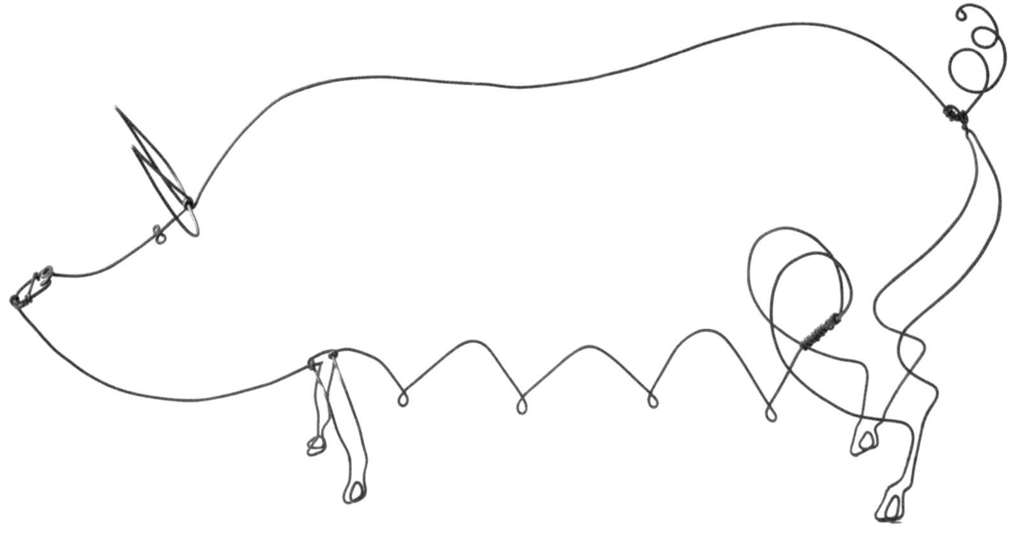

Sow. 1928
Steel wire, 7½ × 17 × 3 in. (19.1 × 43.2 × 7.6 cm)
The Museum of Modern Art, New York.
Gift of the artist

Cow (Vache). c. 1929
Steel wire, 6½ × 16 × 4¼ in. (16.5 × 40.6 × 10.8 cm)
The Museum of Modern Art, New York.
Gift of Edward M. M. Warburg

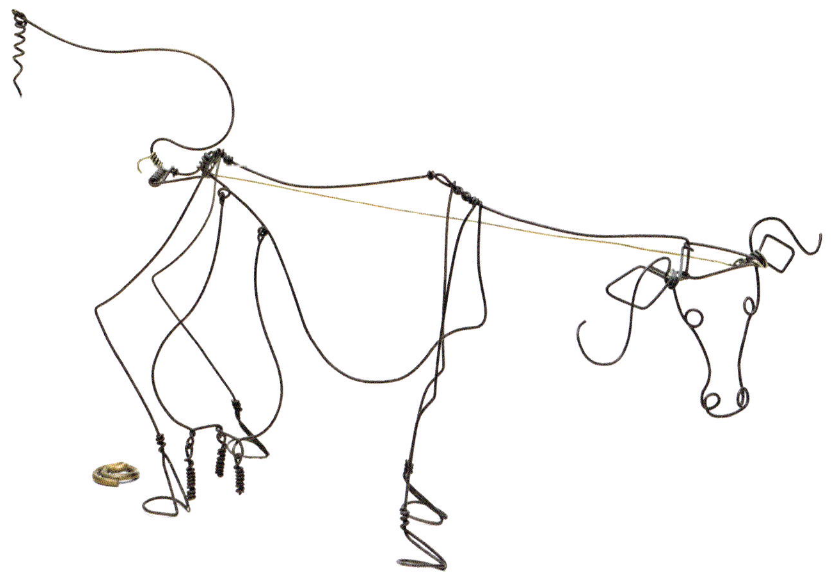

Josephine Baker III. c. 1927
Steel wire, 39 × 22 ⅜ × 9 ¾ in. (99.1 × 56.8 × 24.8 cm)
The Museum of Modern Art, New York.
Gift of the artist

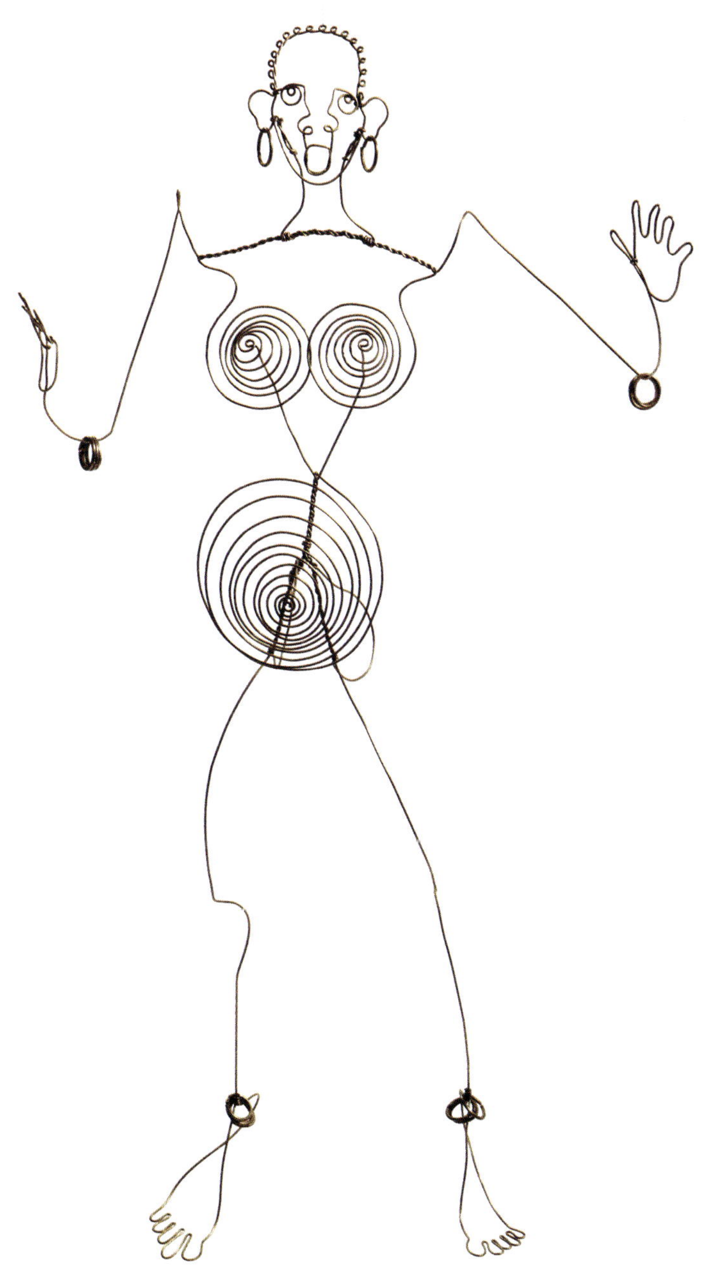

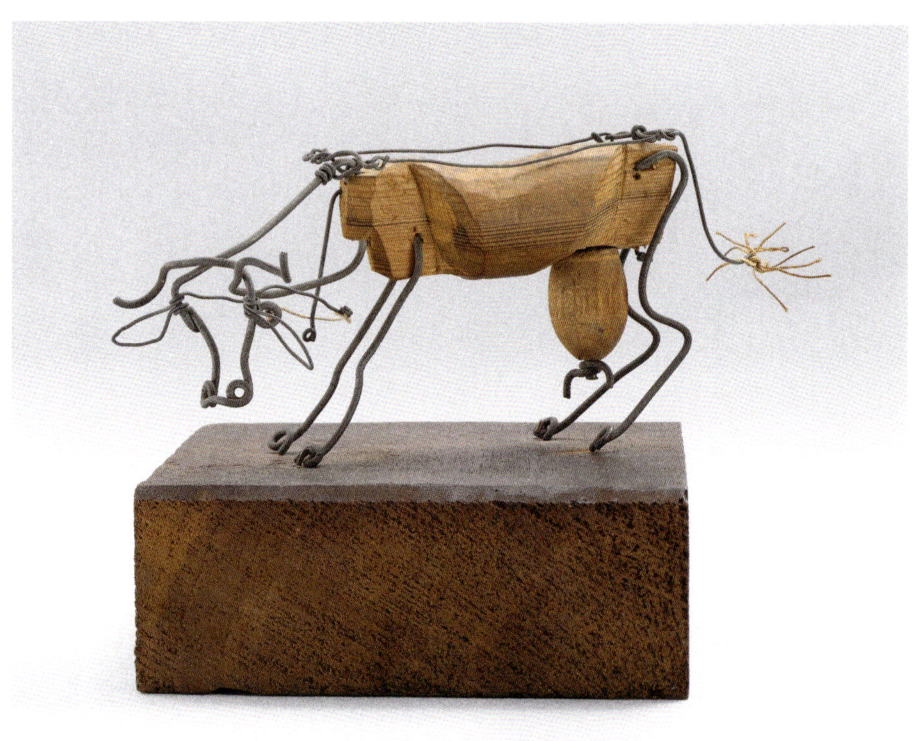

Cow. c. 1926
Wire, wood, and string, 5 ¾ × 8 ⅛ × 6 in. (14.6 × 20.6 × 15.2 cm)
The Museum of Modern Art, New York. Gift of Edward M. M. Warburg

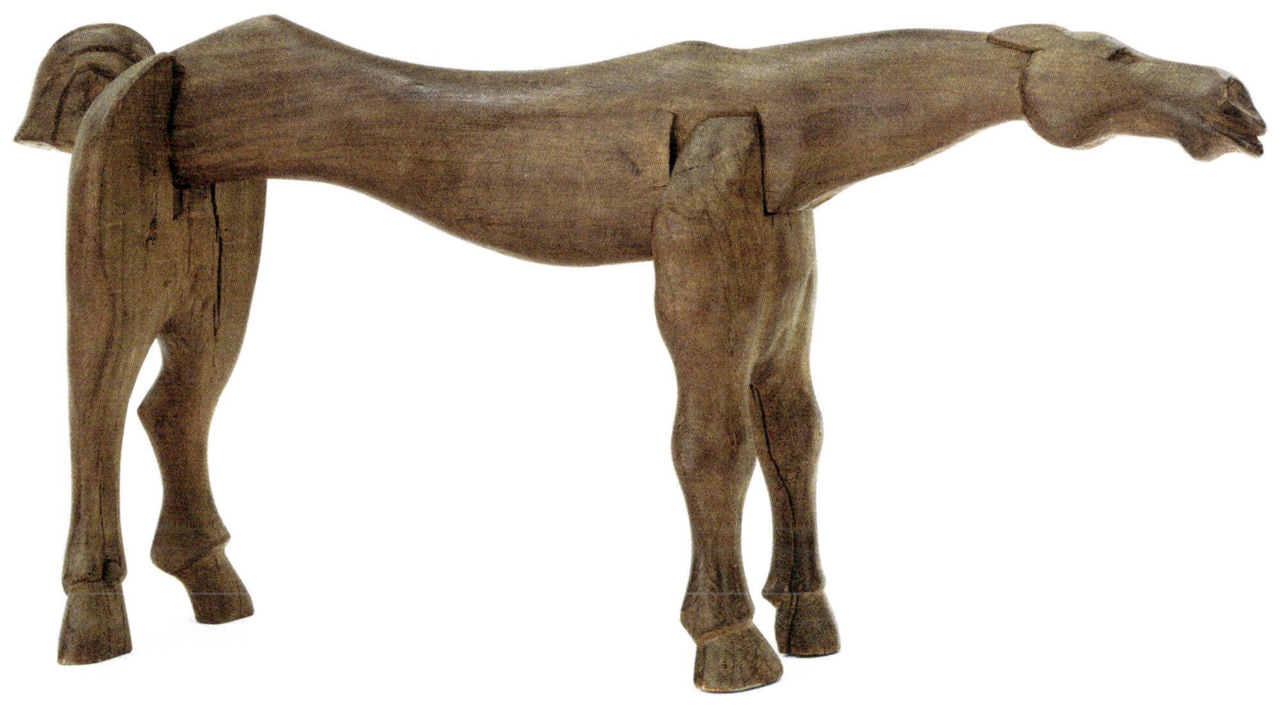

The Horse. 1928
Wood, 15 ½ × 34 ¾ × 8 ⅛ in. (39.4 × 88.3 × 20.6 cm)
The Museum of Modern Art, New York. Acquired through the Lillie P. Bliss Bequest (by exchange)

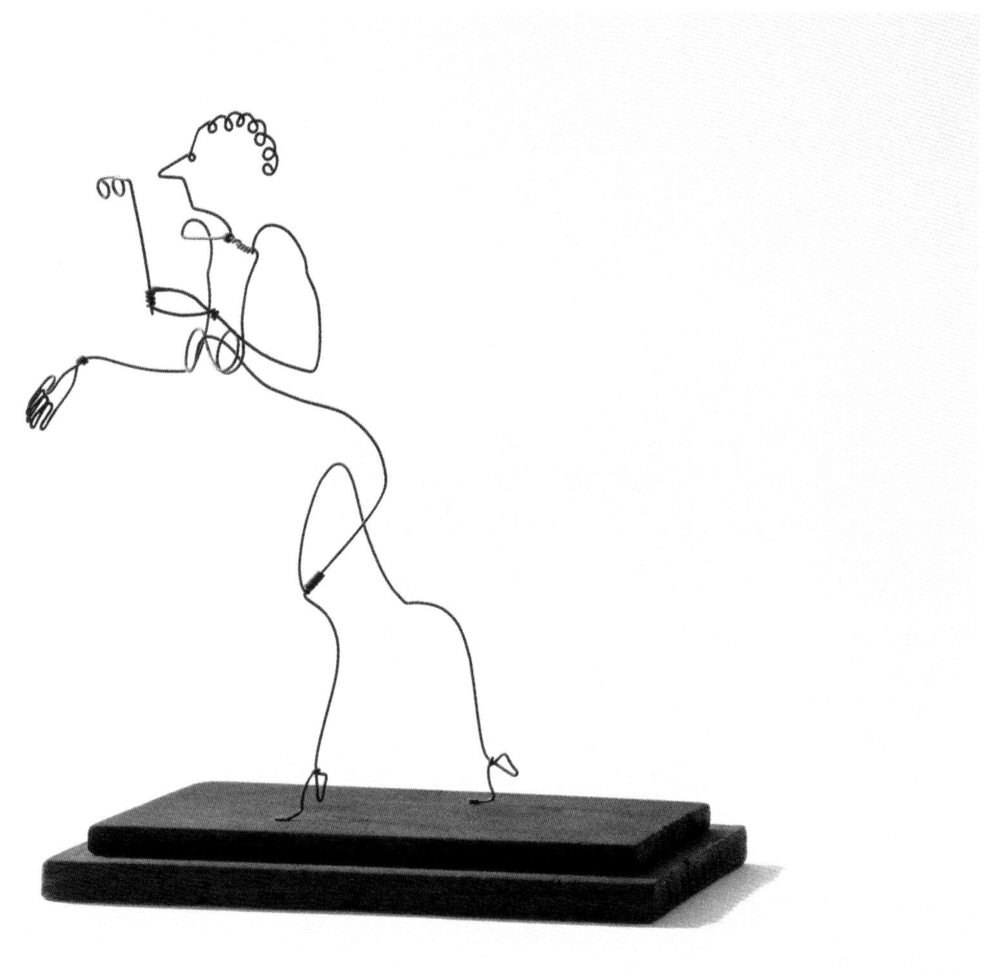

The Hostess (Dowager). 1928
Steel wire and wood, 12 × 4 × 12 in. (30.5 × 10.2 × 30.5 cm)
The Museum of Modern Art, New York. Gift of Edward M. M. Warburg

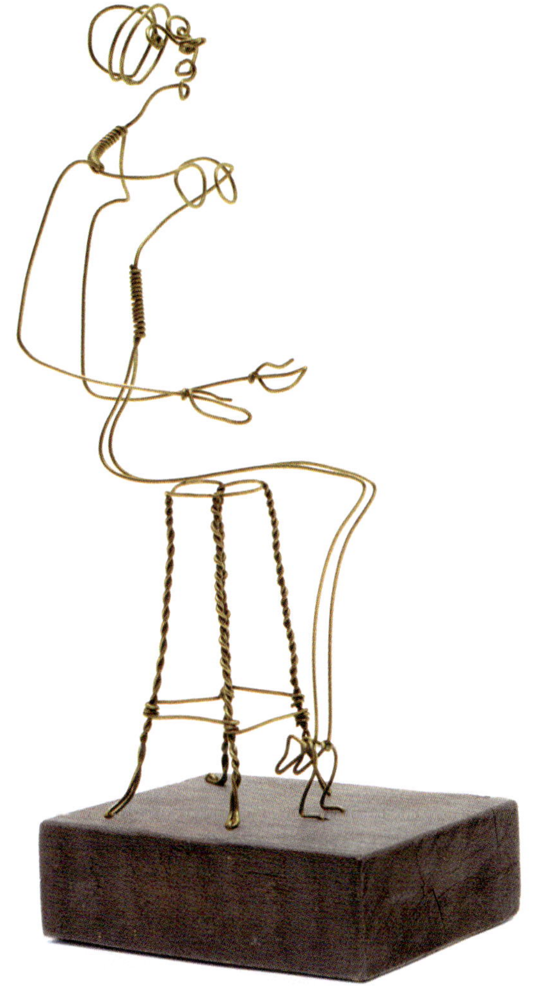

Soda Fountain. c. 1927
Steel wire and wood, 12 ½ × 6 ¼ × 3 ½ in. (31.8 × 15.9 × 8.9 cm)
The Museum of Modern Art, New York. Gift of the artist

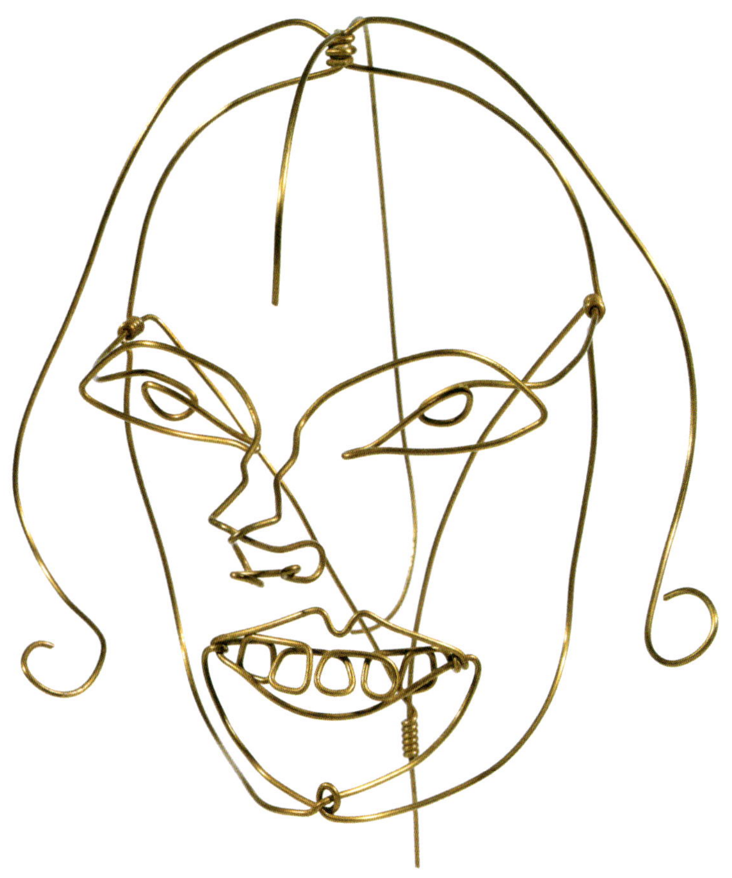

Marion Greenwood. 1928
Brass wire, 12 ⅝ × 11⅛ × 11⅜ in. (32.1 × 28.3 × 28.9 cm)
The Museum of Modern Art, New York. Gift of the artist

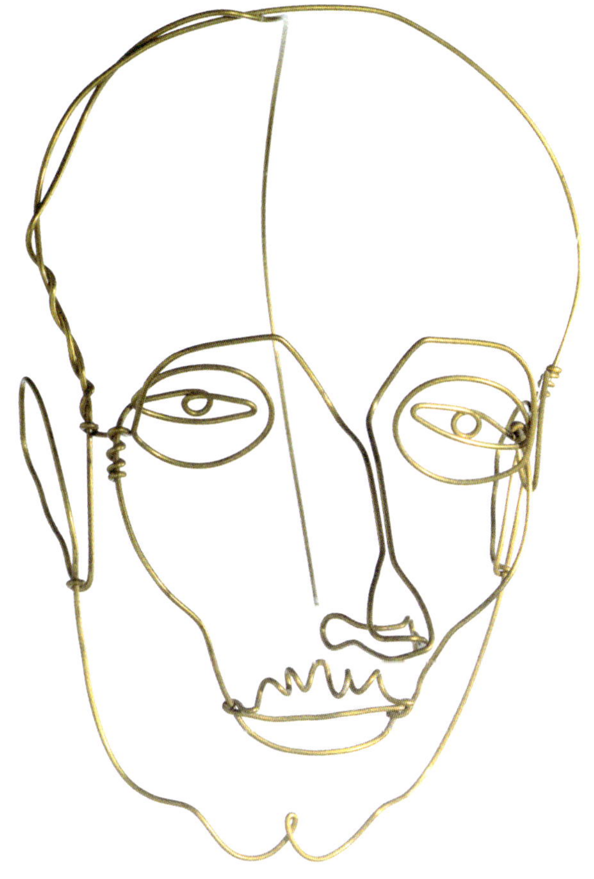

Portrait of a Man. c. 1928
Brass wire, 12 ⅞ × 8 ¾ × 13 ½ in. (32.7 × 22.2 × 34.3 cm)
The Museum of Modern Art, New York. Gift of the artist

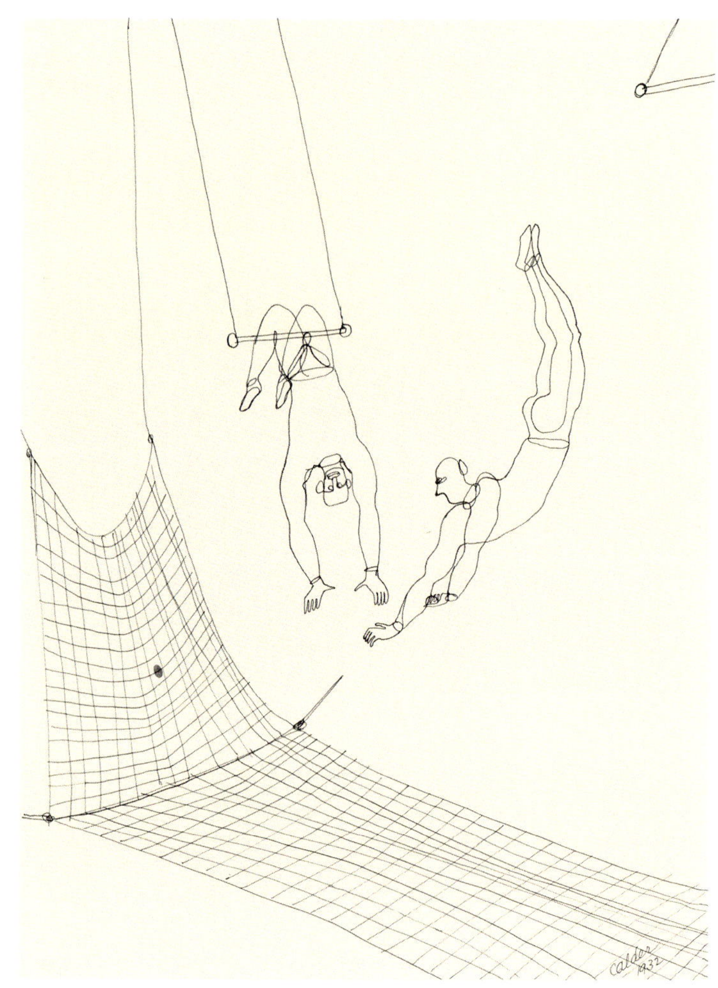

The Catch II. 1932
Ink on paper, 19 ⅛ × 14 ⅛ in. (48.6 × 35.9 cm)
The Museum of Modern Art, New York.
Gift of Mr. and Mrs. Peter A. Rübel

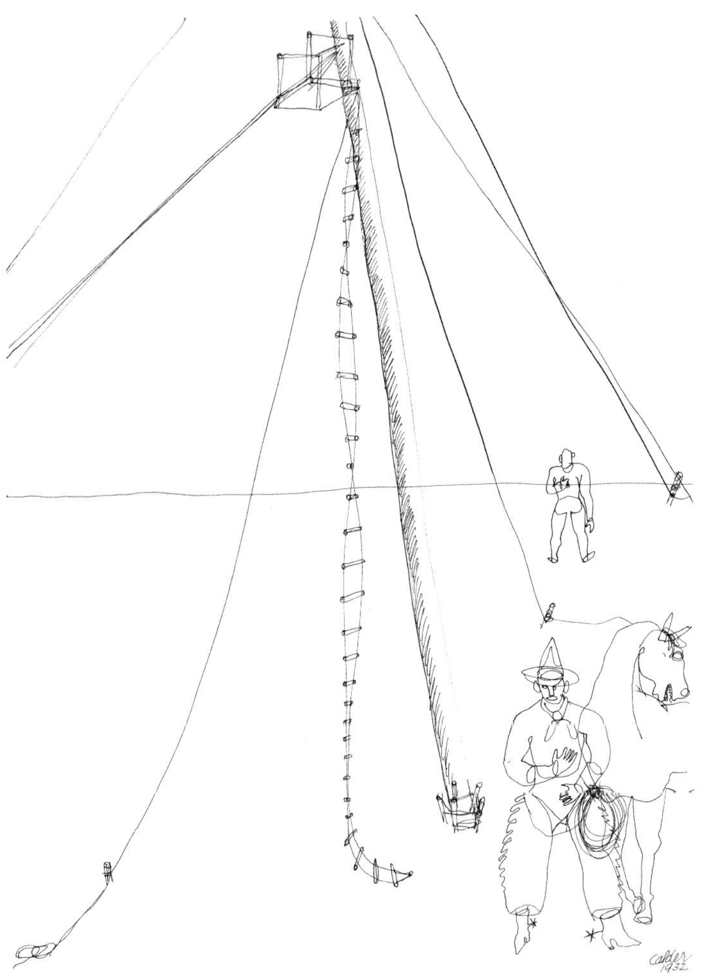

Cowboy and Rope Ladder. 1932
Ink on paper, 19 × 14 ⅛ in. (48.3 × 35.9 cm)
The Museum of Modern Art, New York.
Gift of Mr. and Mrs. Peter A. Rübel

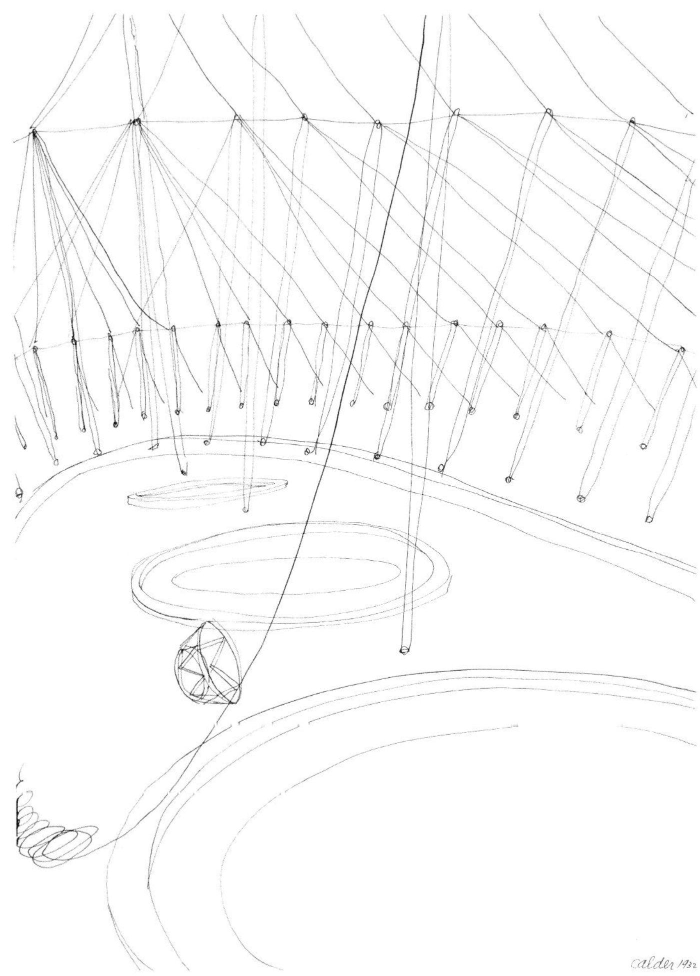

Circus Interior. 1932
Ink on paper, 19 × 14 in. (48.3 × 35.6 cm)
The Museum of Modern Art, New York.
Gift of Mr. and Mrs. Peter A. Rübel

were but answerable to this branching head, I can but think how I should defy all my enemies. The words were hardly out of his mouth, but he discover'd a pack of dogs coming full-cry towards him. Away he scours cross the fields, casts off the dogs, and gains a wood; but pressing thorough a thicket, the bushes held him by the horns, till the hounds came in, and pluck'd him down. The last thing he said was this. What an unhappy fool was I, to take my friends for my enemies, and my enemies for my friends! I trusted to my head, that has betray'd me, and I found fault with my leggs, that would otherwise have brought me off.

THE MORAL

He that does not thoroughly know himself, may be well allowed to make a false judgment upon other matters that most nearly concern him.

A LYON, ASS AND FOX

AS an ass and a fox were together upon the ramble, a lyon meets them by the way. The foxes heart went pit-a-pat; but however, to make the best of a bad game, he sets a good face on't, and up he goes to the lyon. Sir, says he; I am come to offer your majesty a piece of service, and I'll cast myself upon your honour for my own security. If you have a mind to my companion, the ass here, 'tis but a word speaking, and you shall have him immediately. Let it be done then says the lyon. So the fox trepann'd the ass into the toyl, and the lyon, when he found he had him sure, began with the fox himself, and after that, for his second course, made up his meal with the other.

THE MORAL

We love the treason, but we hate the traytor.

2

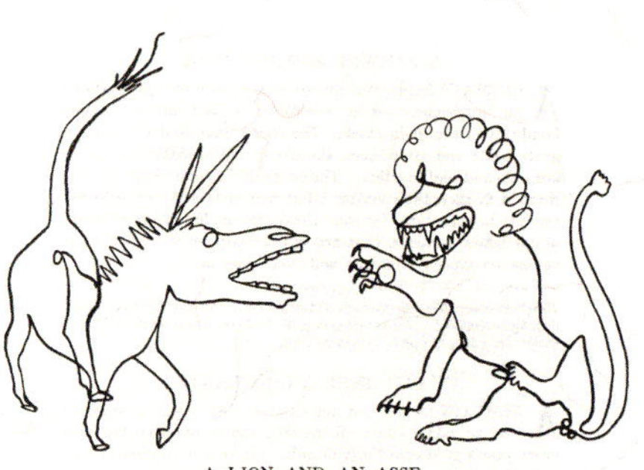

A LION AND AN ASSE

AN asse was so hardy once, as to fall a mopping and braying at a lyon. The lyon began at first to shew his teeth, and to stomack the affront; but upon second thoughts; well! (says he) jeer on, and be an asse still. Take notice only by the way, that 'tis the baseness of your character that has sav'd your carcass.

THE MORAL

It is below the dignity of a great mind to entertain contests with people that have neither quality nor courage: beside the folly of contending with a miserable wretch, where the very competition is a scandal.

3

JUPITER AND A HERDS-MAN

A HERDS-MAN that had lost a calf out of his grounds, sent up and down after it; and when he could get no tydings on't, he betook himself at last to his prayers, according to the custom of the world, when people are brought to a forc'd put. Great Jupiter (says he) do but shew me the thief that stole my calf, and I'll give thee a kid for a sacrifice. The word was no sooner pass'd; but the thief appear'd; which was indeed a lyon. This discovery put him to his prayers once again. I have not forgotten my vow, says he, but now thou hast brought me to the thief, I'll make that kid a bull, if thou'lt but set me quit of him again.

THE MORAL

We cannot be too careful and considerate what vows, and promises we make; for the very granting of our prayers turns many times to our utter raine.

A PIGEON AND A PICTURE

A PIGEON saw the picture of a glass with water in't, and taking it to be water indeed, flew rashly and eagerly up to't, for a soup to quench her thirst. She broke her feathers against the frame of the picture, and falling to the ground upon't, was taken up by the by-standers.

THE MORAL

Rash men do many things in hast that they repent of at leisure.

A BOY AND COCKLES

SOME people were roasting of cockles, and they hiss'd in the fire. Well (says a block-headed boy) these are villanous creatures sure, to sing when their houses are a-fire over their heads.

THE MORAL

Nothing can be well that's out of season.

6

A FOX AND A CARV'D HEAD

AS a fox was rummidging among a great many carv'd figures, there was one very extraordinary piece among the rest. He took it up, and when he had consider'd it a while, well, (says he) what pity 'tis, that so exquisite an outside of a head should not have one grain of sense in't.

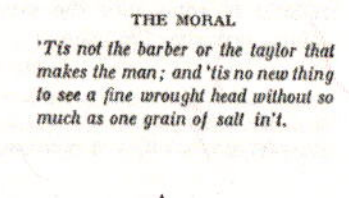

THE MORAL

'Tis not the barber or the taylor that makes the man; and 'tis no new thing to see a fine wrought head without so much as one grain of salt in't.

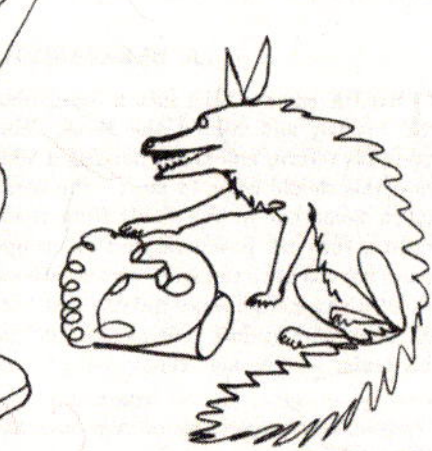

7

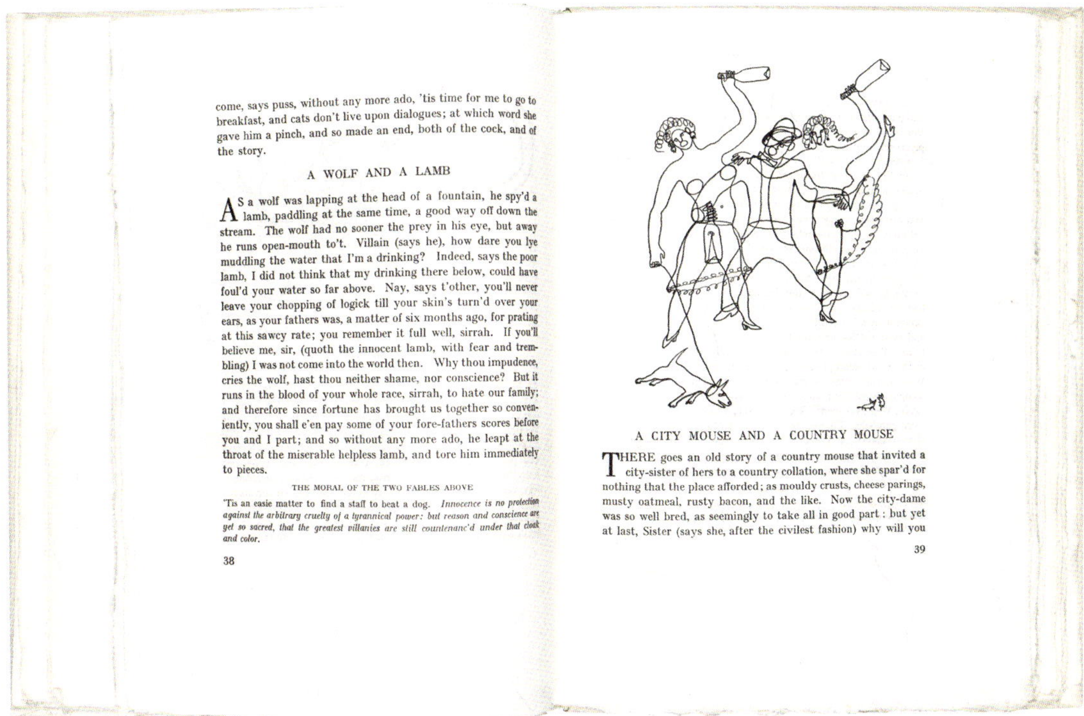

come, says puss, without any more ado, 'tis time for me to go to breakfast, and cats don't live upon dialogues; at which word she gave him a pinch, and so made an end, both of the cock, and of the story.

A WOLF AND A LAMB

As a wolf was lapping at the head of a fountain, he spy'd a lamb, paddling at the same time, a good way off down the stream. The wolf had no sooner the prey in his eye, but away he runs open-mouth to't. Villain (says he), how dare you lye muddling the water that I'm a drinking? Indeed, says the poor lamb, I did not think that my drinking there below, could have foul'd your water so far above. Nay, says t'other, you'll never leave your chopping of logick till your skin's turn'd over your ears, as your fathers was, a matter of six months ago, for prating at this sawcy rate; you remember it full well, sirrah. If you'll believe me, sir, (quoth the innocent lamb, with fear and trembling) I was not come into the world then. Why thou impudence, cries the wolf, hast thou neither shame, nor conscience? But it runs in the blood of your whole race, sirrah, to hate our family; and therefore since fortune has brought us together so conveniently, you shall e'en pay some of your fore-fathers scores before you and I part; and so without any more ado, he leapt at the throat of the miserable helpless lamb, and tore him immediately to pieces.

THE MORAL OF THE TWO FABLES ABOVE

'Tis an easie matter to find a staff to beat a dog. *Innocence is no protection against the arbitrary cruelty of a tyrannical power: but reason and conscience are yet so sacred, that the greatest villanies are still countenanc'd under that cloak and color.*

38

A CITY MOUSE AND A COUNTRY MOUSE

THERE goes an old story of a country mouse that invited a city-sister of hers to a country collation, where she spar'd for nothing that the place afforded; as mouldy crusts, cheese parings, musty oatmeal, rusty bacon, and the like. Now the city-dame was so well bred, as seemingly to take all in good part: but yet at last, Sister (says she, after the civilest fashion) why will you

39

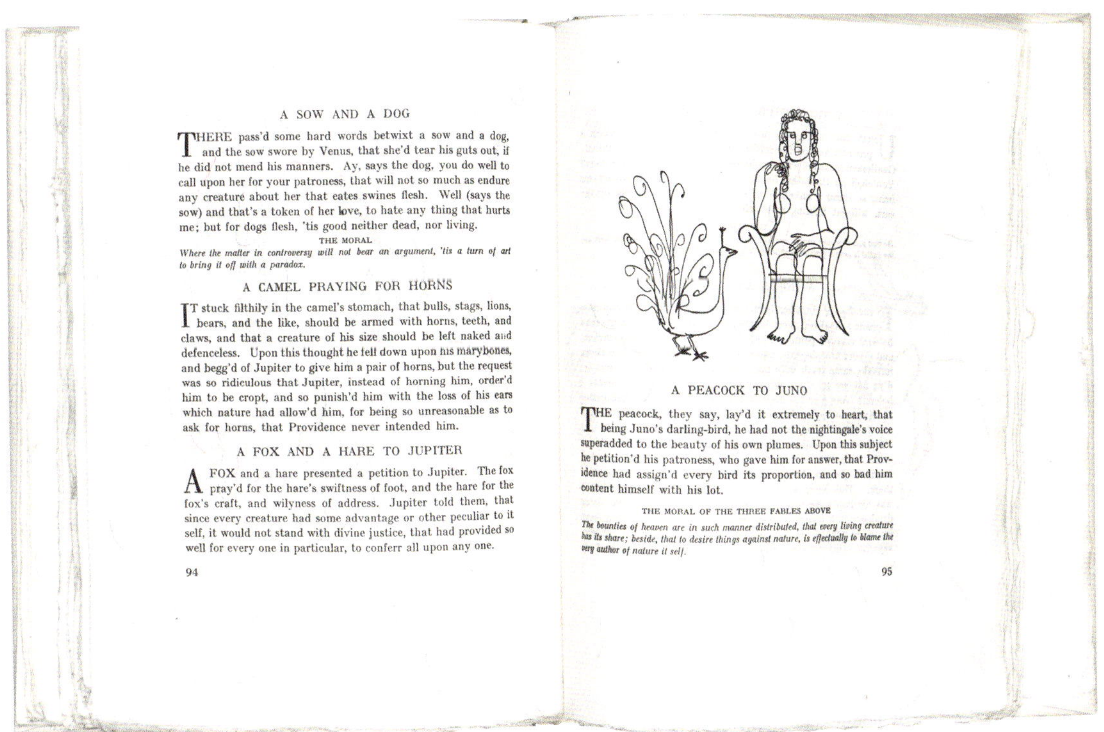

A SOW AND A DOG

THERE pass'd some hard words betwixt a sow and a dog, and the sow swore by Venus, that she'd tear his guts out, if he did not mend his manners. Ay, says the dog, you do well to call upon her for your patroness, that will not so much as endure any creature about her that eates swines flesh. Well (says the sow) and that's a token of her love, to hate any thing that hurts me; but for dogs flesh, 'tis good neither dead, nor living.

THE MORAL

Where the matter in controversy will not bear an argument, 'tis a turn of art to bring it off with a paradox.

A CAMEL PRAYING FOR HORNS

IT stuck filthily in the camel's stomach, that bulls, stags, lions, bears, and the like, should be armed with horns, teeth, and claws, and that a creature of his size should be left naked and defenceless. Upon this thought he fell down upon his marybones, and begg'd of Jupiter to give him a pair of horns, but the request was so ridiculous that Jupiter, instead of horning him, order'd him to be cropt, and so punish'd him with the loss of his ears which nature had allow'd him, for being so unreasonable as to ask for horns, that Providence never intended him.

A FOX AND A HARE TO JUPITER

A FOX and a hare presented a petition to Jupiter. The fox pray'd for the hare's swiftness of foot, and the hare for the fox's craft, and wilyness of address. Jupiter told them, that since every creature had some advantage or other peculiar to it self, it would not stand with divine justice, that had provided so well for every one in particular, to confer all upon any one.

94

A PEACOCK TO JUNO

THE peacock, they say, lay'd it extremely to heart, that being Juno's darling-bird, he had not the nightingale's voice superadded to the beauty of his own plumes. Upon this subject he petition'd his patroness, who gave him for answer, that Providence had assign'd every bird its proportion, and so bad him content himself with his lot.

THE MORAL OF THE THREE FABLES ABOVE

The bounties of heaven are in such manner distributed, that every living creature has its share; beside, that to desire things against nature, is effectually to blame the very author of nature it self.

95

Fables of Aesop. 1931
Illustrated book with fifty-two letterpress prints and one supplementary drawing (ink on paper), page (each, irreg.): 9 13⁄16 × 7 11⁄16 in. (24.9 × 19.5 cm); drawing: 9 13⁄16 × 7 1⁄4 in. (24.9 × 18.4 cm); overall (closed): 10 3⁄16 × 7 7⁄8 × 3⁄4 in. (25.9 × 20 × 2 cm)

Publisher: Harrison of Paris, Paris; Minton Balch and Company, New York. Printer: Aimé Jourde. Edition: 665
The Museum of Modern Art, New York. Gift of Monroe Wheeler

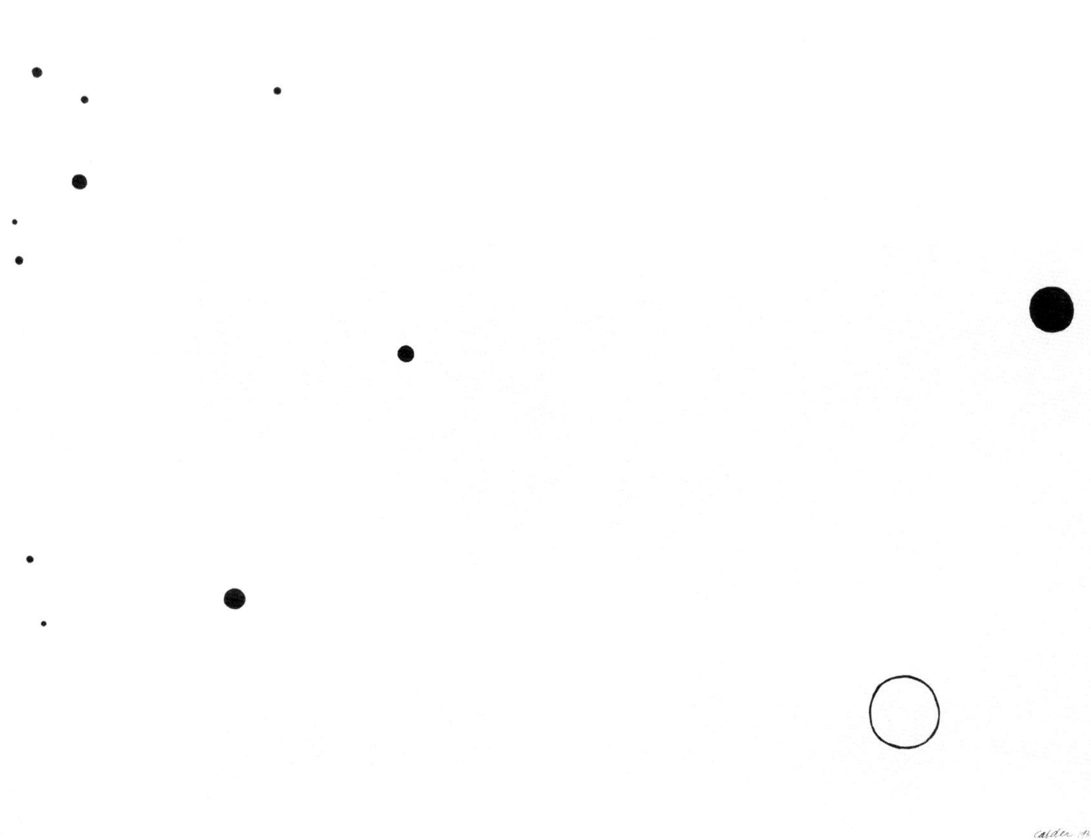

Many. 1931
Ink on paper, 19 ⅝ × 25 ½ in. (49.9 × 64.8 cm)
The Museum of Modern Art, New York.
Gift of Mr. and Mrs. Klaus G. Perls

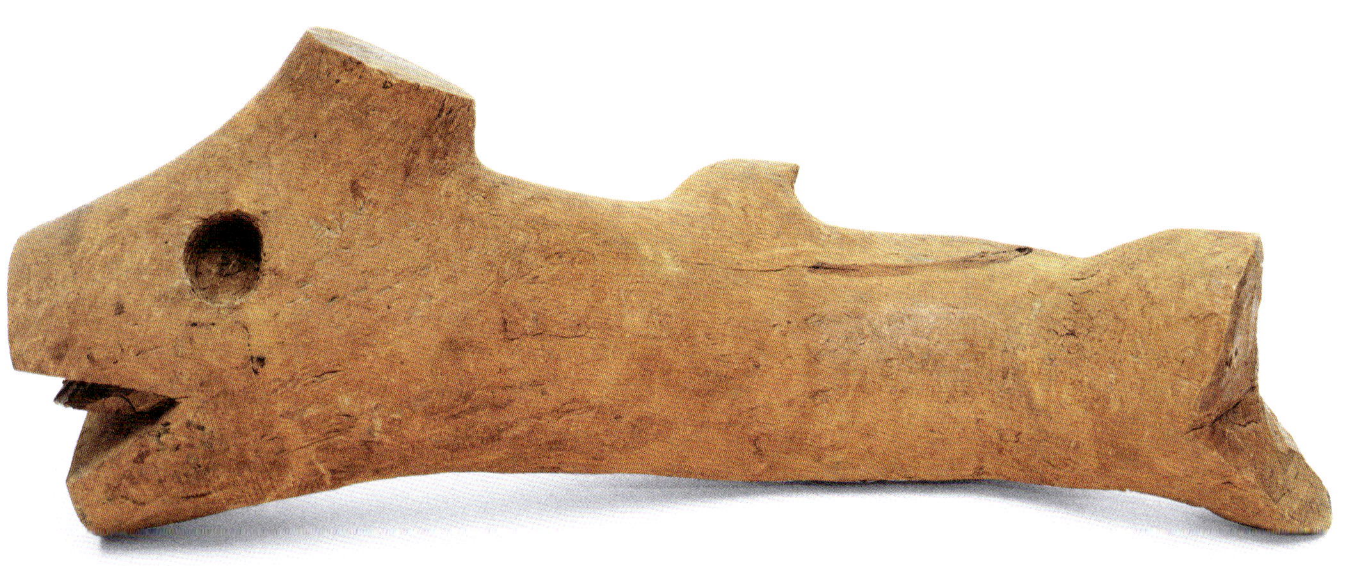

Shark Sucker. 1930
Wood, 10 ¾ × 30 ⅞ × 10 ¼ in. (27.3 × 78.4 × 26 cm)
The Museum of Modern Art, New York.
Gift of the artist

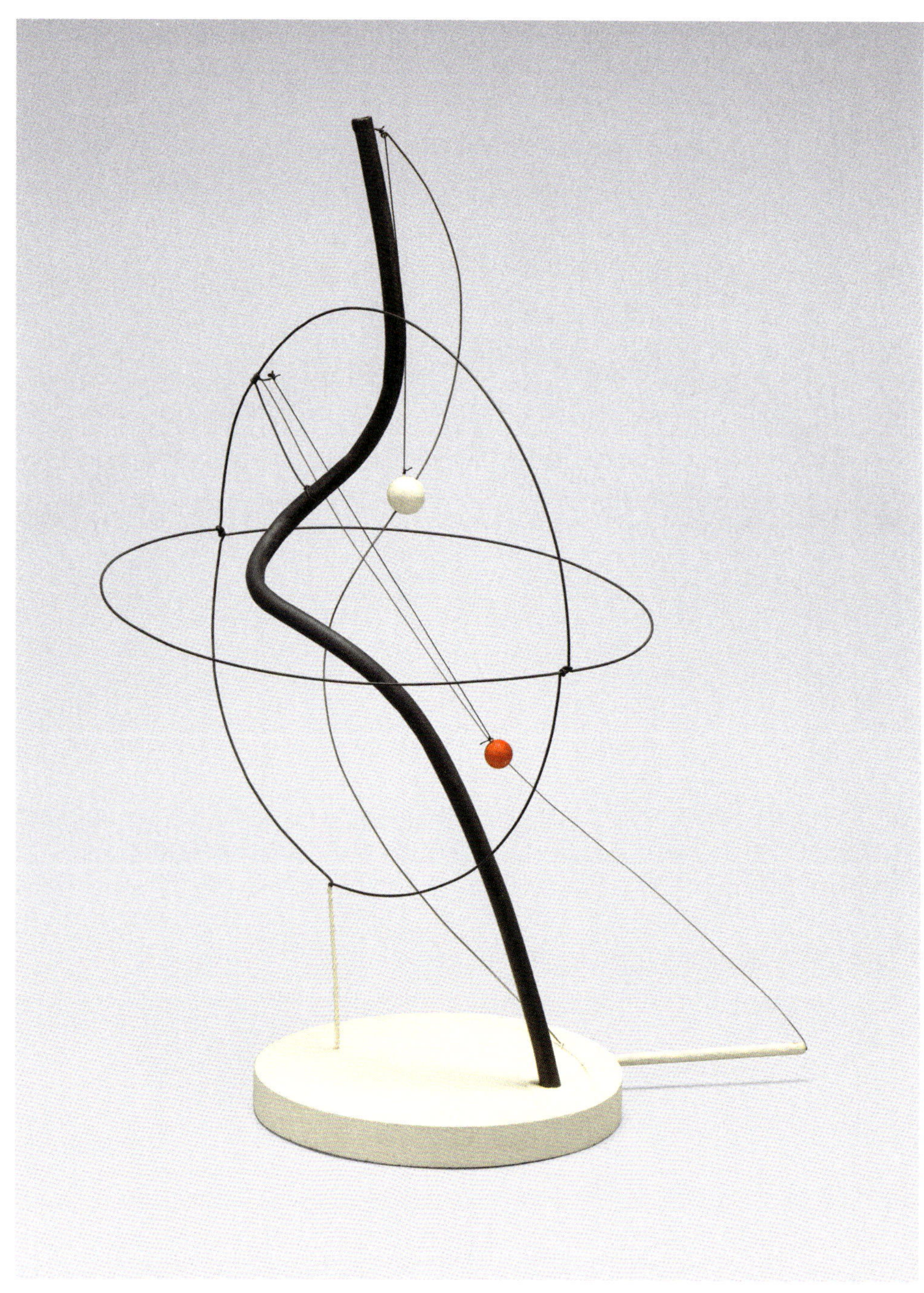

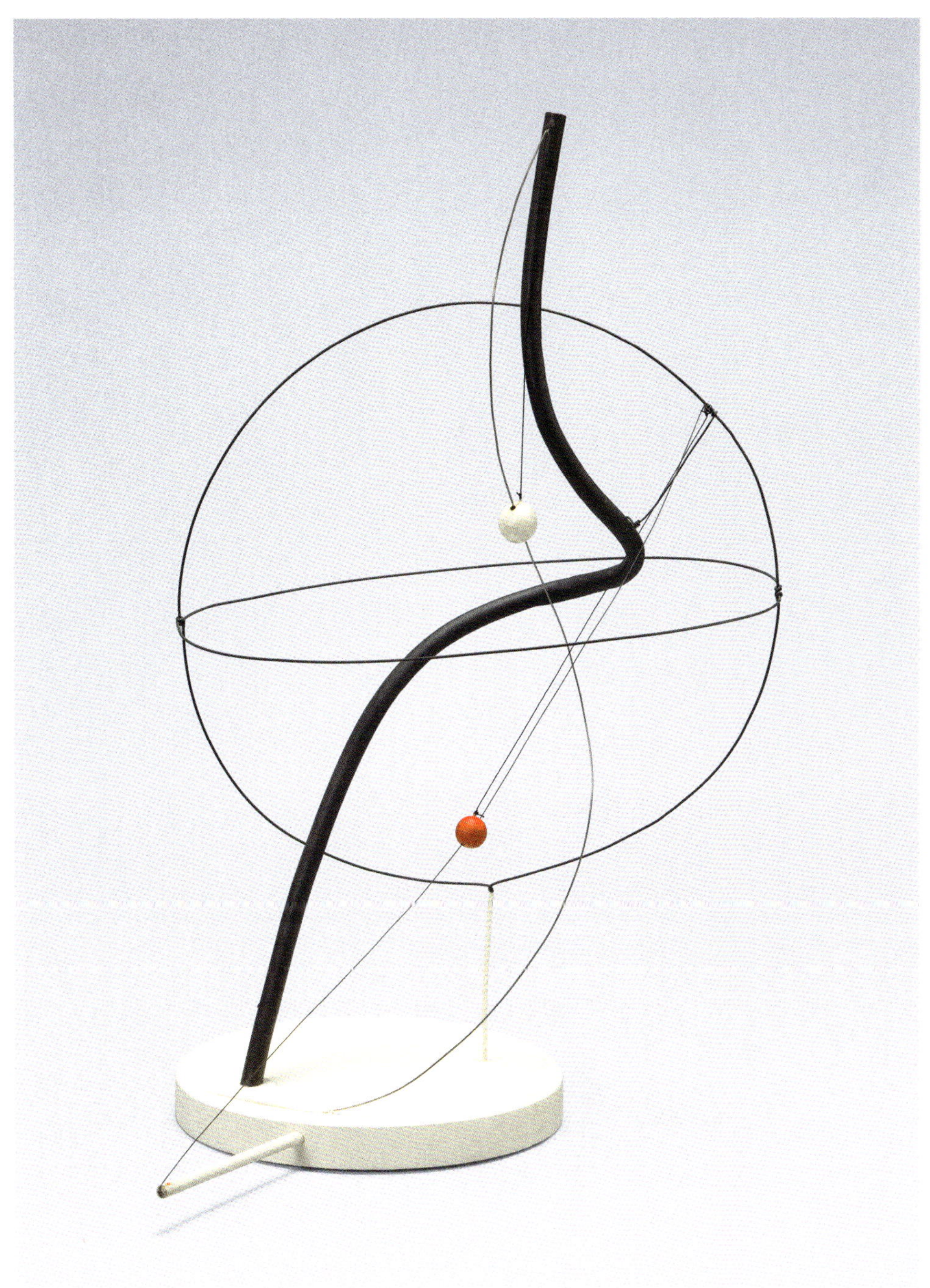

A Universe. 1934
Iron pipe, steel wire, wood, paint, and thread, with motor, 40 ½ × 30 in. (102.9 × 76.2 cm)
The Museum of Modern Art, New York.
Gift of Abby Aldrich Rockefeller (by exchange)

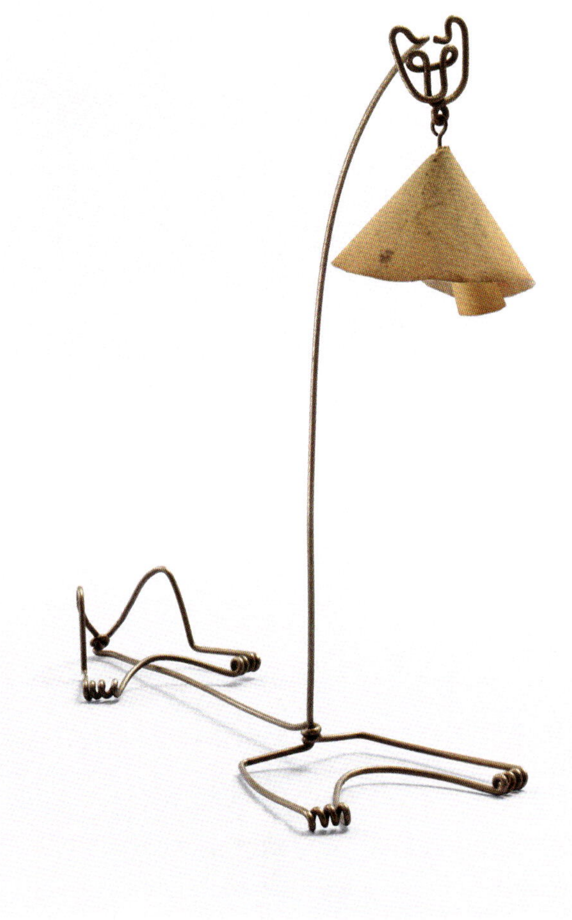

Cat Lamp. 1928
Steel wire and paper, 8 ¾ × 10 ⅛ × 3 ⅛ in. (22.2 × 25.7 × 7.9 cm)
The Museum of Modern Art, New York. Gift of the artist

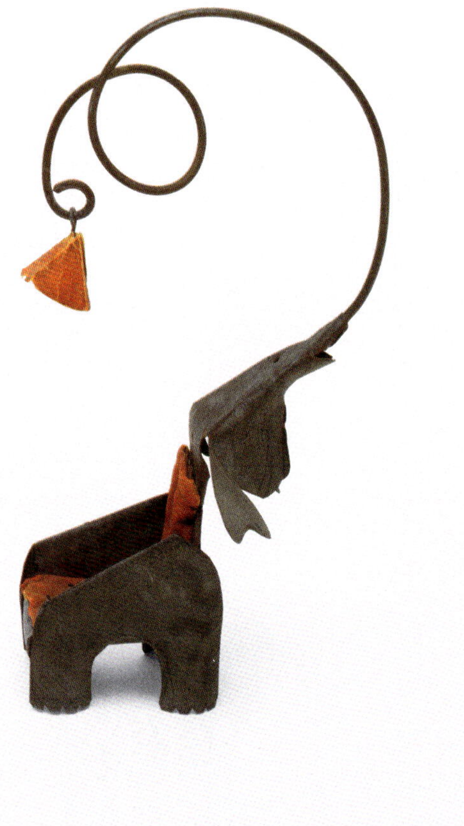

Elephant Chair with Lamp (**The Elephant Hunter's Chair**). 1928
Galvanized steel, steel wire, lead, cloth, paper, and paint,
7 ⅞ × 3 ½ × 4 ⅛ in. (20 × 8.9 × 10.5 cm)
The Museum of Modern Art, New York. Gift of the artist

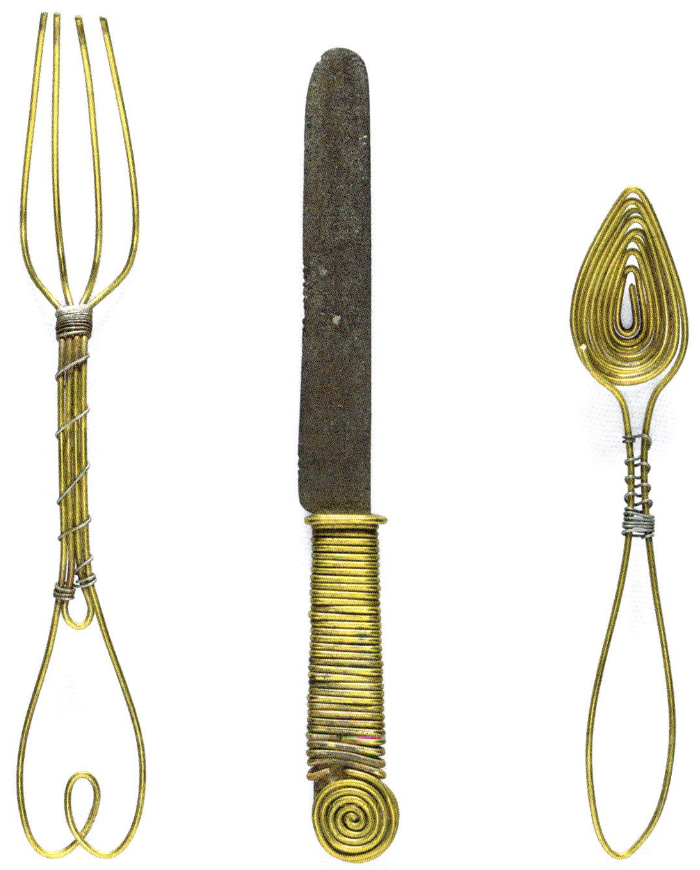

Cutlery. 1936
Brass, iron, and silver, fork: 9 ¾ × 1 ¾ × 1 ½ in. (24.8 × 4.5 × 3.8 cm);
knife: 9 ½ × 1 × ½ in. (24.1 × 2.5 × 1.3 cm); spoon: 7 ¾ × 1 ½ × ½ in. (19.7 × 3.8 × 1.3 cm)
The Museum of Modern Art, New York. James Thrall Soby Bequest

Well Sweep. 1935
Steel, stainless steel, and paint, 22 ft. (670.6 cm) high × 15 ft. (475.2 cm) diam.
The Museum of Modern Art, New York. James Thrall Soby Bequest
Commissioned by James Thrall Soby
Installation view, Farmington, Connecticut, 1936. Photograph by
James Thrall Soby

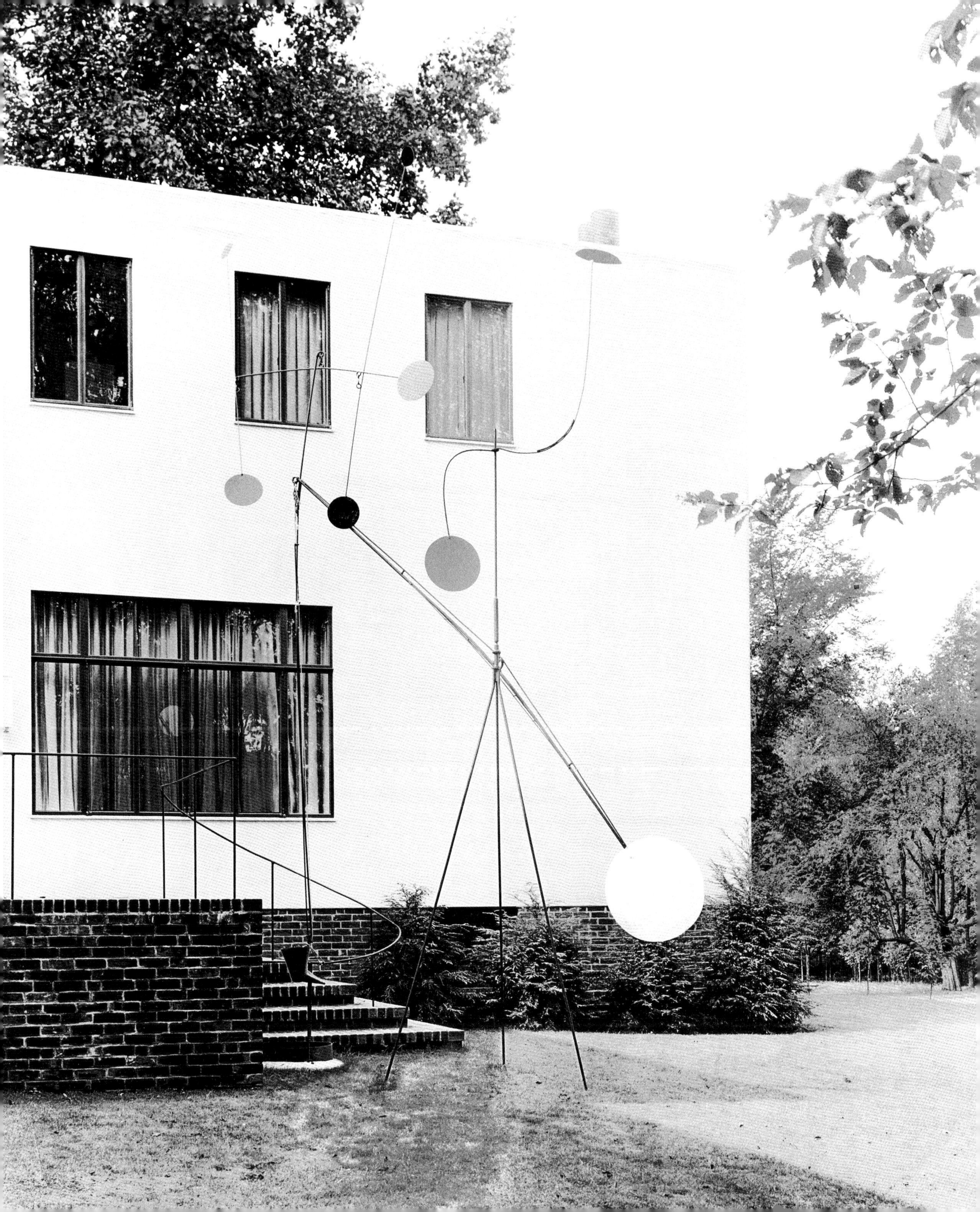

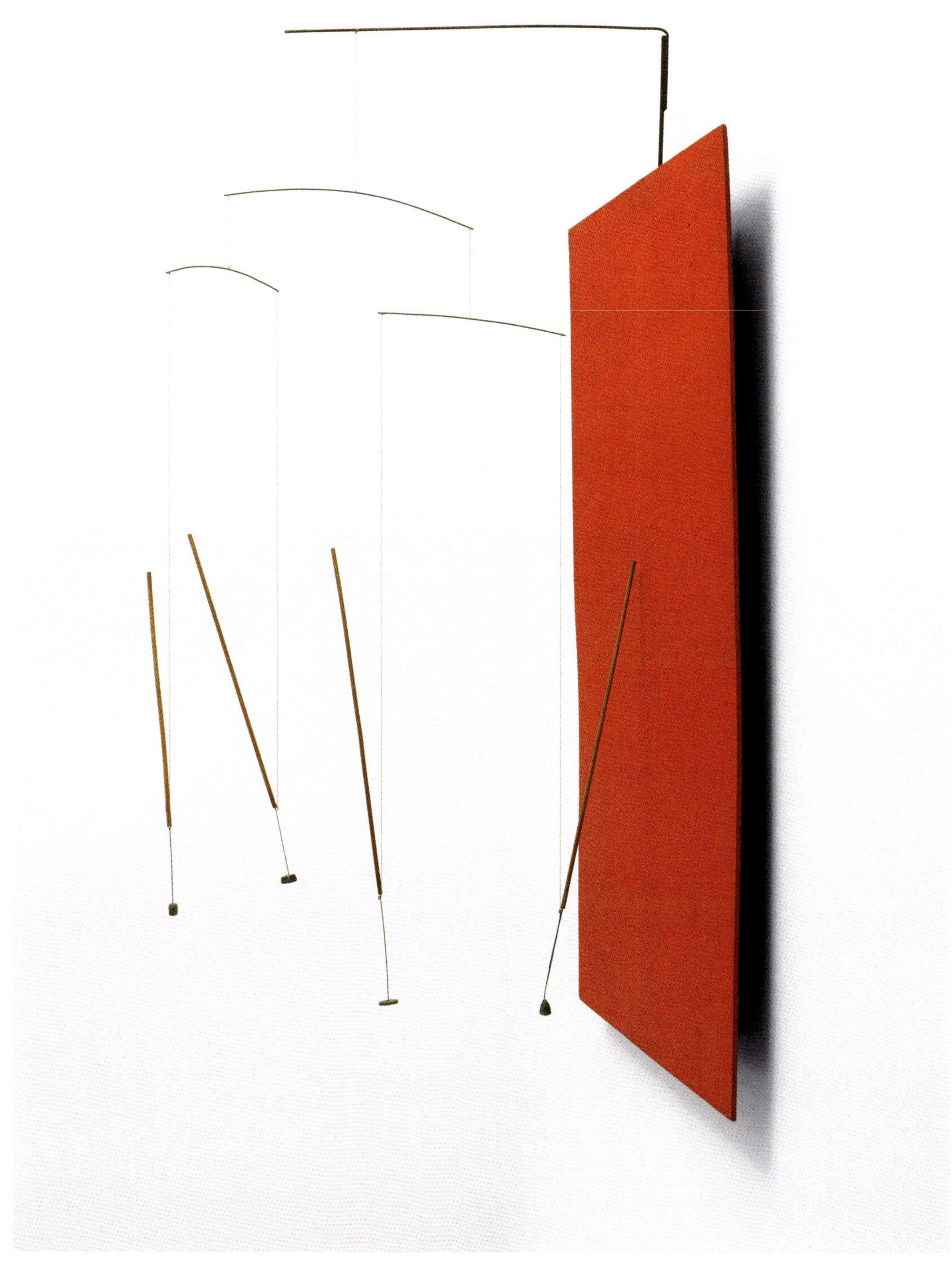

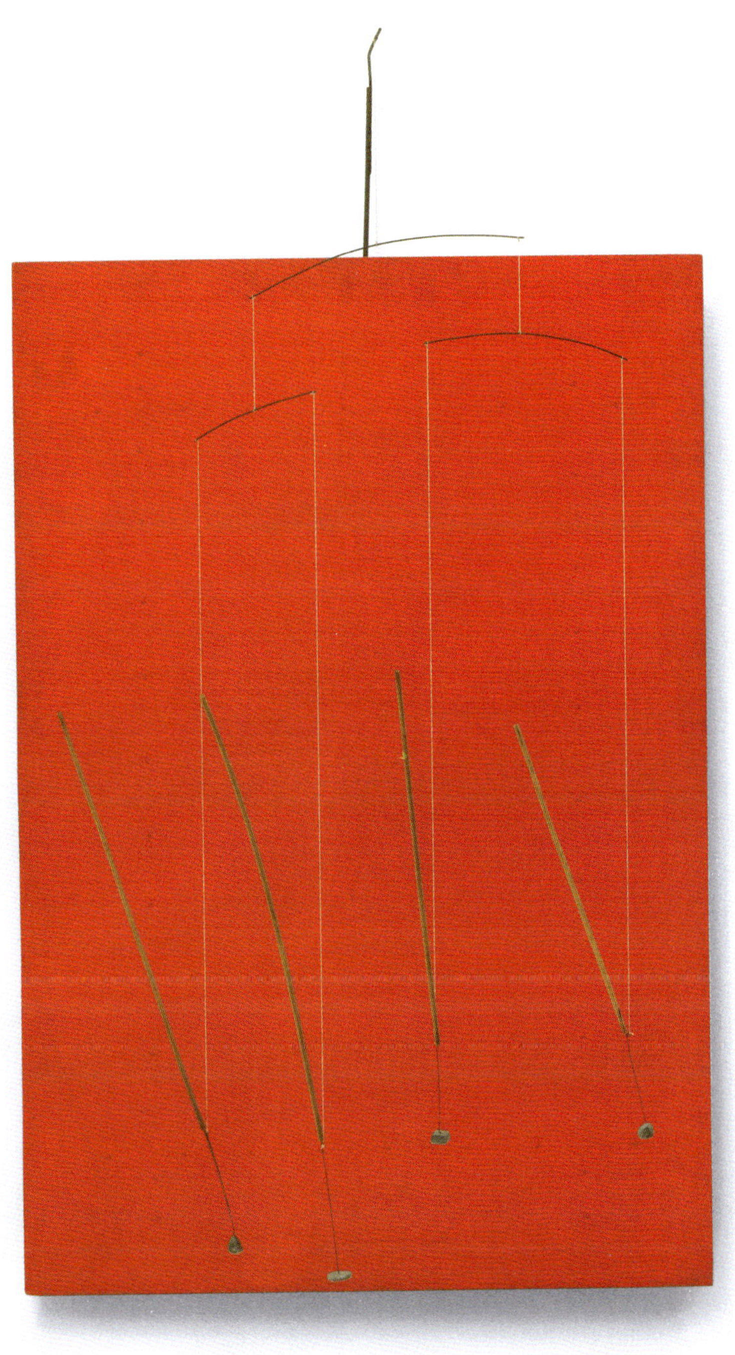

Swizzle Sticks. 1936
Plywood, paint, steel rod, string, wood, wire, and lead,
56⅜ × 45⅝ × 48½ in. (143.2 × 115.9 × 123.2 cm)
The Museum of Modern Art, New York.
James Thrall Soby Bequest

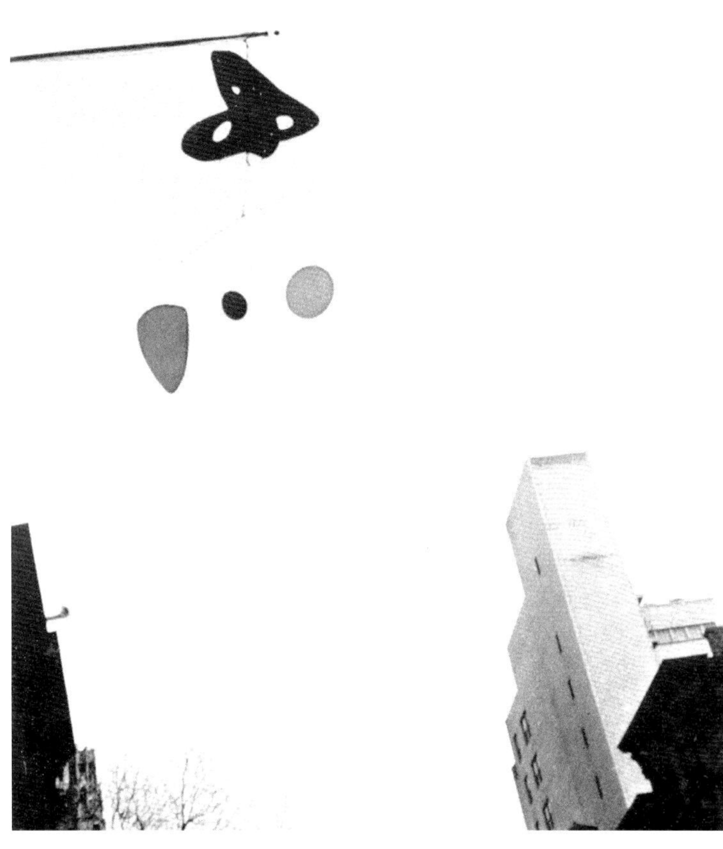

Objet volant (Flying object). 1935
Cloth, rod, wire, and rope, 15 ft. 8 ¼ in. × 10 ft. 4 in. × 7 ft. 5 in. (478.2 × 315 × 226.1 cm)
The Museum of Modern Art, New York
Commissioned for the exhibition **Cubism and Abstract Art**, The Museum of Modern Art, New York, March 2–April 19, 1936

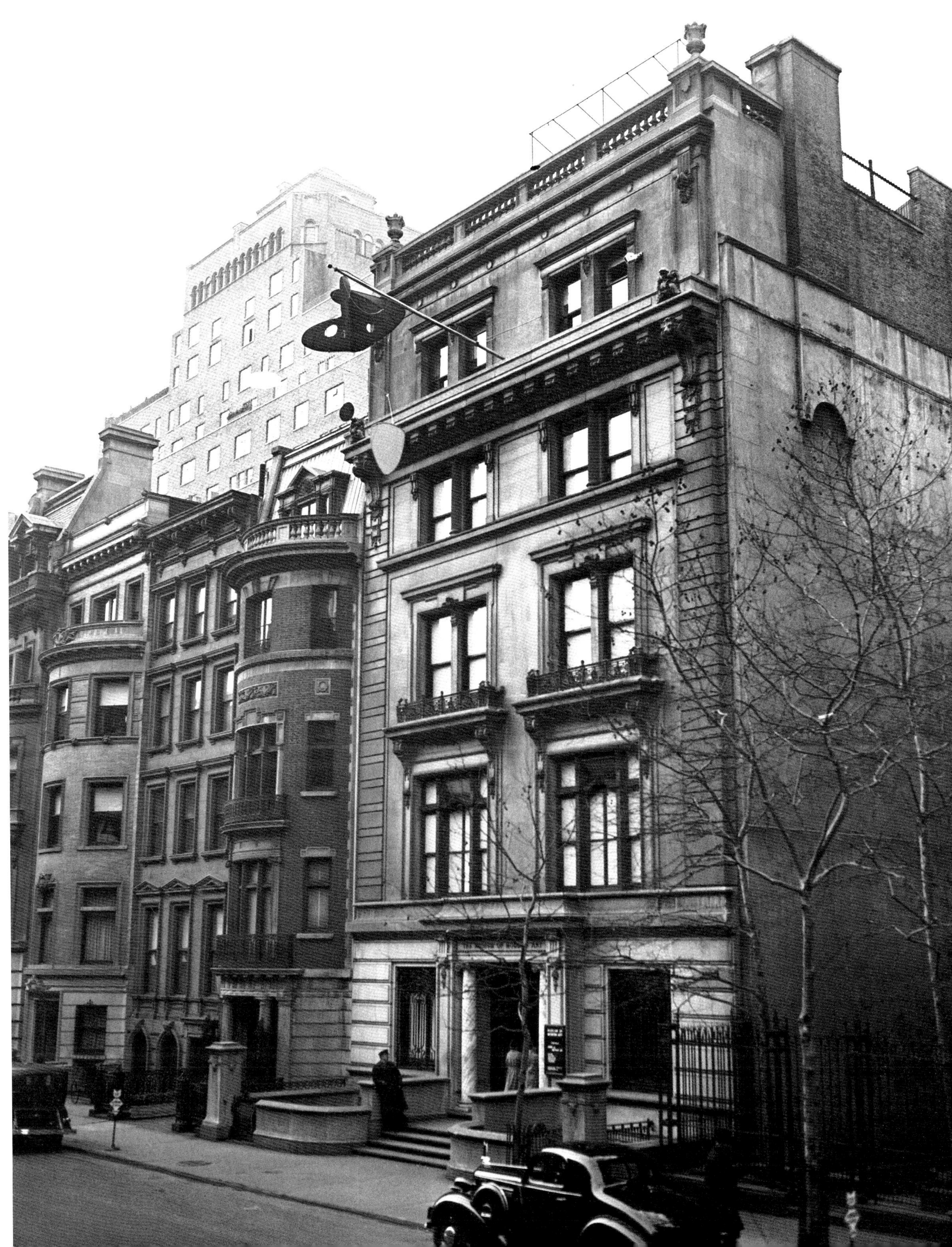

Gibraltar. 1936
Lignum vitae, walnut, wood, paint, and steel rods,
51⅞ × 24¼ × 11⅜ in. (131.8 × 61.6 × 28.9 cm.)
The Museum of Modern Art, New York. Gift of the artist

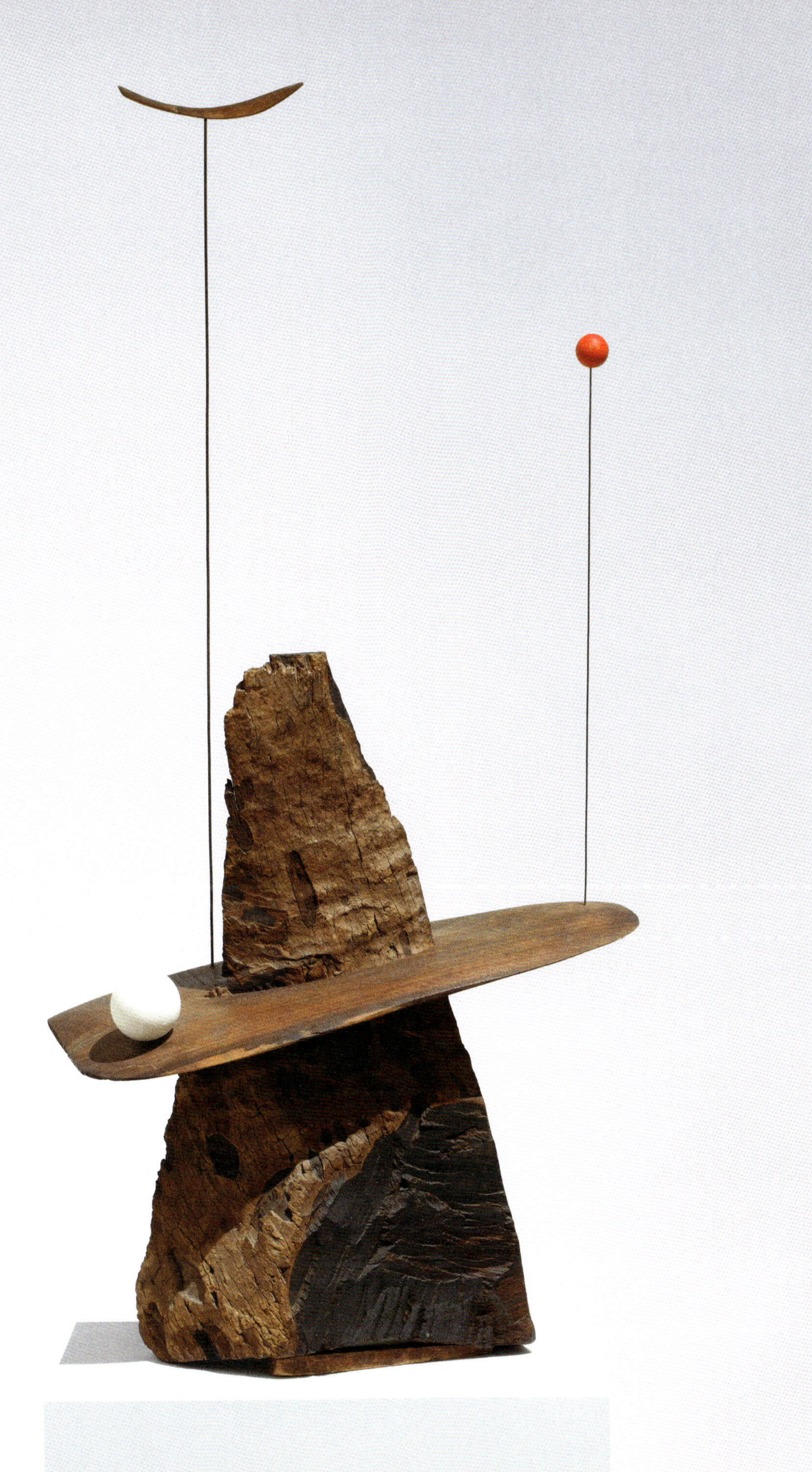

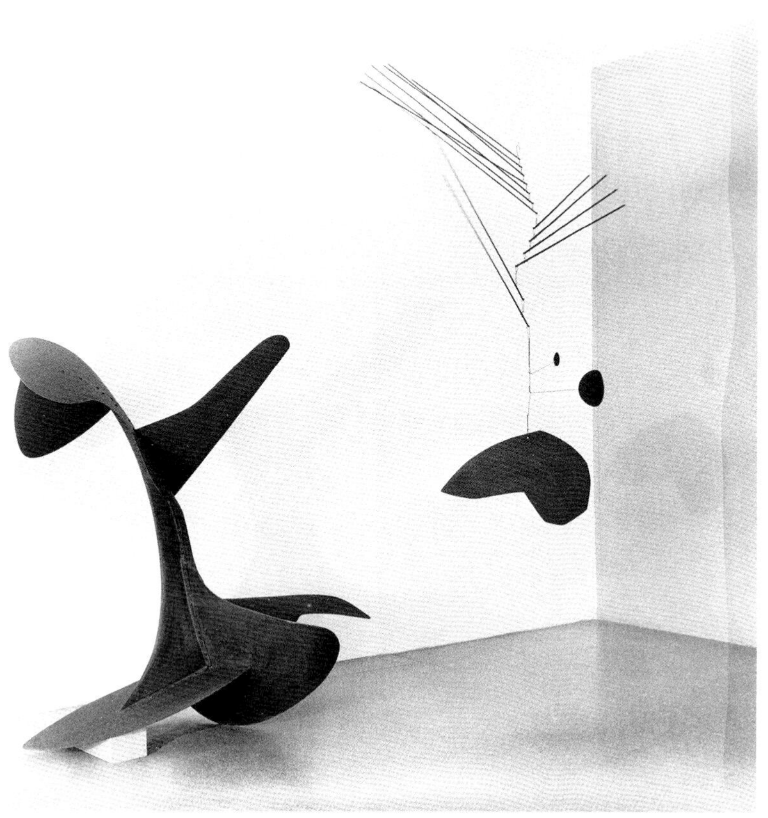

Whale II. 1964 (after **Devil Fish**. 1937)
Sheet steel, wood, and paint, 68 × 69 ½ × 45 ⅜ in. (172.7 × 176.5 × 115.3 cm)
The Museum of Modern Art, New York. Gift of the artist (by exchange)
Opposite: Installation view in The Abby Aldrich Rockefeller Sculpture Garden, The Museum of Modern Art, New York, 1965
Above: Installation view of the original 1937 sculpture in **Alexander Calder: Sculptures and Constructions**, 1943. It is now in the collection of the Calder Foundation, New York.

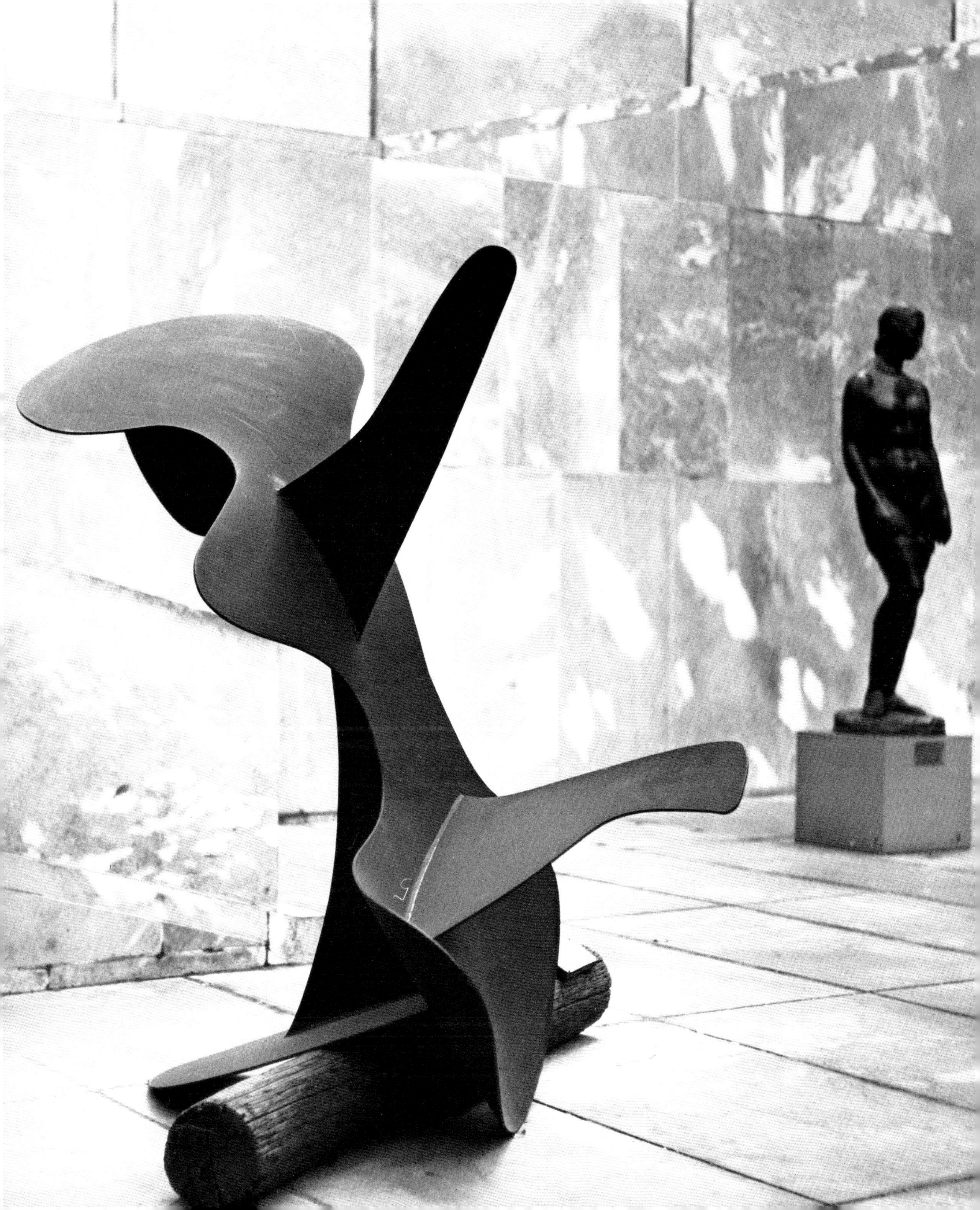

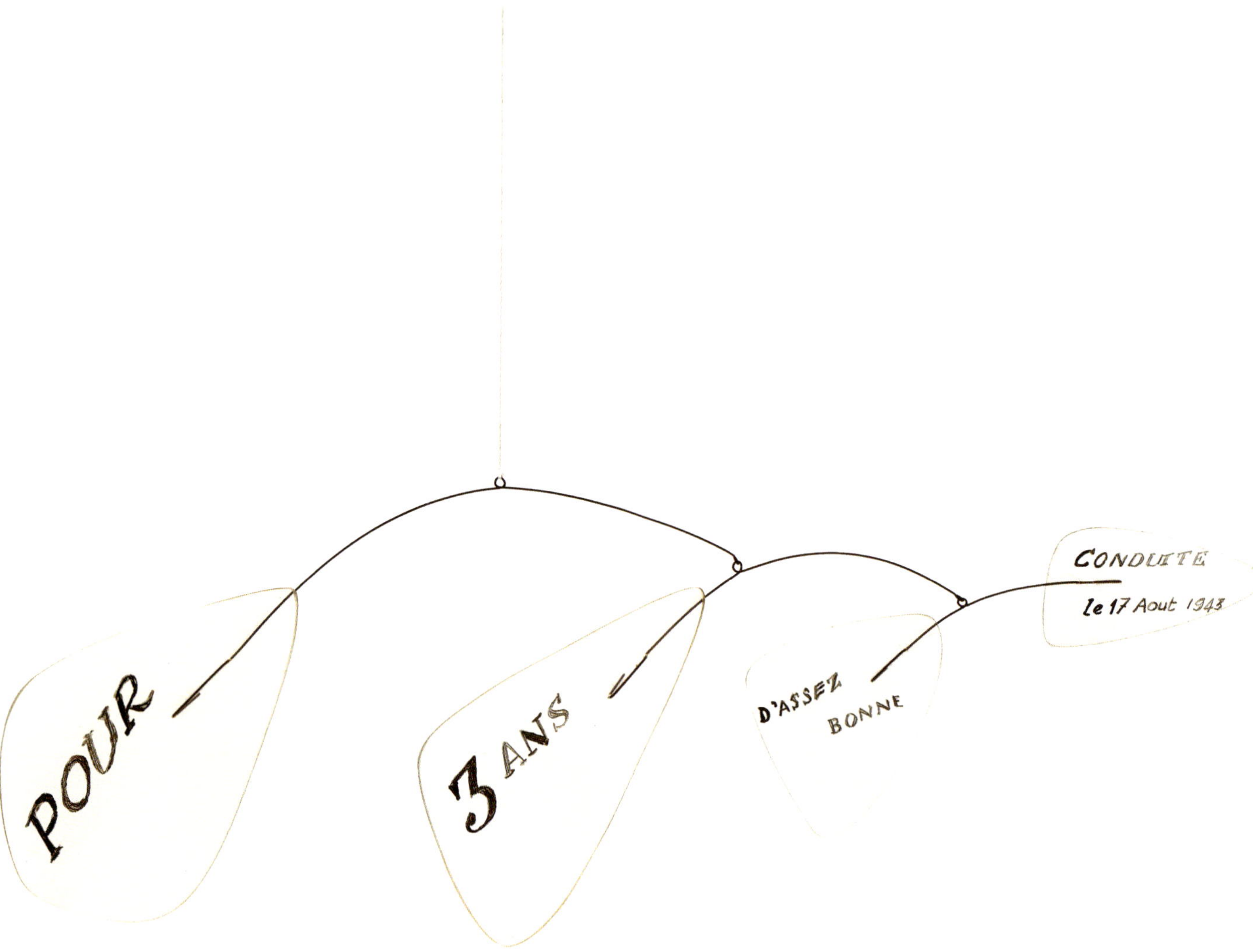

For 3 Years of Fairly Good Behavior (**Pour 3 ans d'assez bonne conduite**). 1941–43
Plexiglas, wire, and paint, 10 ¼ in. (26 cm) high × 29 in. (73.7 cm) diam.
The Museum of Modern Art, New York. Kay Sage Tanguy Bequest

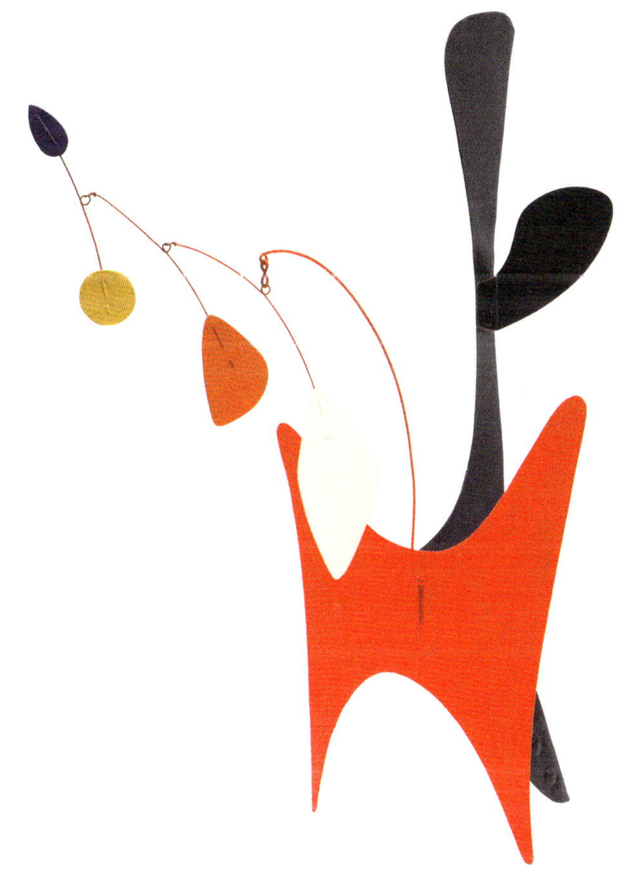

Untitled. 1939
Sheet aluminum, steel wire, and paint,
14 ⅝ × 9 × 10 ⅞ in. (37.2 × 22.9 × 27.6 cm)
The Museum of Modern Art, New York.
Kay Sage Tanguy Bequest

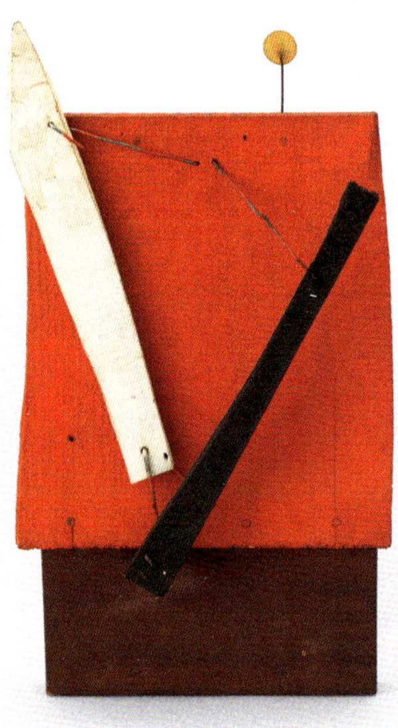

Untitled. c. 1934
Wood, wire, sheet metal, paint, and motor,
11 ¾ × 8 × 7 in. (29.9 × 20.3 × 17.8 cm)
The Museum of Modern Art, New York.
Kay Sage Tanguy Bequest

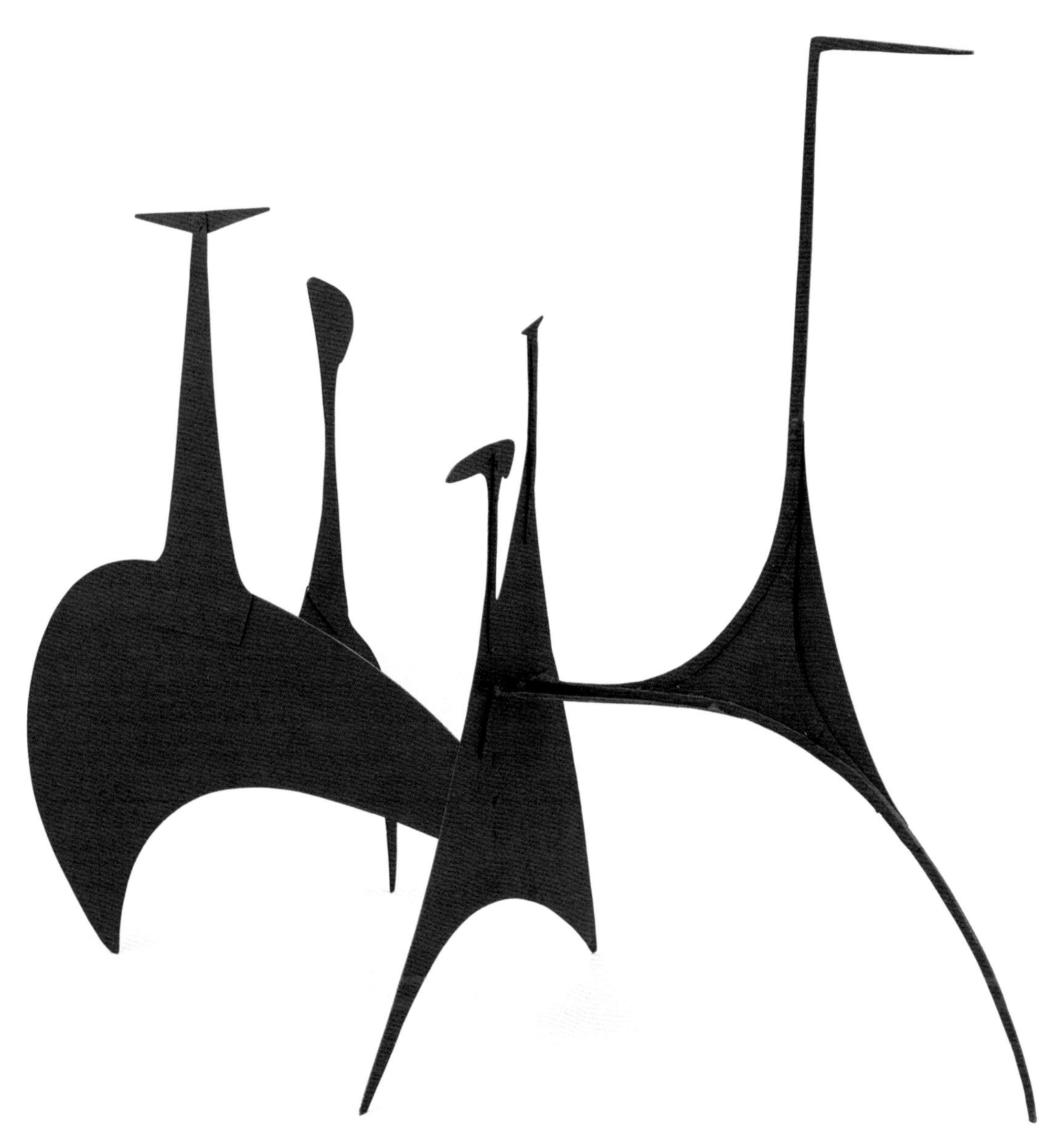

Spiny (maquette). c. 1939
Sheet aluminum and paint, 26 × 30 × 14 ⅜ in. (66 × 76.2 × 36.5 cm)
The Museum of Modern Art, New York. Nelson A. Rockefeller Bequest

Spider. 1939
Sheet aluminum, steel rod, steel wire, and paint,
6 ft. 8 ½ in. × 7 ft. 4 ½ in. × 36 ½ in. (204.5 × 224.8 × 92.7 cm)
The Museum of Modern Art, New York. Gift of the artist

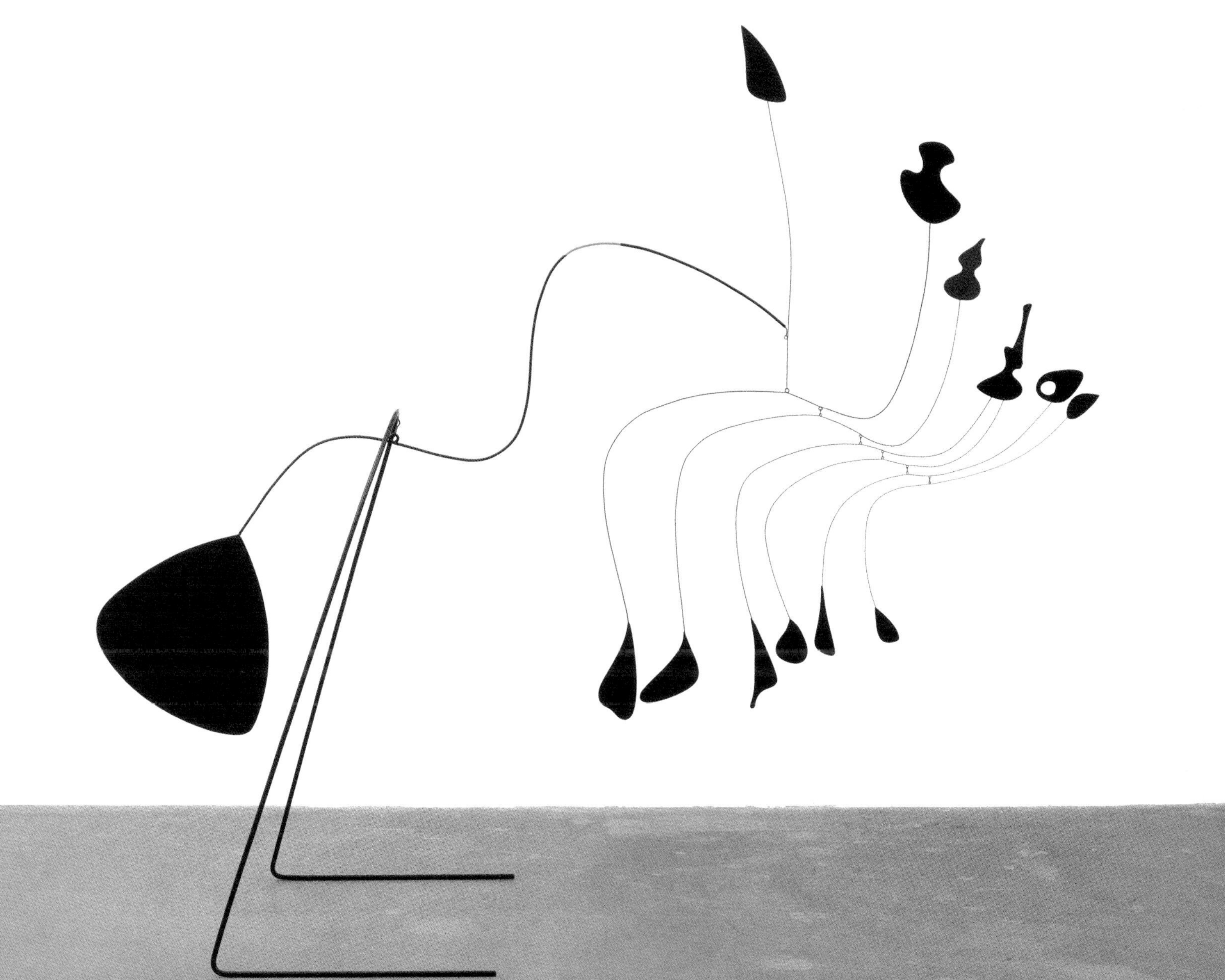

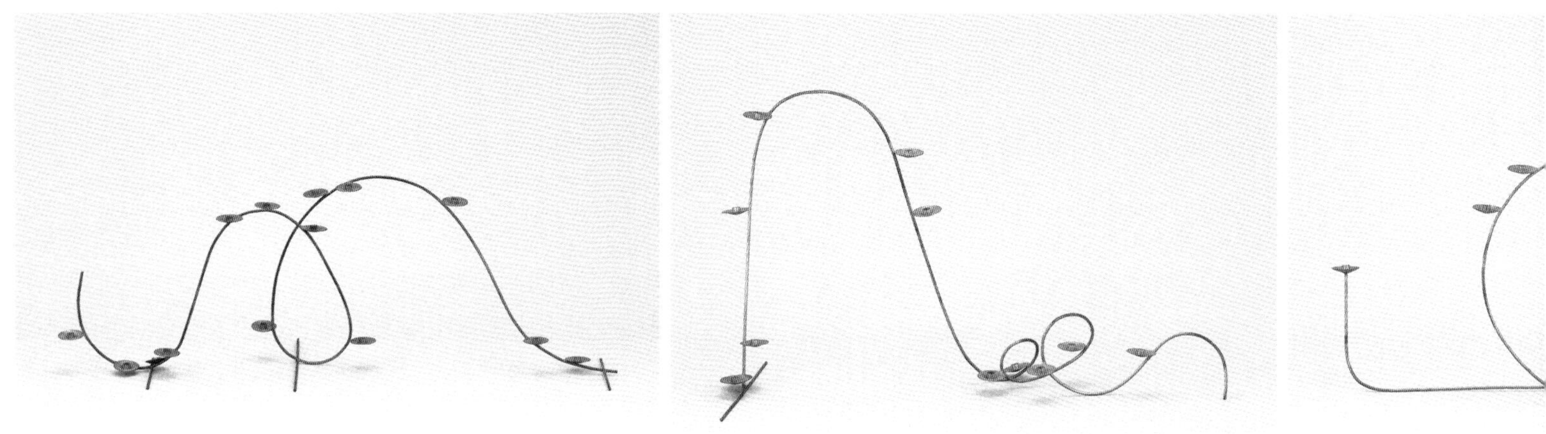

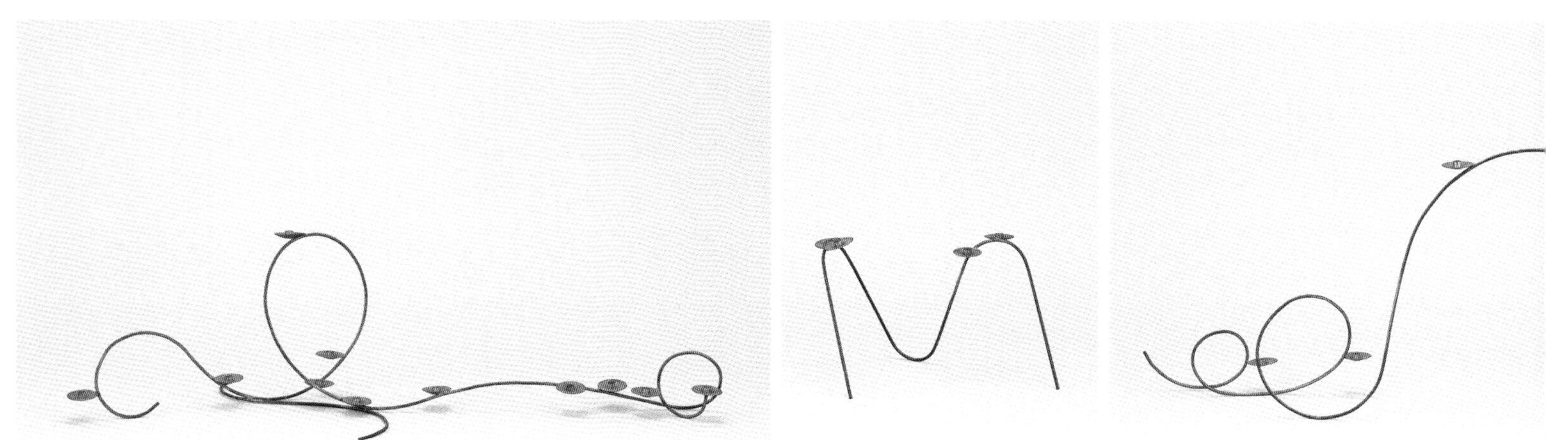

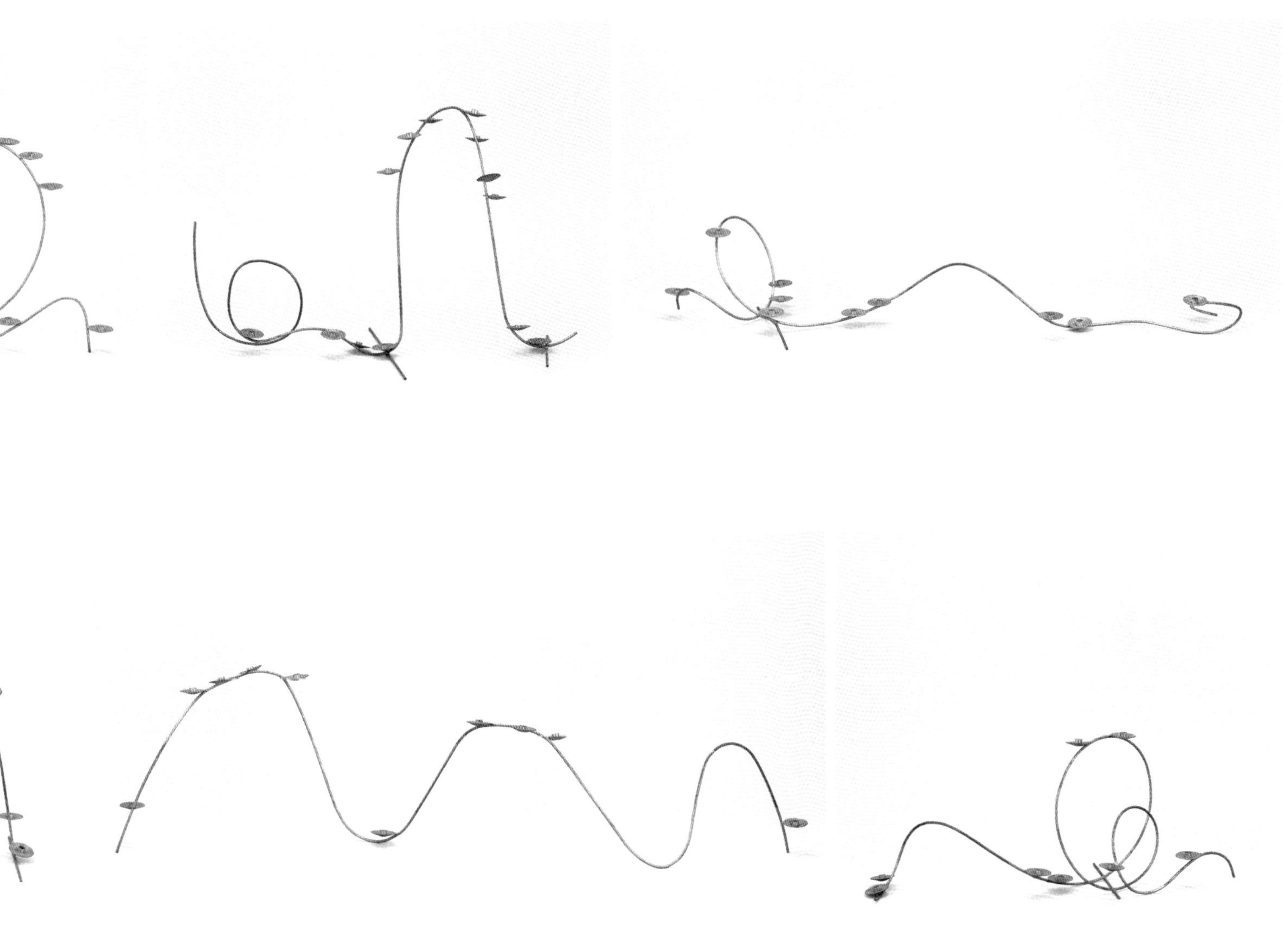

Candelabra. 1939
Rolled-steel tubing and sheet-iron candle holders, ten sections, dimensions variable
The Museum of Modern Art, New York
Commissioned for The Museum of Modern Art's tenth-anniversary dinner, May 8, 1939

Lobster Trap and Fish Tail. 1939
Sheet aluminum, steel wire, and paint, 8 ft. 6 in. (259.1 cm) high × 9 ft. 6 in. (289.5 cm) diam.
The Museum of Modern Art, New York
Commissioned by the Advisory Committee of The Museum of Modern Art, New York, for the stairwell of MoMA's new building, designed by Philip L. Goodwin and Edward Durrell Stone

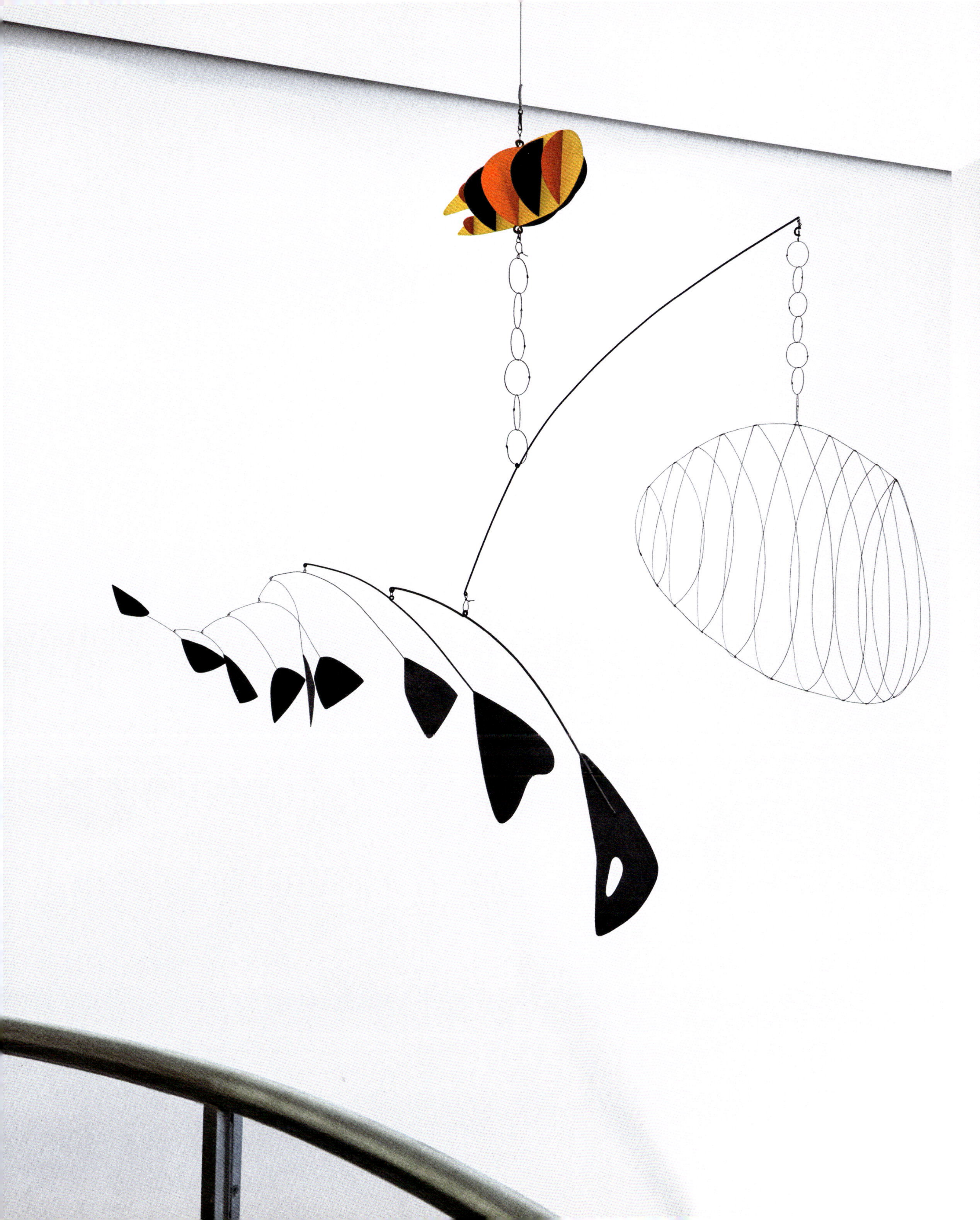

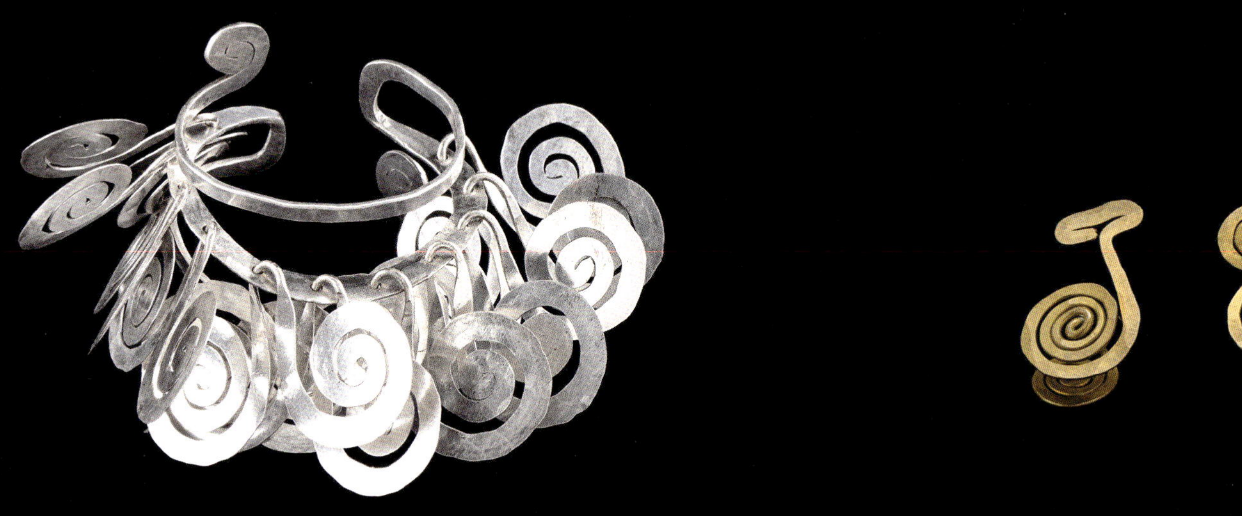

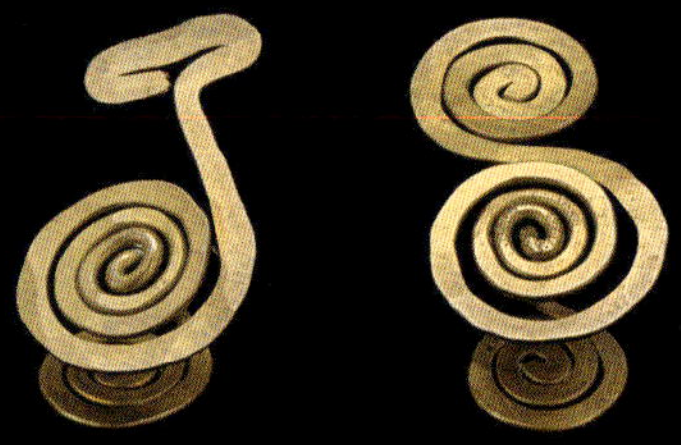

Bracelet. c. 1940
Silver, 4 ¾ × 4 × 2 in. (12.1 × 10.2 × 5.1 cm)
The Museum of Modern Art, New York. Purchase

J and *S* cuff links. c. 1935
Brass, 1 ¾ × 1 ¼ × 1 in. (4.5 × 3.2 × 2.5 cm)
and 2 × 1 ⅛ × ¾ in. (4.9 × 2.8 × 1.9 cm)
The Museum of Modern Art, New York.
James Thrall Soby Bequest

Flying-bird brooch. c. 1940
Silver and steel, 12 ¼ × 11 ⅞ in. (31.1 × 30.2 cm)
The Museum of Modern Art, New York.
Gift of the artist

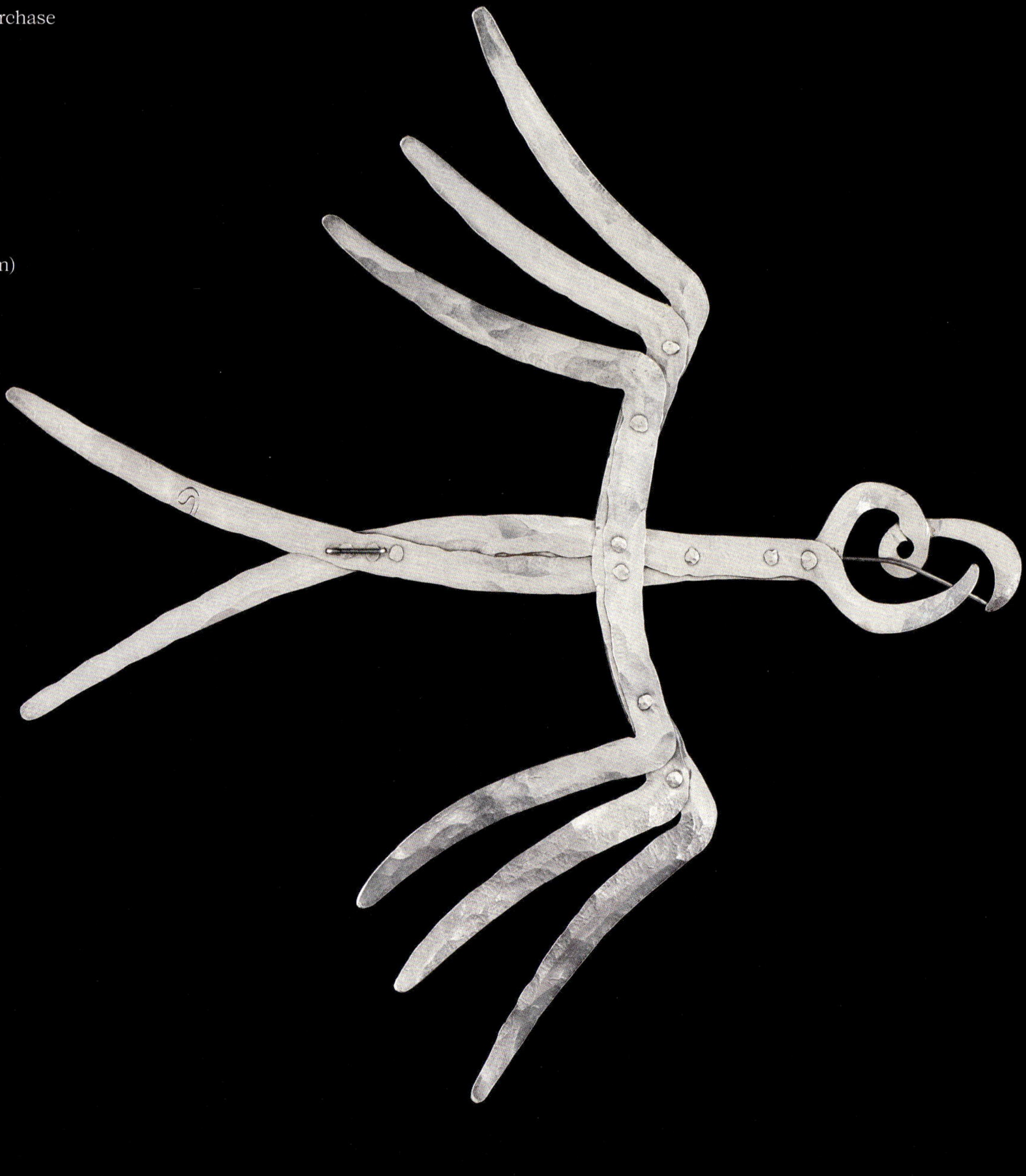

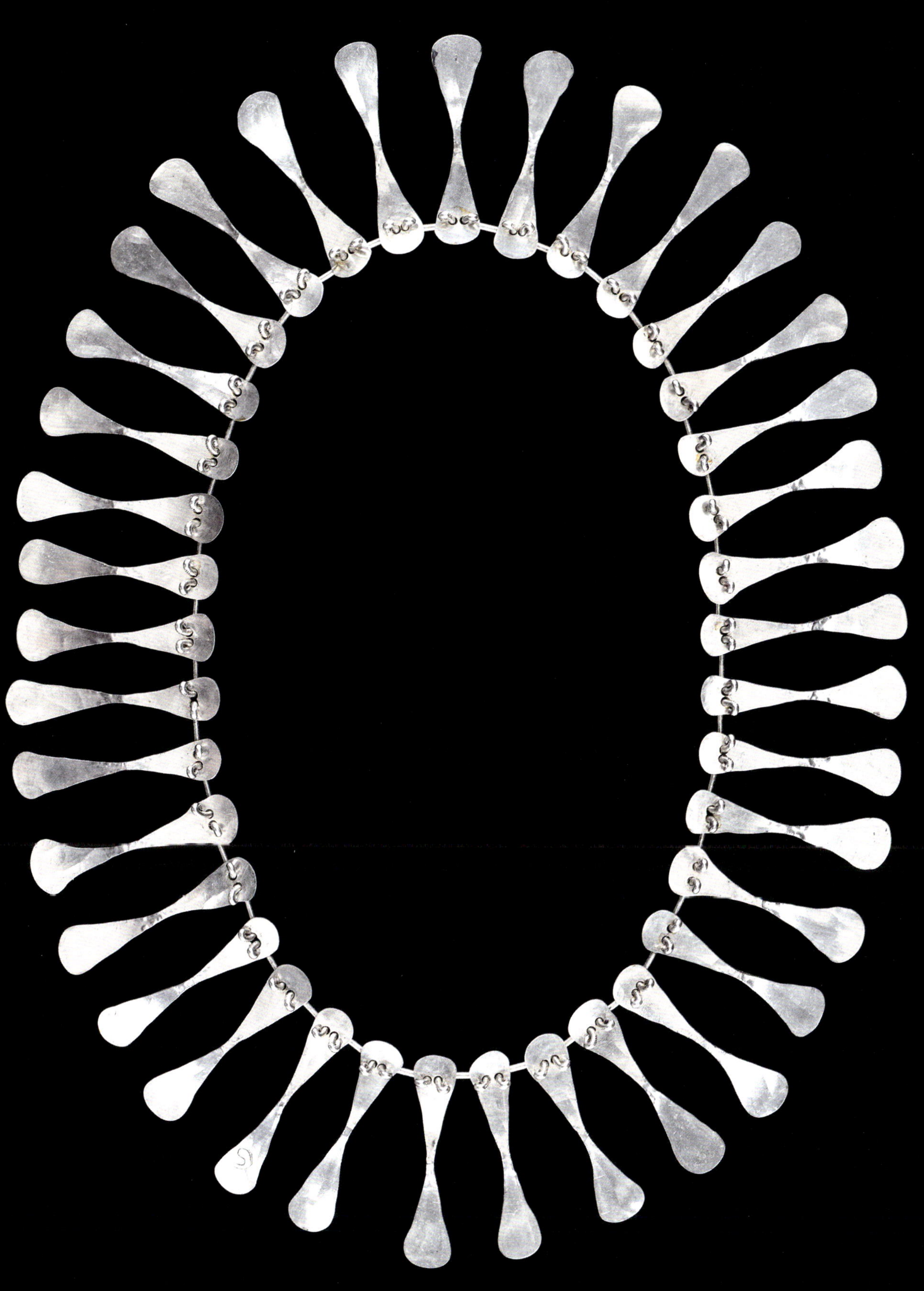

Necklace. 1941
Silver, inner circumference: 26 in. (66 cm);
outer circumference: 34 in. (86.4 cm)
The Museum of Modern Art, New York. James Thrall Soby Fund

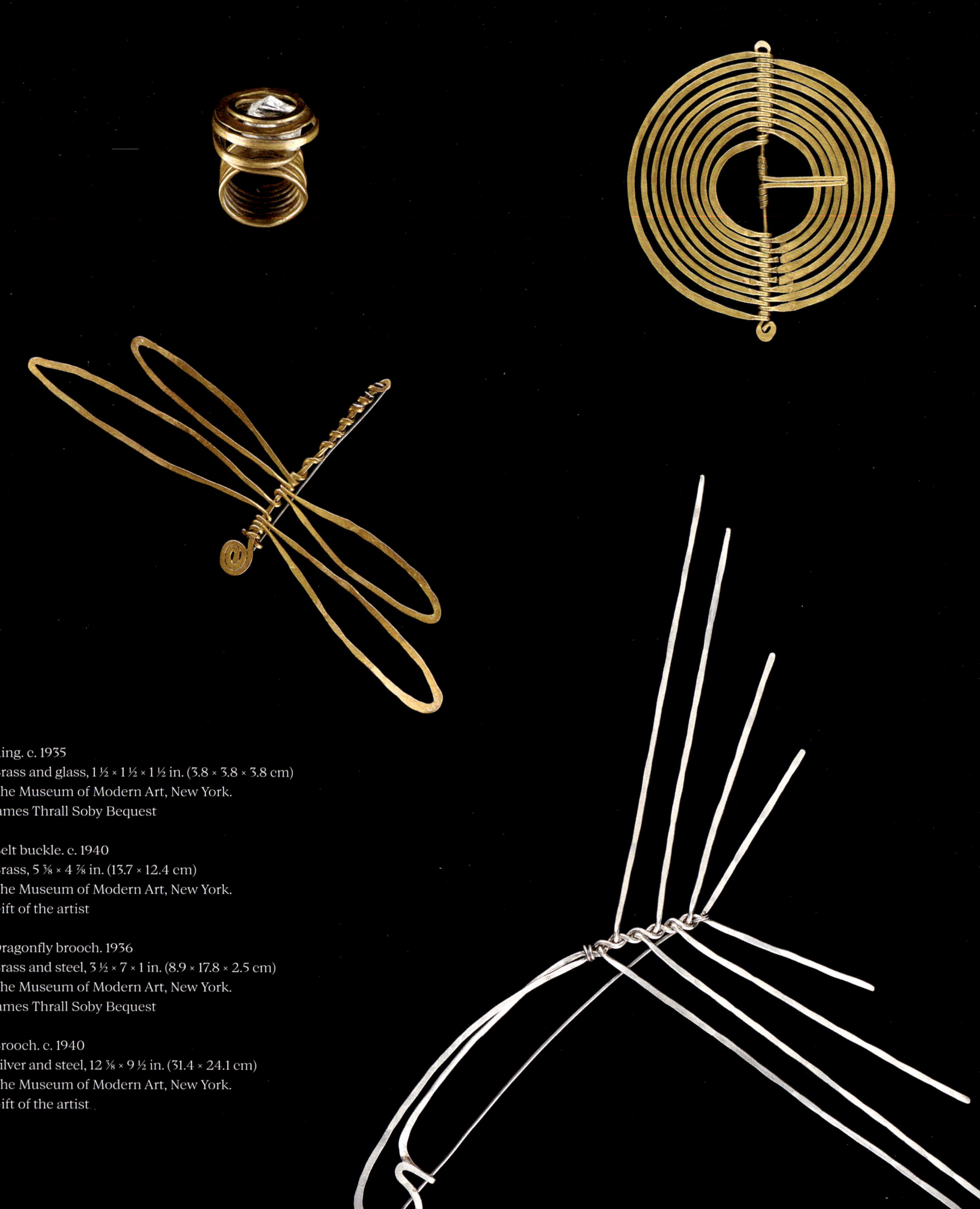

Ring. c. 1935
Brass and glass, 1 ½ × 1 ½ × 1 ½ in. (3.8 × 3.8 × 3.8 cm)
The Museum of Modern Art, New York.
James Thrall Soby Bequest

Belt buckle. c. 1940
Brass, 5 ⅜ × 4 ⅞ in. (13.7 × 12.4 cm)
The Museum of Modern Art, New York.
Gift of the artist

Dragonfly brooch. 1936
Brass and steel, 3 ½ × 7 × 1 in. (8.9 × 17.8 × 2.5 cm)
The Museum of Modern Art, New York.
James Thrall Soby Bequest

Brooch. c. 1940
Silver and steel, 12 ⅜ × 9 ½ in. (31.4 × 24.1 cm)
The Museum of Modern Art, New York.
Gift of the artist

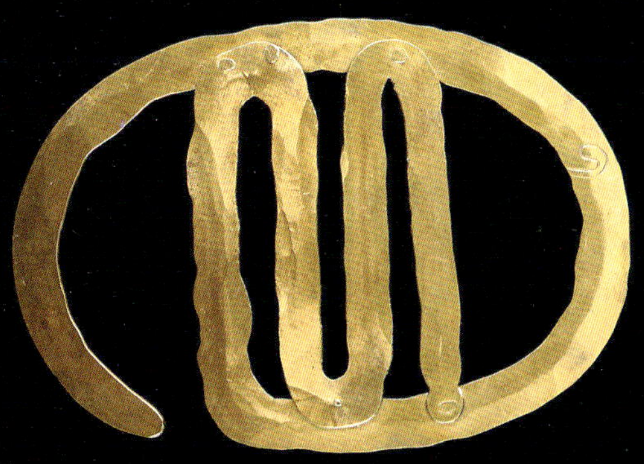

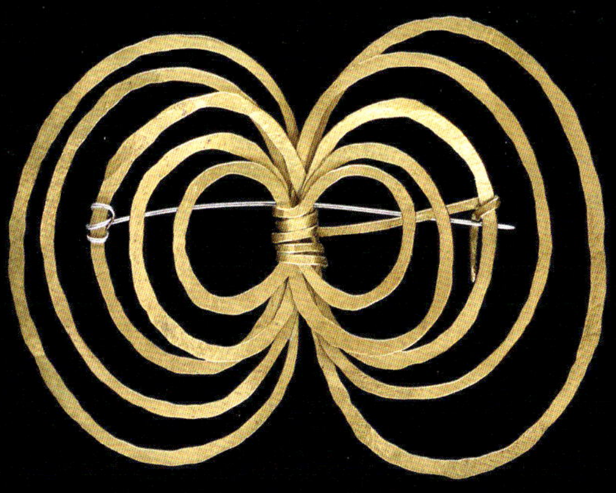

Belt buckle. c. 1945
Brass, 3 ⅛ × 4 7⁄16 × ⅜ in. (7.9 × 11.3 × 1 cm)
The Museum of Modern Art, New York.
Gift of the artist

Brooch. c. 1936
Brass and steel, 3 ⅝ × 4 ¾ in. (9.2 × 12.1 cm)
The Museum of Modern Art, New York.
Gift of Mrs. Katharine Kuh

Comb. c. 1940
Brass, 6 ½ × 3 ⅞ × ¾ in. (16.5 × 9.8 × 2 cm)
The Museum of Modern Art, New York.
Gift of the artist

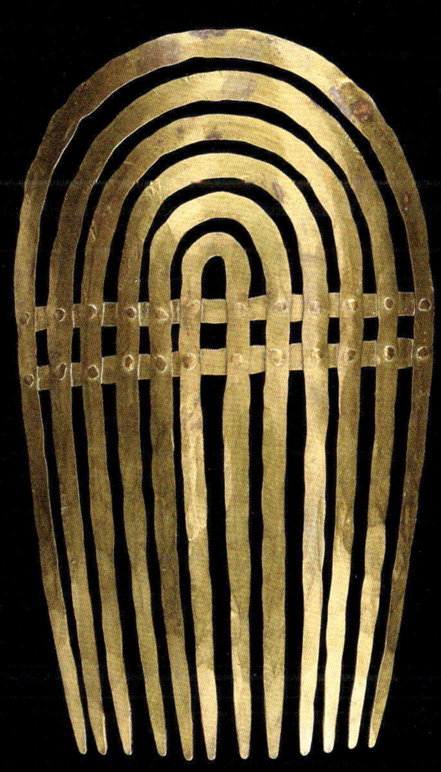

Morning Star. 1943
Sheet steel, steel wire, wood, and paint,
6 ft. 4 ¾ in. × 48 ⅜ in. × 45 ¾ in. (195 × 122.9 × 116.2 cm)
The Museum of Modern Art, New York. Gift of the artist

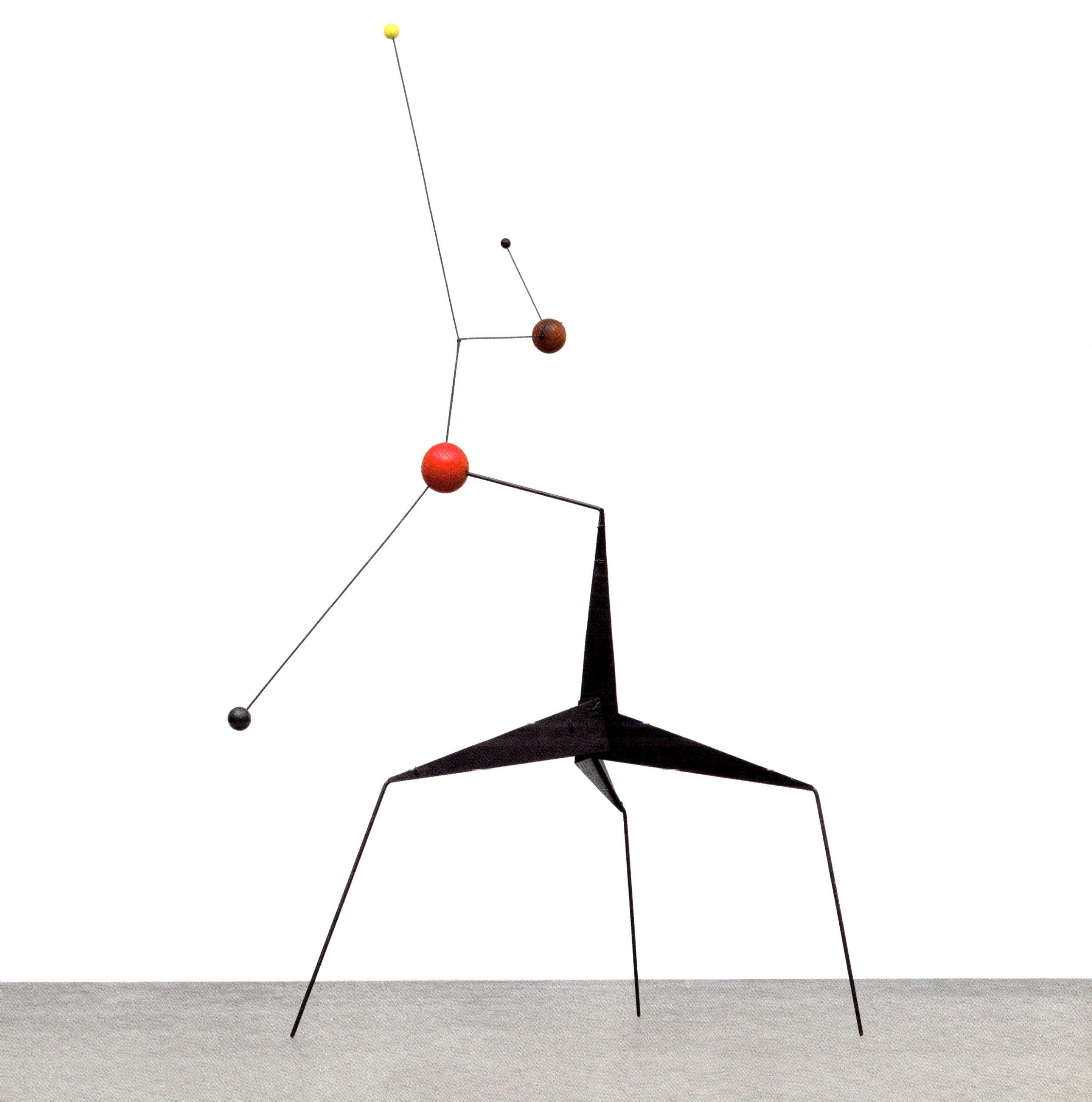

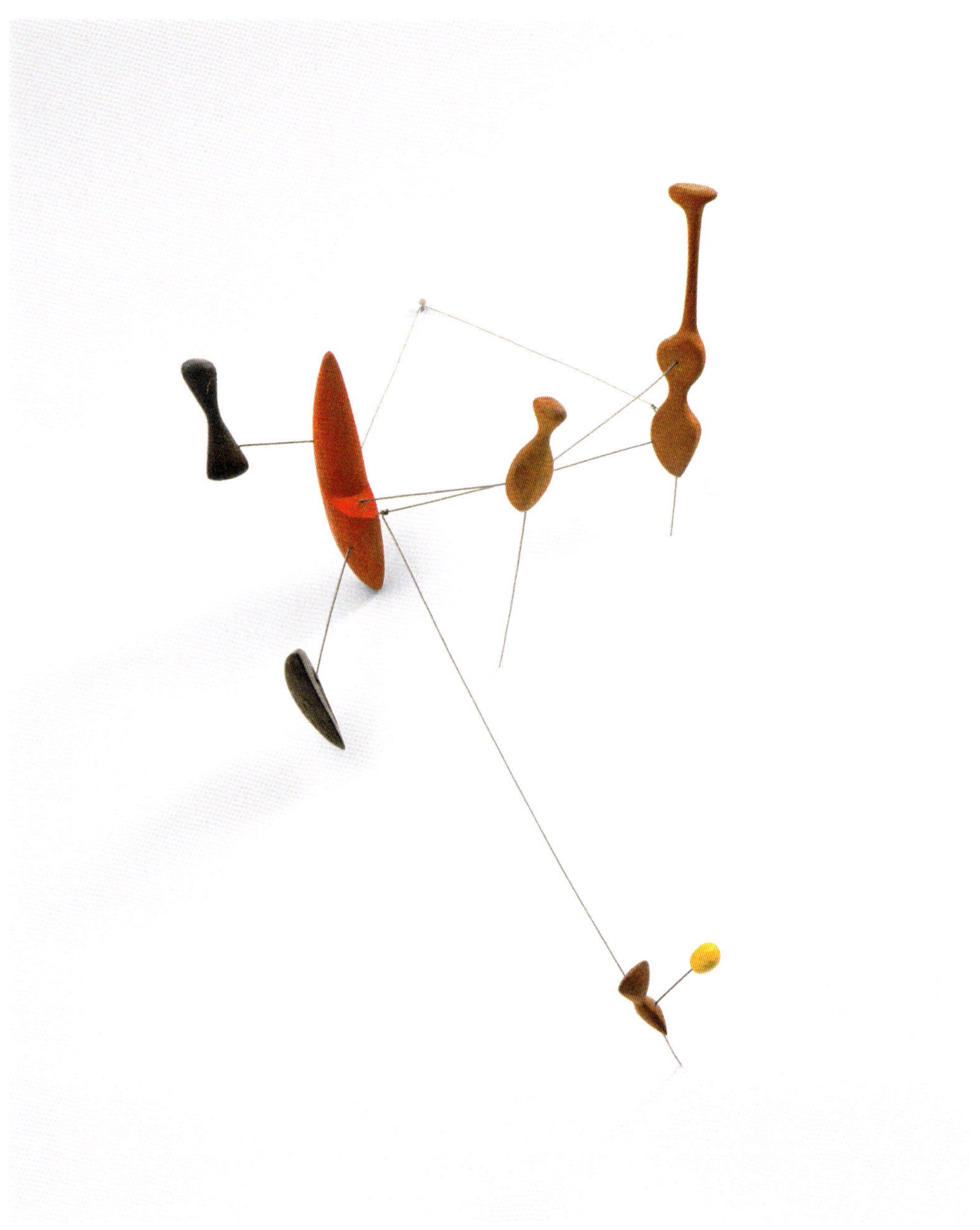

Wall Constellation with Red Object. 1943
Wood, steel wire, and paint, 24 ½ × 15 ¼ × 9 ½ in. (62.2 × 38.7 × 24.1 cm)
The Museum of Modern Art, New York. James Thrall Soby Fund

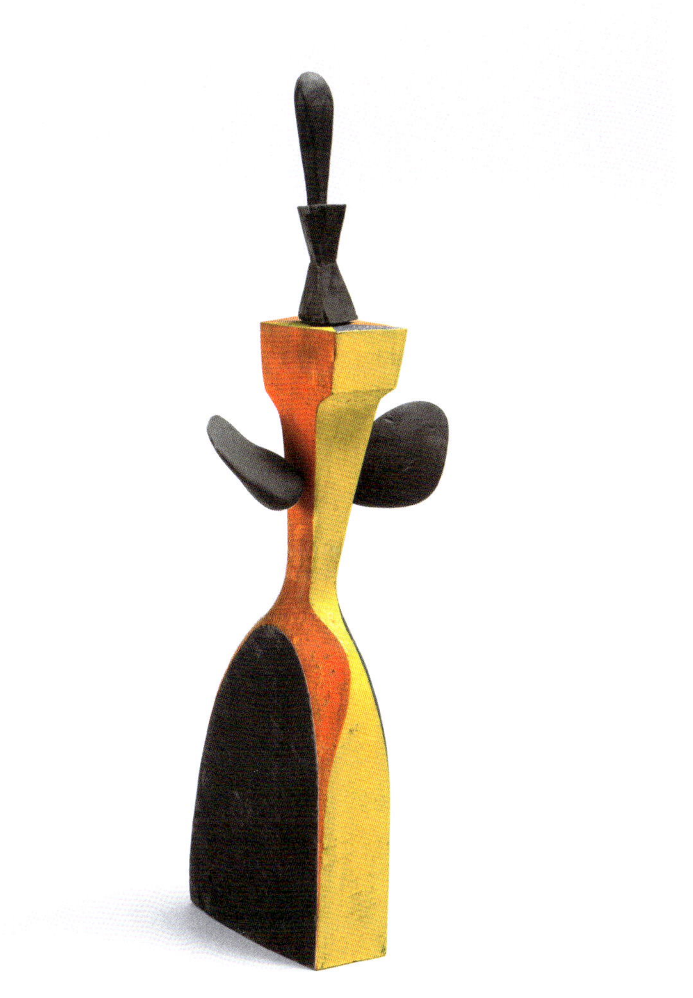

Untitled. 1943
Wood and paint, 28 ⅞ × 10 × 8 ¾ in. (73.3 × 25.4 × 22.2 cm)
The Museum of Modern Art, New York. Gift of Pierre Matisse in memory of Patricia Kane Matisse

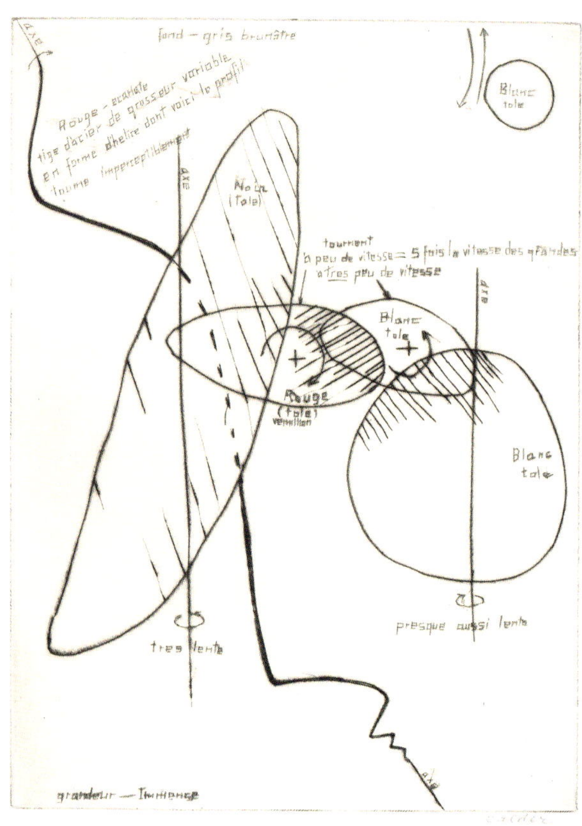

Grandeur–Immense (plate, folio 7), from **23 Gravures**, by Anatole Jakovski. 1935
Drypoint from an illustrated book with twelve etchings (one with aquatint and drypoint), five drypoints, three engravings (one with drypoint), two lithographs, and one woodcut, plate: 10 7/16 × 7 3/4 in. (26.5 × 19.7 cm); sheet: 12 9/16 × 9 3/4 in. (31.9 × 24.8 cm)
Publisher: Éditions Orobitz et Cie, Paris. Printer: Tanneur, Paris. Edition: 50
The Museum of Modern Art, New York. Purchase Fund

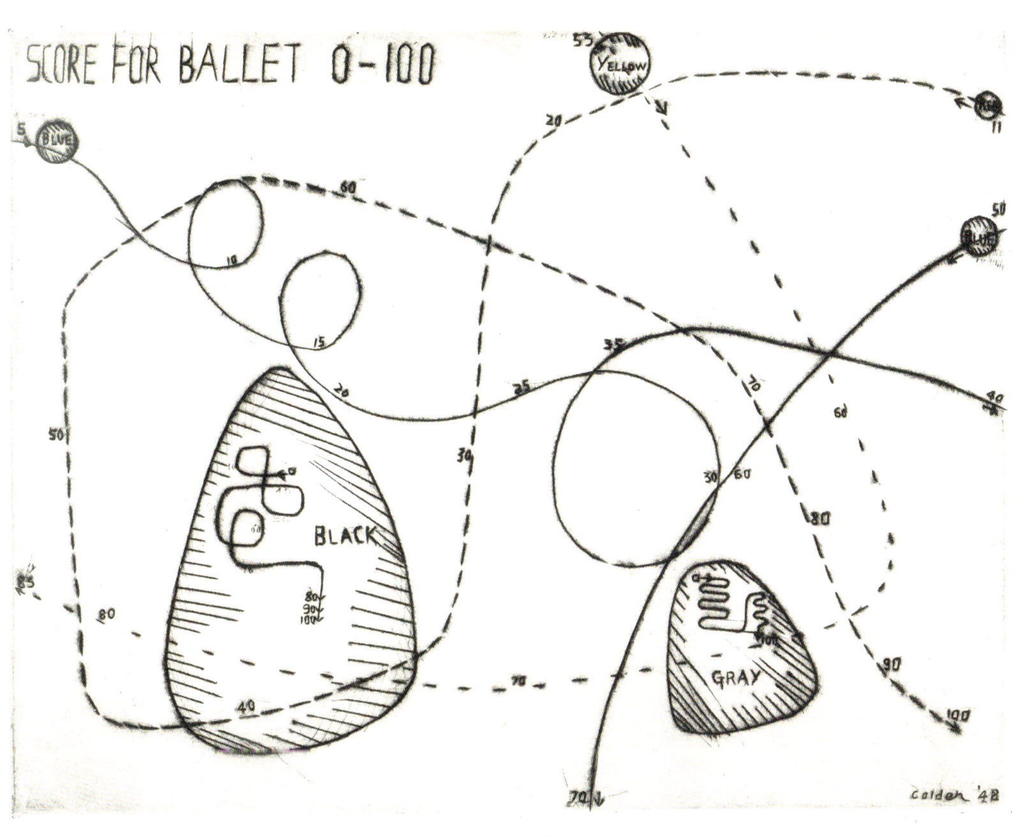

Score for Ballet 0–100, from **VVV Portfolio**. 1942, published 1943
Etching from a portfolio of five etchings (one with aquatint), three duplicated drawings (two watercolor on paper and one crayon on paper), one collage, one engraving, and one gelatin silver print, plate: 11 5/16 × 14 13/16 in. (28.7 × 37.6 cm); sheet: 14 × 17 15/16 in. (35.6 × 45.6 cm)
Publisher: VVV, New York. Printer: Atelier 17, New York. Edition: 50
The Museum of Modern Art, New York. The Louis E. Stern Collection

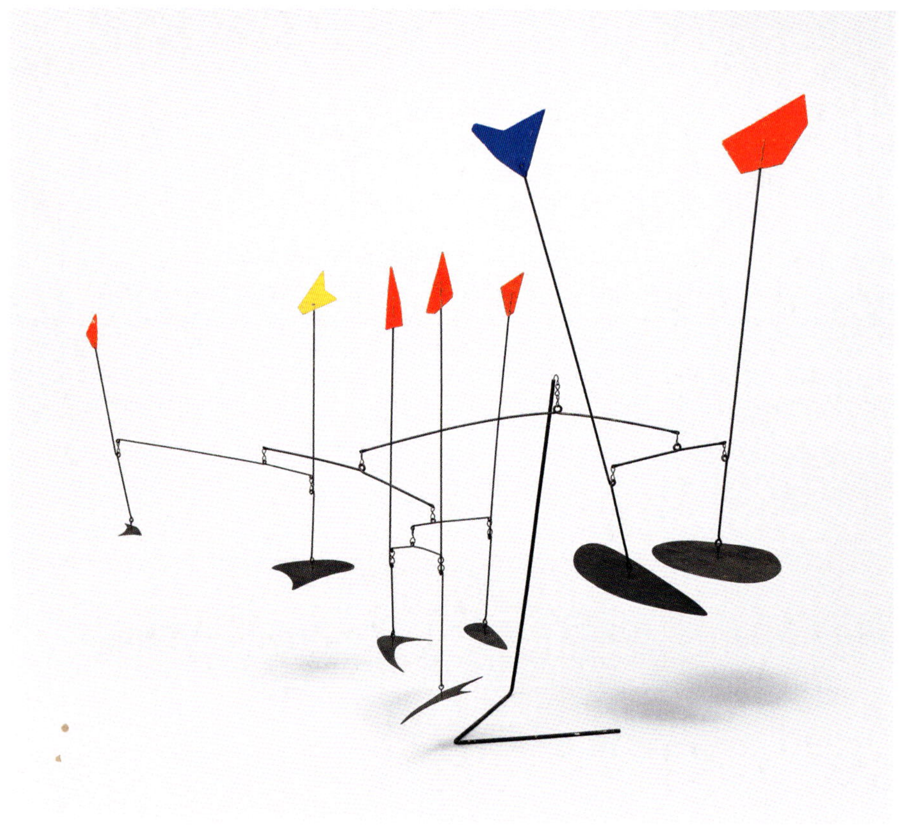

Mobile with 14 Flags (model for **Man-Eater with Pennants**). 1945
Sheet aluminum, copper rod, and paint, 53 in. (134.6 cm) high × approx. 50 in. (127 cm) diam.
The Museum of Modern Art, New York. Gift of the artist

Man-Eater with Pennants. 1945
Sheet iron, steel rods, and paint, 14 ft. (426.7 cm) high × approx. 30 ft. (914.4 cm) diam.
The Museum of Modern Art, New York. Purchase
Installation view in The Abby Aldrich Rockefeller Sculpture Garden,
The Museum of Modern Art, New York, c. 1948

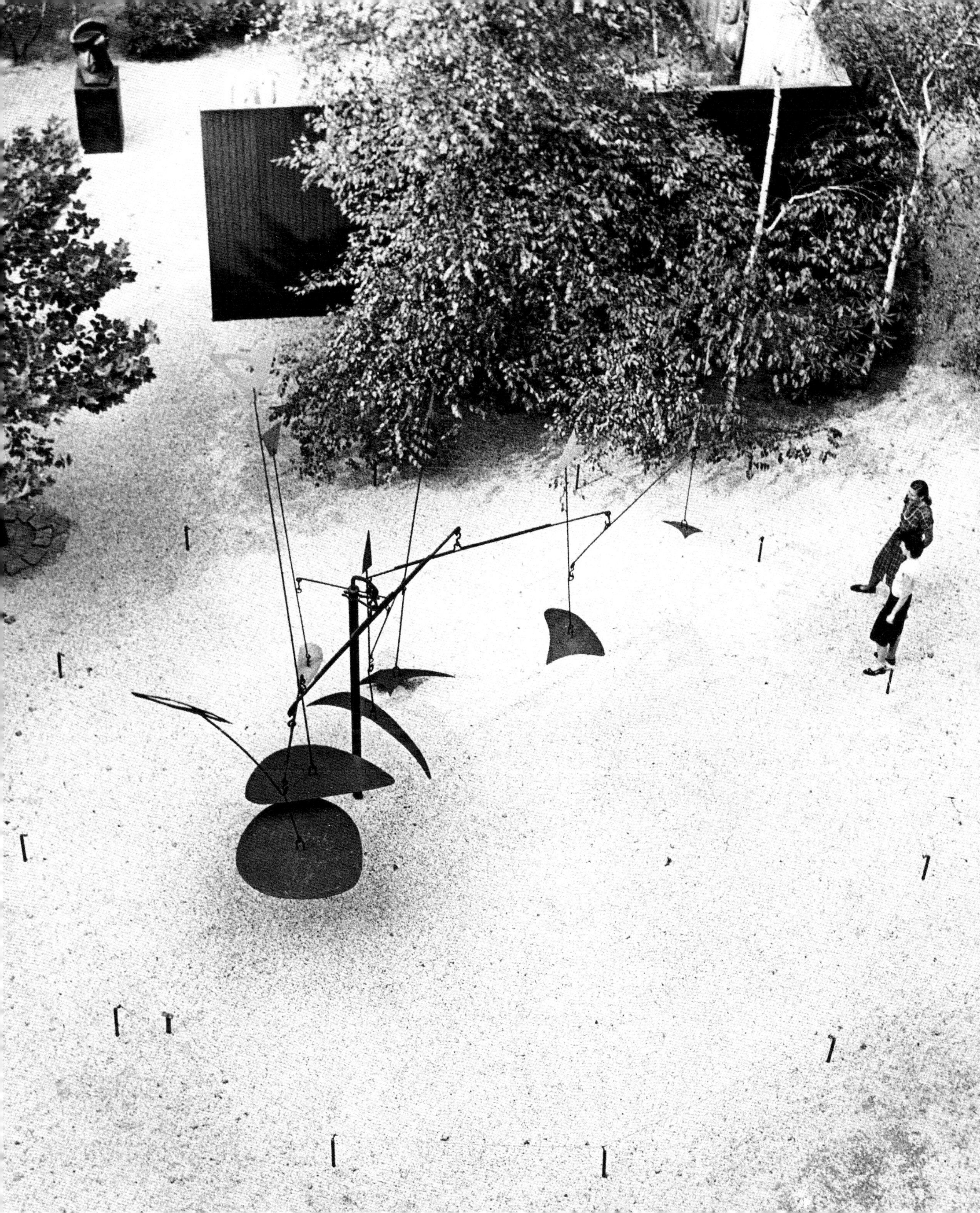

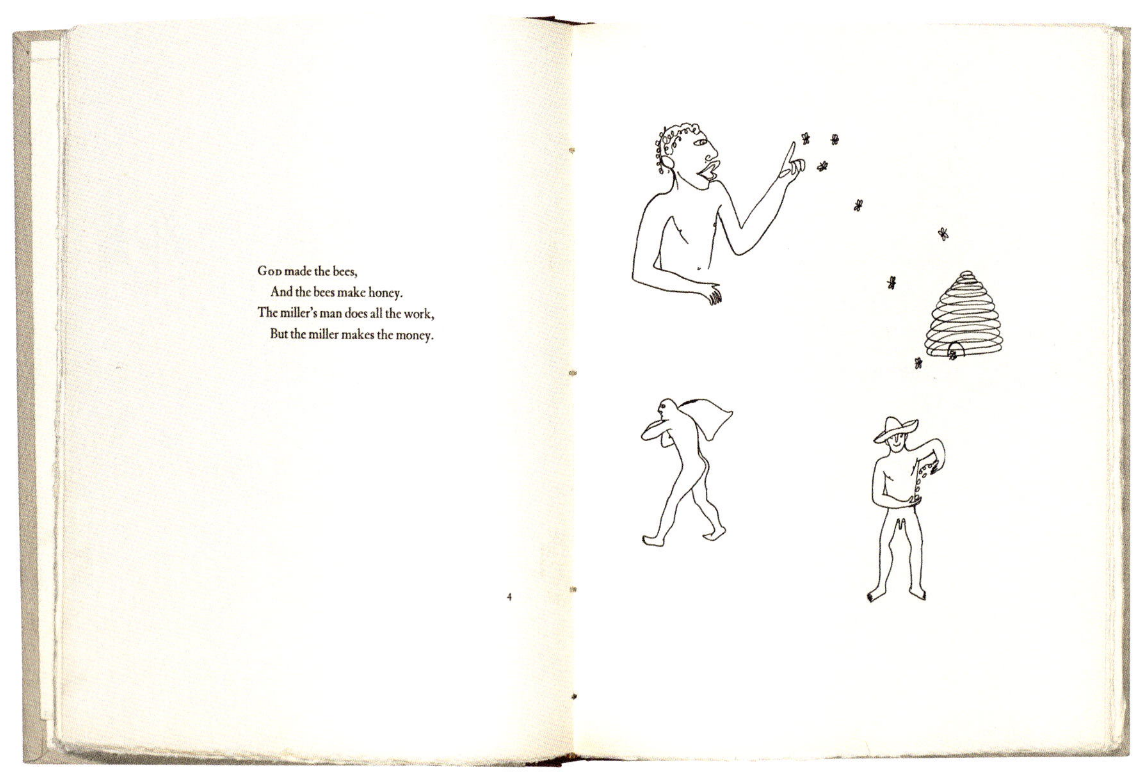
GOD made the bees,
And the bees make honey.
The miller's man does all the work,
But the miller makes the money.

4

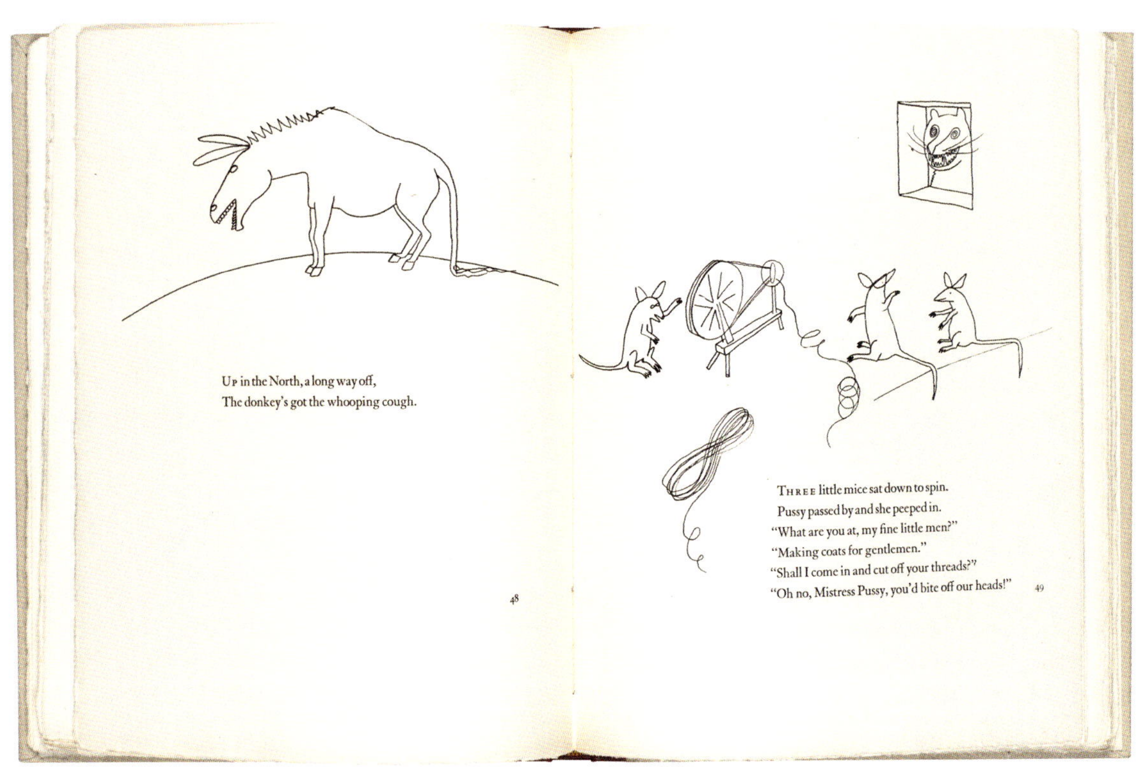
UP in the North, a long way off,
The donkey's got the whooping cough.

48

THREE little mice sat down to spin.
Pussy passed by and she peeped in.
"What are you at, my fine little men?"
"Making coats for gentlemen."
"Shall I come in and cut off your threads?"
"Oh no, Mistress Pussy, you'd bite off our heads!"

49

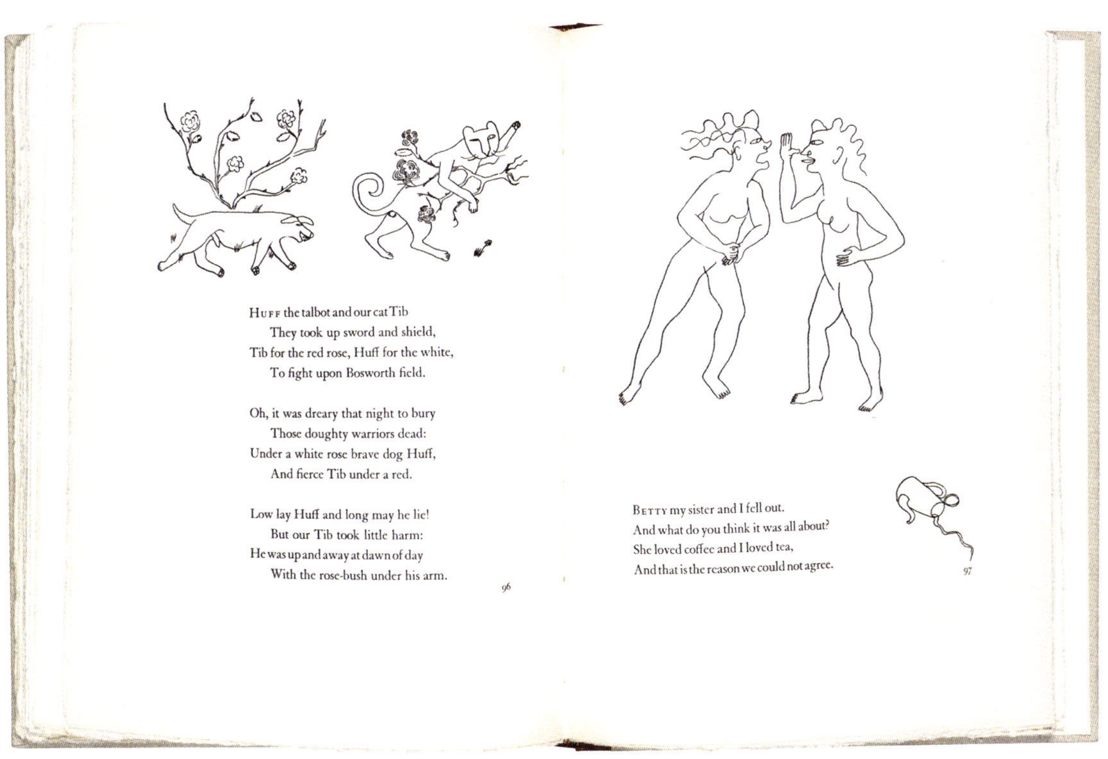

Huff the talbot and our cat Tib
They took up sword and shield,
Tib for the red rose, Huff for the white,
To fight upon Bosworth field.

Oh, it was dreary that night to bury
Those doughty warriors dead:
Under a white rose brave dog Huff,
And fierce Tib under a red.

Low lay Huff and long may he lie!
But our Tib took little harm:
He was up and away at dawn of day
With the rose-bush under his arm.

96

Betty my sister and I fell out.
And what do you think it was all about?
She loved coffee and I loved tea,
And that is the reason we could not agree.

97

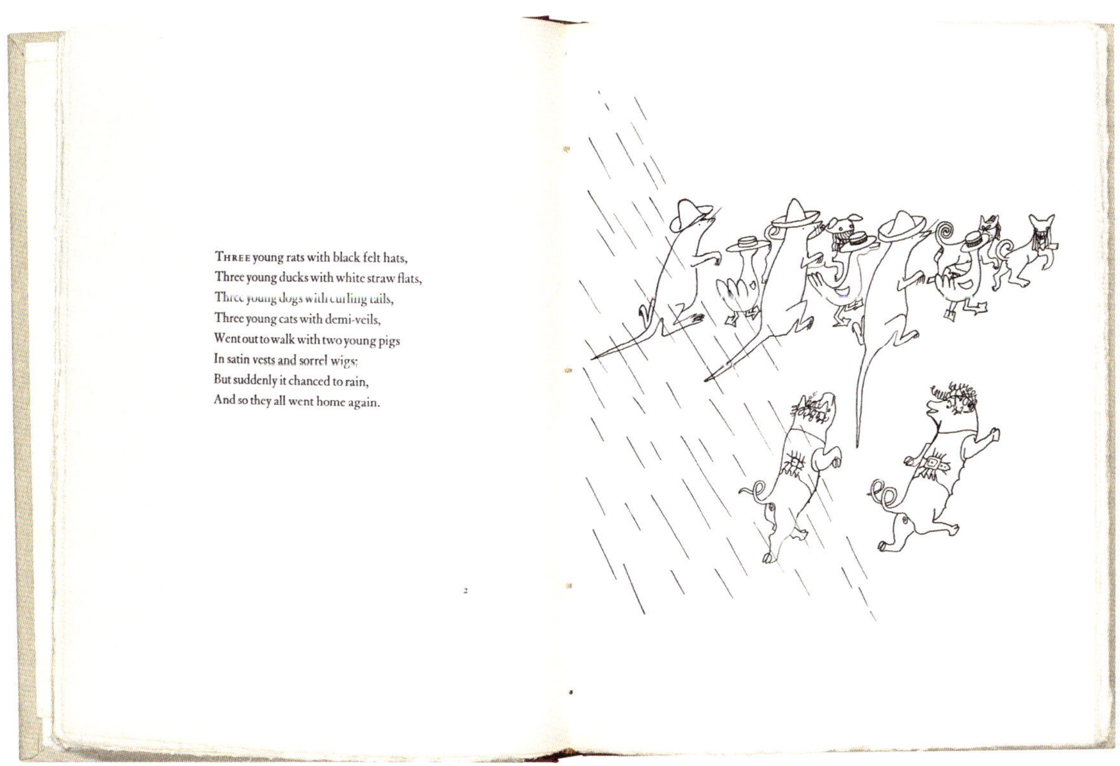

Three young rats with black felt hats,
Three young ducks with white straw flats,
Three young dogs with curling tails,
Three young cats with demi-veils,
Went out to walk with two young pigs
In satin vests and sorrel wigs;
But suddenly it chanced to rain,
And so they all went home again.

2

Three Young Rats and Other Rhymes, compiled by James Johnson Sweeney. 1944
Illustrated book with eighty-five letterpress prints and one supplementary drawing (ink on paper), page (each, irreg.): $12\frac{3}{16} \times 9\frac{7}{16}$ in. (31 × 24 cm); overall (closed): $12\frac{11}{16} \times 9\frac{13}{16} \times 1\frac{1}{16}$ in. (32.2 × 24.9 × 2.7 cm)
Publisher: Curt Valentin, New York. Printer: Golden Eagle Press, Mount Vernon, New York. Edition: 700
The Museum of Modern Art, New York. The Louis E. Stern Collection

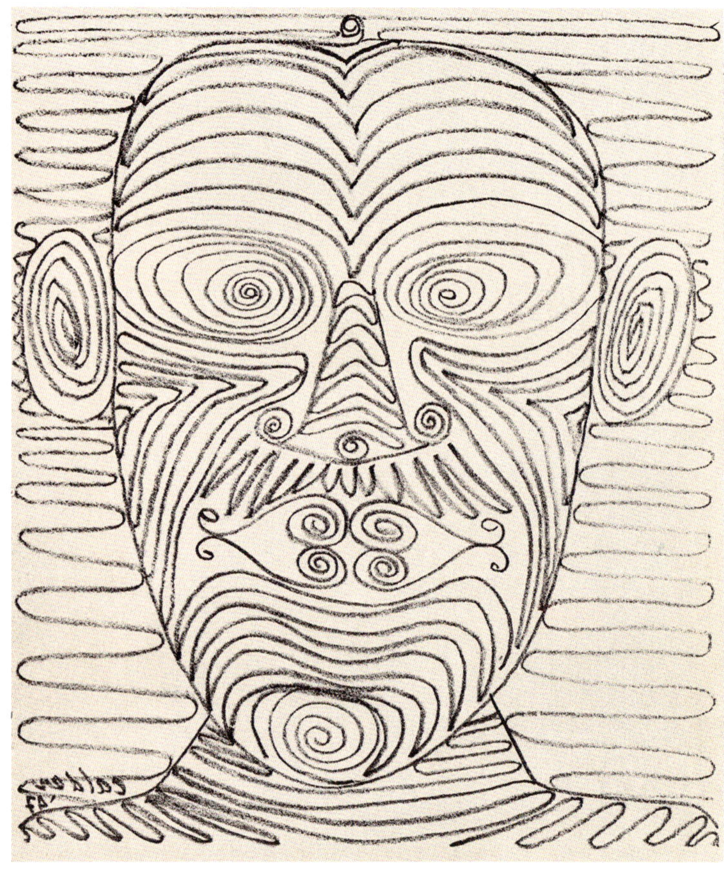

Plate from **Le Surréalisme en 1947**, edited by André Breton. 1947
Lithograph from an illustrated book with eighteen lithographs, four etchings (two with aquatint), two woodcuts, one photogravure, and one ready-made object, comp. (irreg.): $9\frac{1}{8} \times 8$ in. (23.2×20.3 cm); page: $9\frac{7}{16} \times 8$ in. (24×20.3 cm)
Publisher: Pierre à Feu (Maeght Éditeur), Paris. Printer: Mourlot, Paris.
Edition: 950
The Museum of Modern Art, New York. Henry Church Fund

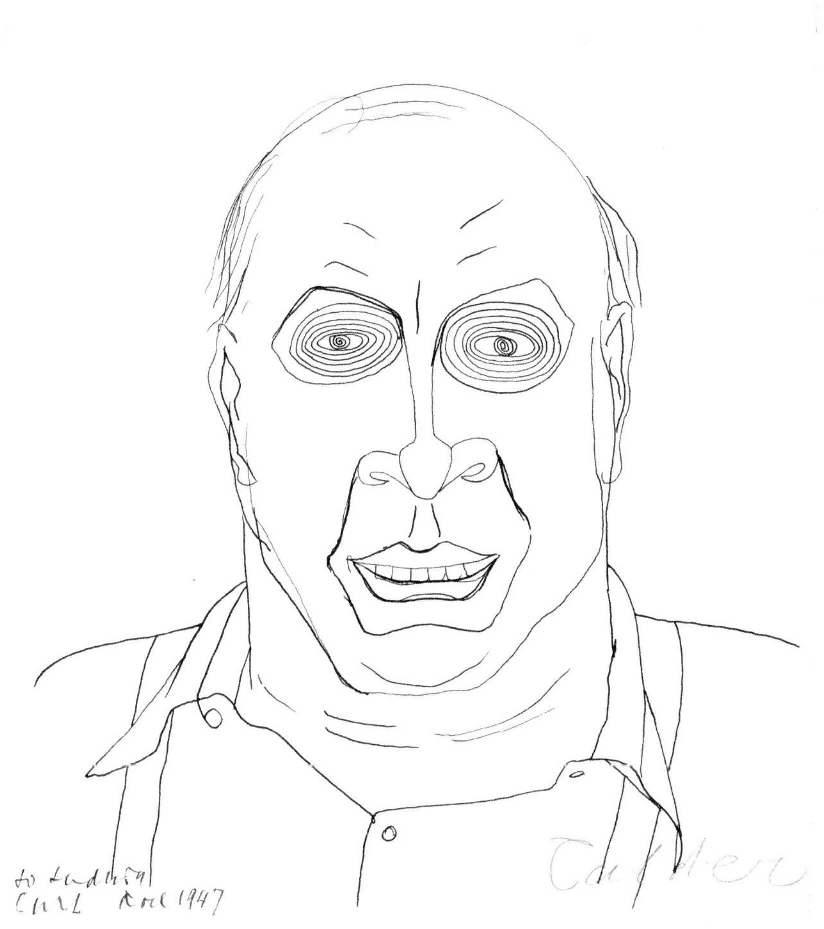

Portrait of Curt Valentin. 1944
Ink on paper, 11 ⅝ × 10 ⅛ in. (29.5 × 25.7 cm)
The Museum of Modern Art, New York.
Gift of Ludwig Charell

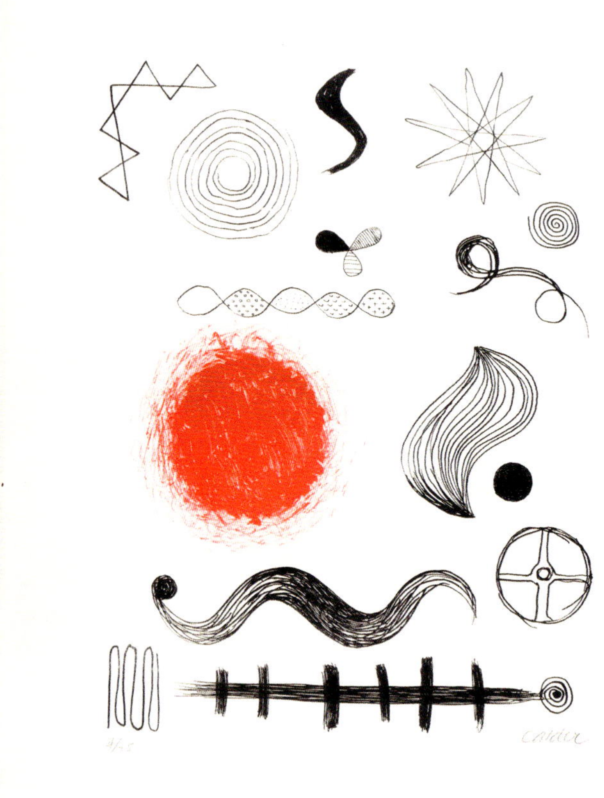

Untitled. 1946
Lithograph, comp.: 14 13⁄16 × 11 ¼ in. (37.6 × 28.6 cm);
sheet: 19 5⁄16 × 15 11⁄16 in. (49.1 × 39.8 cm)
Publisher: Buchholz Gallery, New York.
Printer: Mourlot, Paris. Edition: 25
The Museum of Modern Art, New York.
Gift of the artist

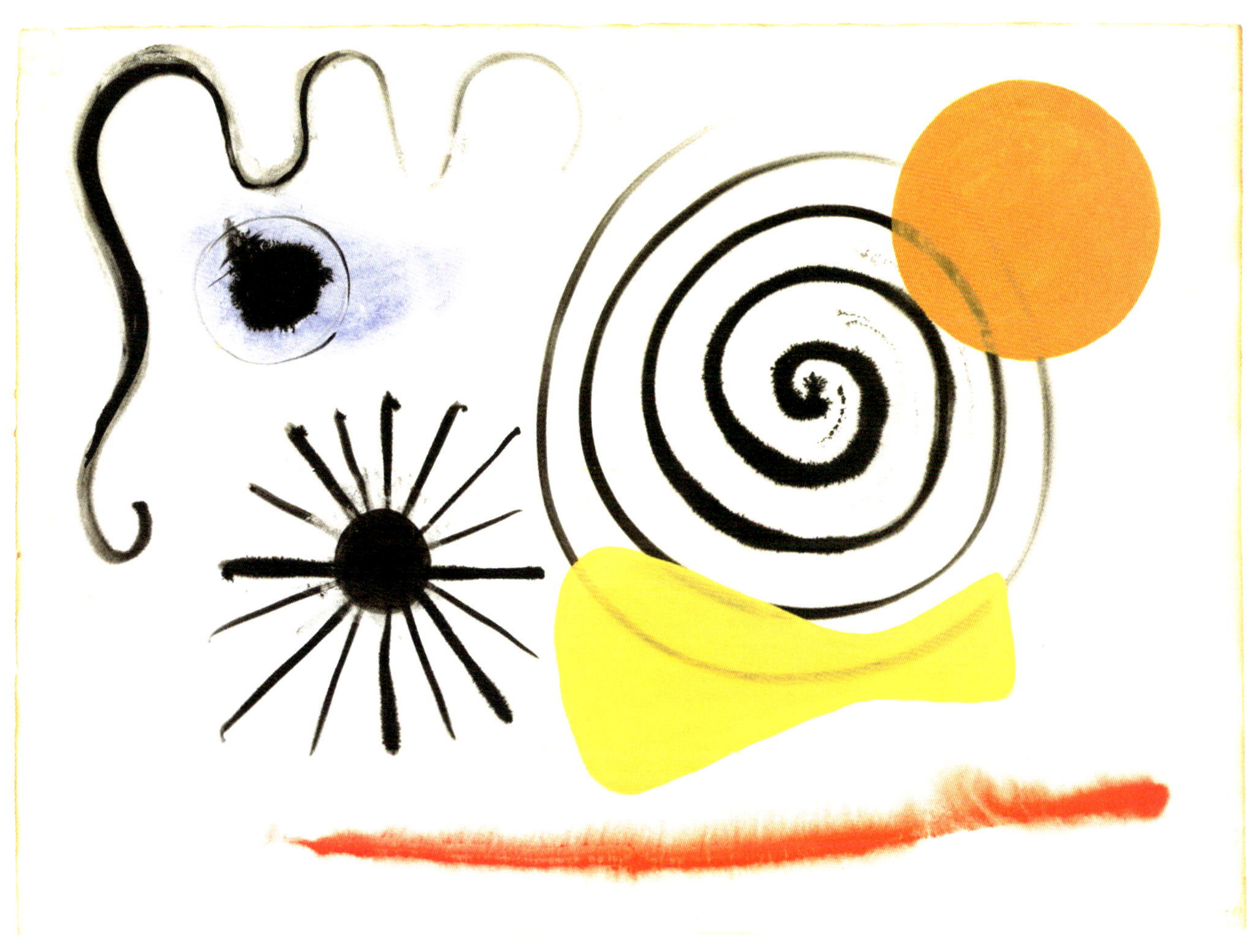

Untitled. 1941
Gouache and ink on paper, 22 ¼ × 30 ⅞ in. (56.5 × 78.4 cm)
The Museum of Modern Art, New York.
James Thrall Soby Bequest

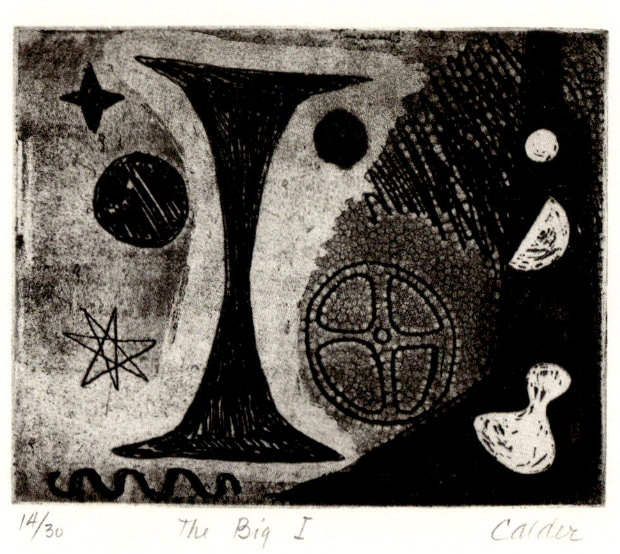

The Big I. 1944
Etching, plate: $6\frac{7}{8} \times 8\frac{7}{8}$ in. (17.5 × 22.5 cm);
sheet: $11\frac{7}{16} \times 15\frac{15}{16}$ in. (29.1 × 40.5 cm)
Publisher: Wittenborn & Co., New York.
Printer: Atelier 17, New York. Edition: 30
The Museum of Modern Art, New York.
Gift of Wittenborn & Co.

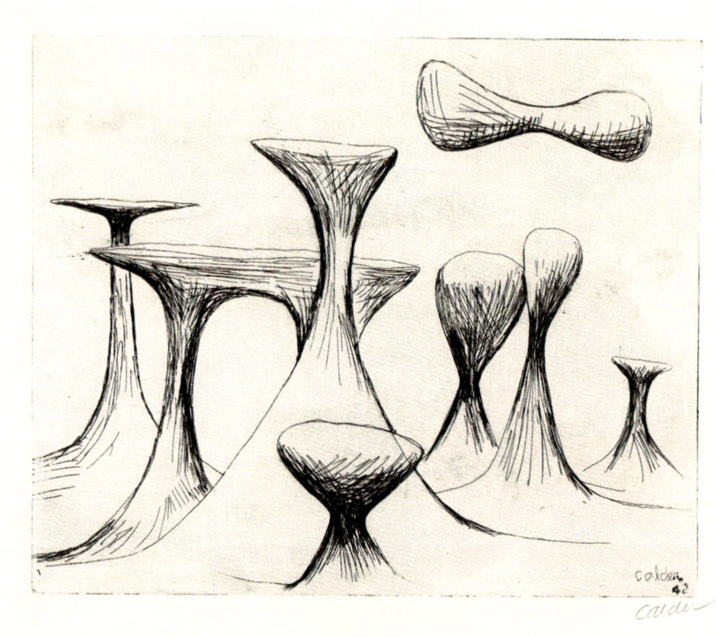

Untitled. 1942
Etching, plate: $11\frac{3}{16} \times 13\frac{15}{16}$ in. (28.4 × 35.4 cm);
sheet: $14\frac{15}{16} \times 19\frac{1}{8}$ in. (37.9 × 48.6 cm)
Edition: unknown
The Museum of Modern Art, New York. Gift of the artist

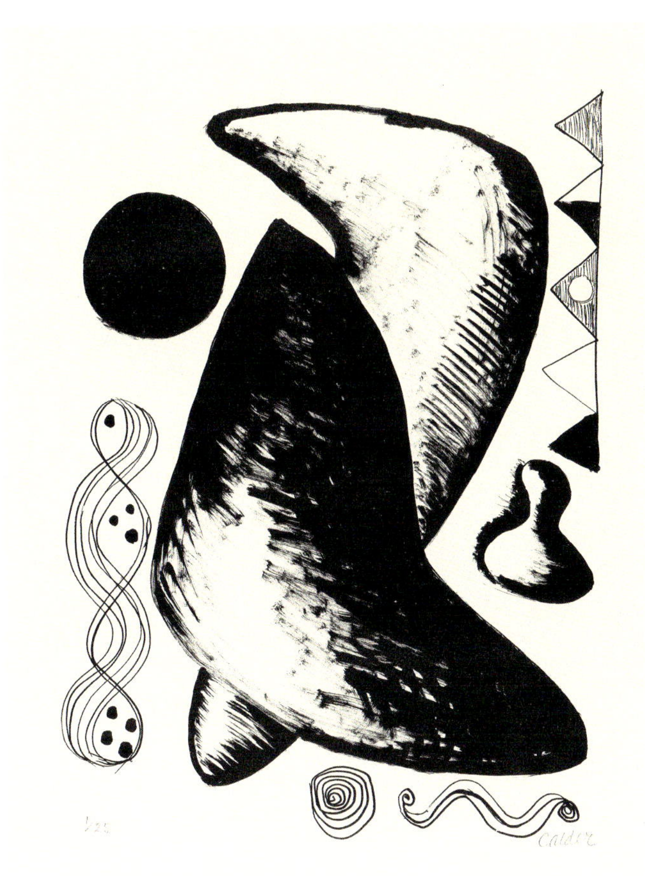

Untitled. 1946
Lithograph, comp.: 16 ¼ × 12 in. (41.3 × 30.5 cm);
sheet: 19 ¾ × 15 ¾ in. (50.2 × 40 cm)
Printer: Mourlot, Paris. Edition: 25
The Museum of Modern Art, New York.
Gift of the artist

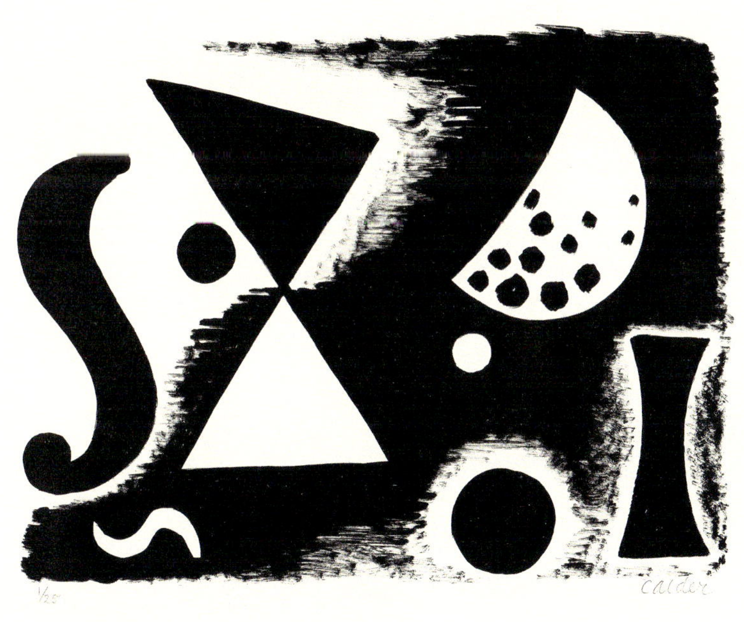

Untitled. 1946
Lithograph, comp.: 11 13/16 × 15 11/16 in. (30 × 39.8 cm);
sheet: 15 11/16 × 19 ¾ in. (39.8 × 50.2 cm)
Printer: Mourlot, Paris. Edition: 25
The Museum of Modern Art, New York. Gift of the artist

Snow Flurry I. 1948
Sheet steel, steel wire, and paint,
7 ft. 10 in. (238.8 cm) high × 6 ft. 10 ¼ in. (208.9 cm) diam.
The Museum of Modern Art, New York. Gift of the artist

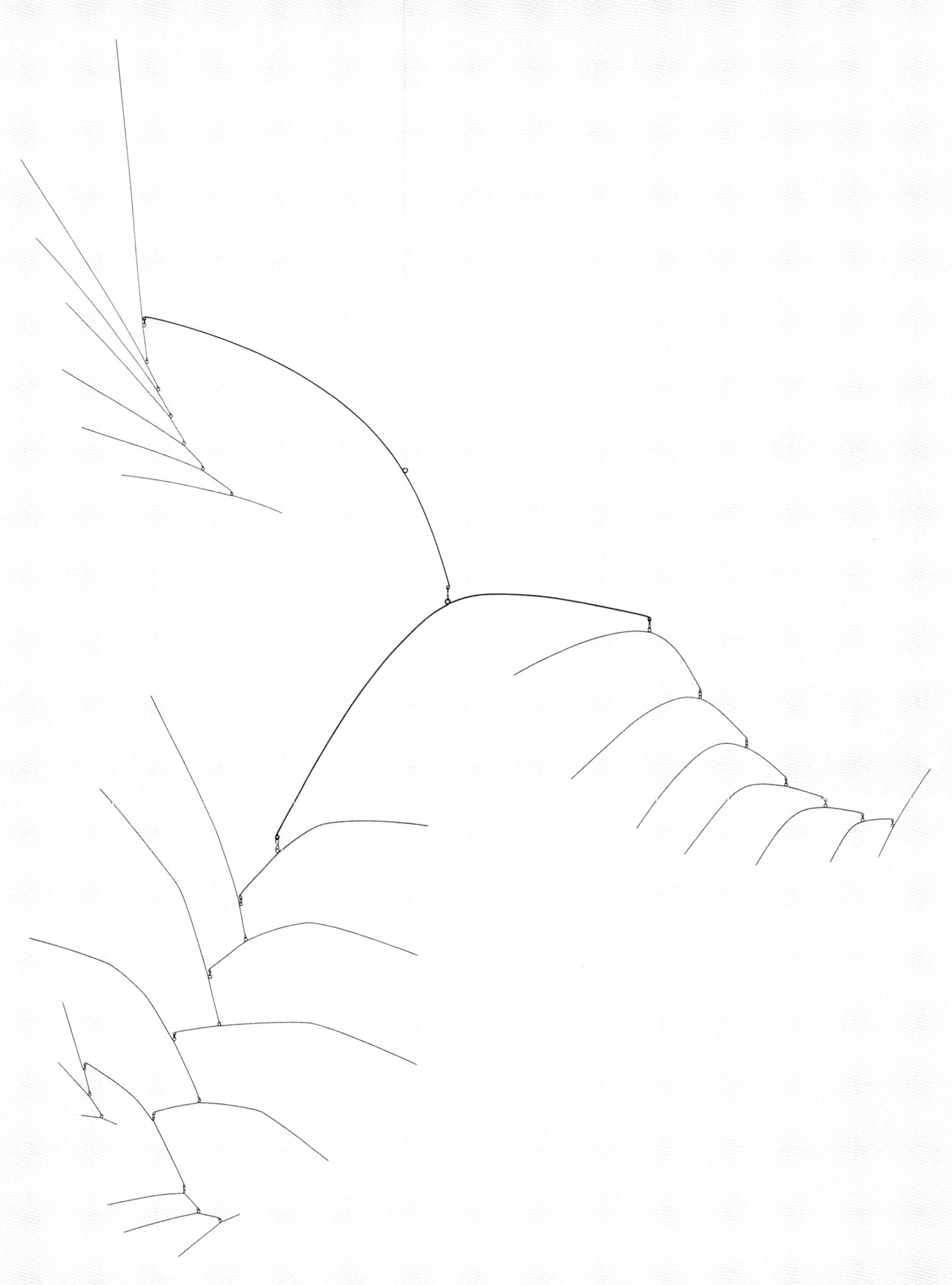

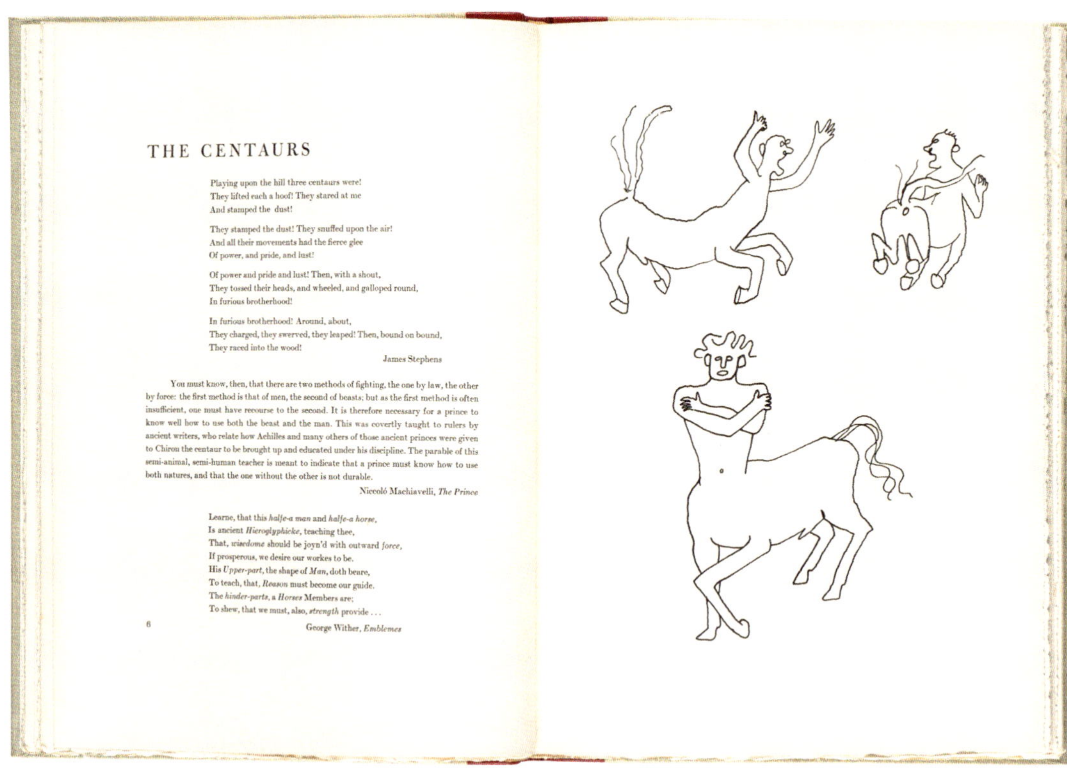

THE CENTAURS

Playing upon the hill three centaurs were!
They lifted each a hoof! They stared at me
And stamped the dust!

They stamped the dust! They snuffed upon the air!
And all their movements had the fierce glee
Of power, and pride, and lust!

Of power and pride and lust! Then, with a shout,
They tossed their heads, and wheeled, and galloped round,
In furious brotherhood!

In furious brotherhood! Around, about,
They charged, they swerved, they leaped! Then, bound on bound,
They raced into the wood!

James Stephens

You must know, then, that there are two methods of fighting, the one by law, the other by *force*: the first method is that of men, the second of beasts; but as the first method is often insufficient, one must have recourse to the second. It is therefore necessary for a prince to know well how to use both the beast and the man. This was covertly taught to rulers by ancient writers, who relate how Achilles and many others of those ancient princes were given to Chiron the centaur to be brought up and educated under his discipline. The parable of this semi-animal, semi-human teacher is meant to indicate that a prince must know how to use both natures, and that the one without the other is not durable.

Niccoló Machiavelli, *The Prince*

Learne, that this *halfe-a man* and *halfe-a horse*,
Is ancient *Hieroglyphicke*, teaching thee,
That, *wisedome* should be joyn'd with outward *force*,
If prosperous, we desire our workes to be.
His *Upper-part*, the shape of *Man*, doth beare,
To teach, that, *Reason* must become our guide.
The *hinder-parts*, a *Horses* Members are;
To shew, that we must, also, *strength* provide . . .

6

George Wither, *Emblemes*

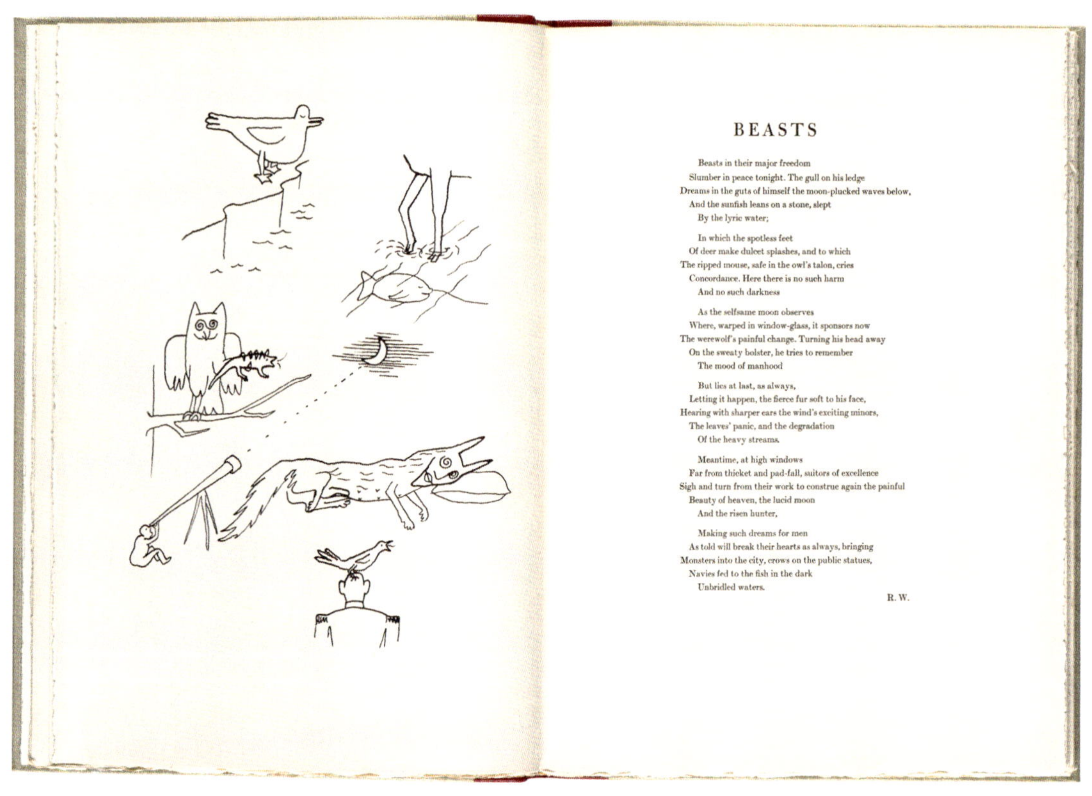

BEASTS

Beasts in their major freedom
Slumber in peace tonight. The gull on his ledge
Dreams in the guts of himself the moon-plucked waves below,
And the sunfish leans on a stone, slept
By the lyric water;

In which the spotless feet
Of deer make dulcet splashes, and to which
The ripped mouse, safe in the owl's talon, cries
Concordance. Here there is no such harm
And no such darkness

As the selfsame moon observes
Where, warped in window-glass, it sponsors now
The werewolf's painful change. Turning his head away
On the sweaty bolster, he tries to remember
The mood of manhood

But lies at last, as always,
Letting it happen, the fierce fur soft to his face,
Hearing with sharper ears the wind's exciting minors,
The leaves' panic, and the degradation
Of the heavy streams.

Meantime, at high windows
Far from thicket and pad-fall, suitors of excellence
Sigh and turn from their work to construe again the painful
Beauty of heaven, the lucid moon
And the risen hunter,

Making such dreams for men
As told will break their hearts as always, bringing
Monsters into the city, crows on the public statues,
Navies fed to the fish in the dark
Unbridled waters.

R. W.

THE OWL

Waterton's childhood was spent at Walton Hall, and in his old age he used sometimes to recall the songs of his nurses. "One of them," he said, "is the only poem in which the owl is pitied. She sang it to the tune of 'Cease, rude Boreas, blustering railer,' and the words are affecting: –

'Once I was a monarch's daughter
And sat on a lady's knee;
But am now a nightly rover,
Banished to the ivy tree.

'Crying, Hoo, hoo, hoo, hoo, hoo, hoo,
Hoo, hoo, hoo, my feet are cold!
Pity me, for here you see me
Persecuted, poor, and old.' "

Norman Moore, *Memoir of Charles Waterton*

Owls have very expressive notes; they hoot in a fine vocal sound, much resembling the *vox humana*, and reducible by a pitch-pipe to a musical key. This note seems to express complacency and rivalry among the males: they use also a quick call and an horrible scream; and can snore and hiss when they mean to menace . . .

A neighbor of mine, who is said to have a nice ear, remarks that the owls about this village hoot in three different keys, in G flat, or F sharp, in B flat and A flat. He heard two hooting to each other, the one in A flat, the other in B flat. *Query*: do these different notes proceed from different species, or only from various individuals? . . .

Gilbert White, *Natural History of Selborne*

There is a singular resemblance between the face of an owl and that of a cat, which is the more notable as both these creatures have much the same kind of habits, live on the same prey, and are evidently representatives of the same idea in their different classes. The owl, in fact, is a winged cat, just as the cat is a furred owl.

J. G. Wood, *Natural History*

Everything in the world is strange and marvellous to well-open eyes. This faculty of wonder is the delight . . . which leads the intellectual man through life in the perpetual ecstasy of the visionary. His special attribute is the wonder of the eyes. Hence it was that the ancients gave Minerva her owl, the bird with ever-dazzled eyes.

José Ortega y Gasset, *Revolt of the Masses*

20

Tuesday, 8 February 1870

Miss Child staying at the house again and in great force. She showed me her clever drawings of horses and told me the adventures of the brown wood owl 'Ruth' which she took home from here last year. She wanted to call the owl 'Eve' but Mrs. Bridge said it should be called 'Ruth.' She and her sister stranded in London at night went to London Bridge hotel (having missed the last train) with little money and no luggage except the owl in a basket. The owl hooted all night in spite of their putting her up the chimney, before the looking glass, under the bed-clothes, and in a circle of lighted candles which they hoped it would mistake for the sun. The owl went on hooting, upset the basket, got out and flew about the room. The chambermaid almost frightened to death dared not come inside the door. Miss Child asked the waiter to get some mice for 'Ruth' but none could be got.

Rev. Francis Kilvert, *Diary*

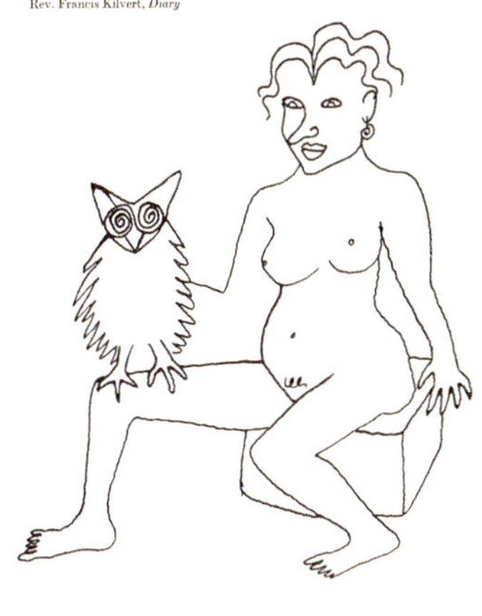

The Mermaide is a sea beast, woonderfully shapen. *Isidore* saith, *Li. II, ca. 3*, where he treateth *De Portentis*, that there be three *Syrenes*, somedeale Maidens, and somedeale foules, with wings & clees. One of them singeth with voice, an other with shamble, and the third with Harpe. Thei please shipmen so greatly with their songe, that they drawe them to peril, and to shipwracke. The cause why they have wings & clees, *Quia Amor & volat, & vulnerat*. . . .

John Bossewell, *Workes of Armorie*

"Do the fishermen along here know anything of the mermaids?" I asked a woman of a village in County Dublin. "Indeed, they don't like to see them at all," she answered, "for they always bring bad weather."

W. B. Yeats, *Irish Fairy and Folk Tales*

These are the seductive voices of the night; the Sirens, too, sang that way. It would be doing them an injustice to think that they wanted to seduce; they knew they had claws and sterile wombs, and they lamented this aloud. They could not help it if their laments sounded so beautiful.

Franz Kafka, *Parables*

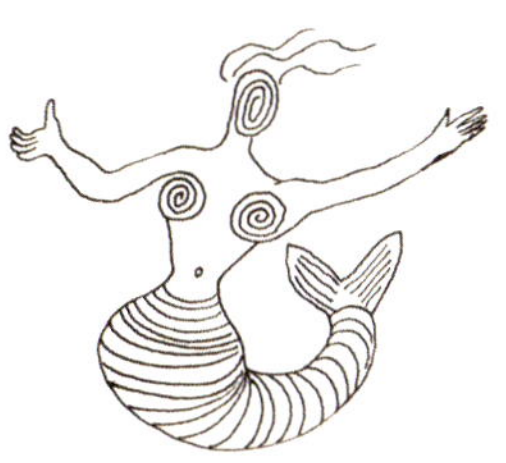

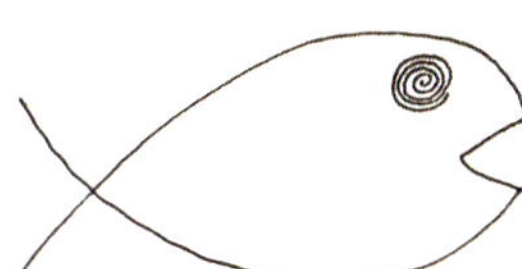

THE FISH

I looked into his eyes
which were far larger than mine
but shallower, and yellowed,
the irises backed and packed
with tarnished tinfoil
seen through the lenses
of old scratched isinglass.
They shifted a little, but not
to return my stare.
– It was more like the tipping
of an object toward the light.

Elizabeth Bishop
from "The Fish"

The fishes in the waters under the earth represent the inhabitants of hell. The waters in Scripture is represented as the place of the dead, the Rephaim, the destroyers; and whales and sea monsters that swim in the great deep are used in Scripture as emblems of devils and the wrath of God, and the miseries of death and God's wrath are there compared to the sea, to the deeps, to floods and billows and the like.

Jonathan Edwards, *Images or Shadows*

27

A Bestiary, compiled by Richard Wilbur. 1955
Illustrated book with fifty-six letterpress plates,
page (each): 12 ½ × 9 3⁄16 in. (31.8 × 23.3 cm);
overall (closed): 12 ¾ × 9 ⅜ × 11⁄16 in. (32.4 × 23.9 × 1.8 cm)

Publisher: Pantheon Books, New York.
Printer: Spiral Press, New York. Edition: 825
The Museum of Modern Art, New York.
The Louis E. Stern Collection

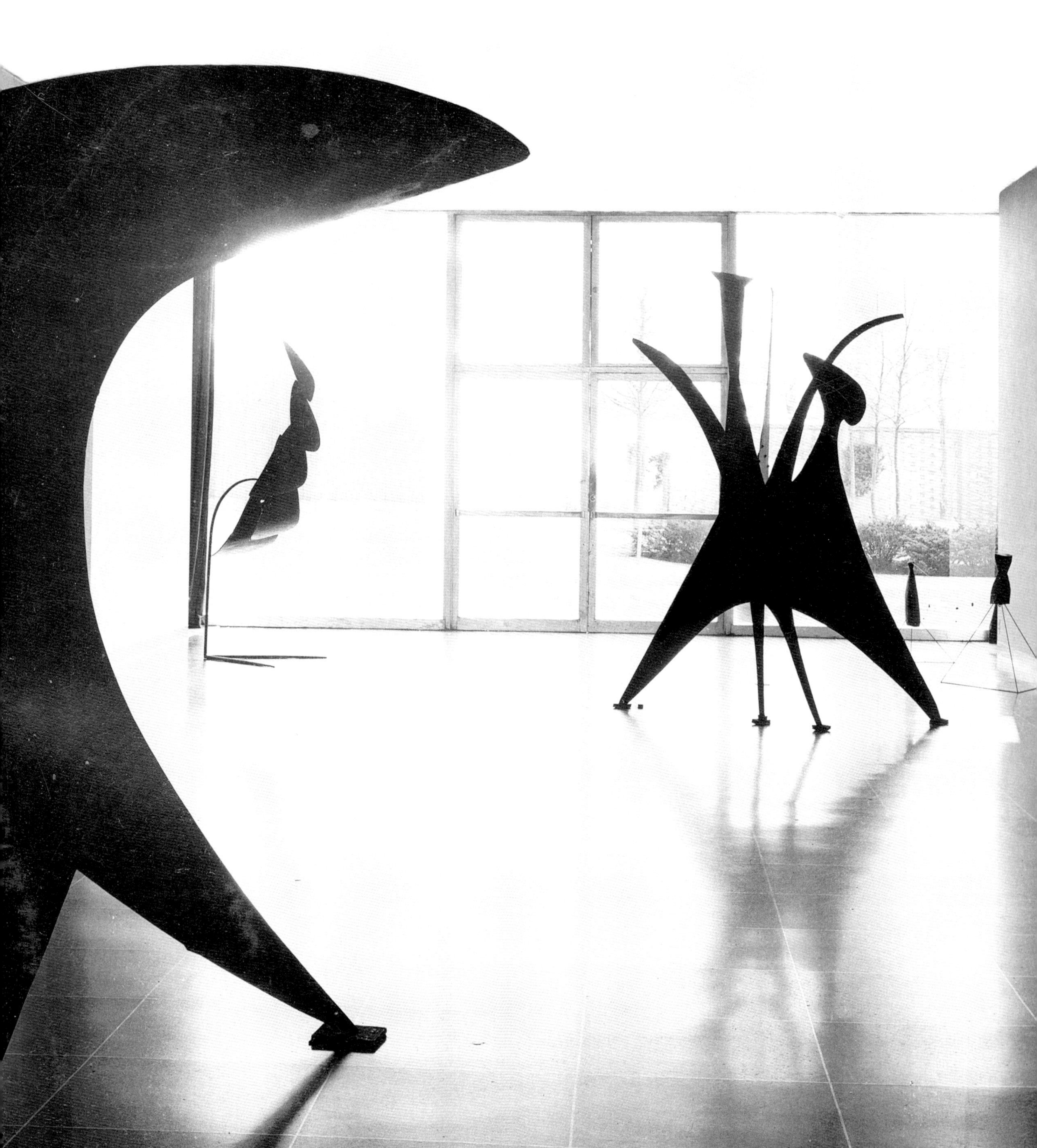

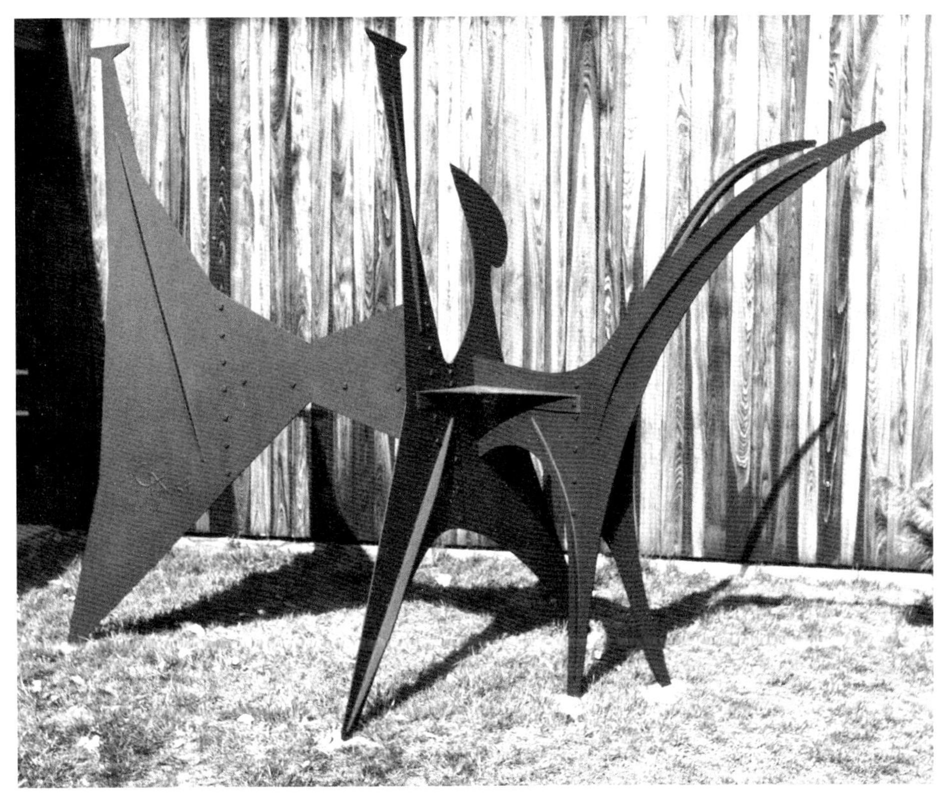

Black Beast II. 1957
Sheet steel and paint, 8 ft. 9 in. × 11 ft. × 6 ft. 5 in. (266.7 × 335.3 × 195.6 cm)
The Museum of Modern Art, New York. Eliot F. Noyes Bequest
Commissioned by Eliot F. Noyes
Above: Installation view at Eliot Noyes House, New Canaan, Connecticut, 1957.
Opposite: Installation view of **Black Beast** (1940), the first version of the sculpture, in **Alexander Calder: Sculpture and Constructions**, The Museum of Modern Art, New York, September 29, 1943–January 16, 1944. This version is now in the collection of the Calder Foundation, New York.

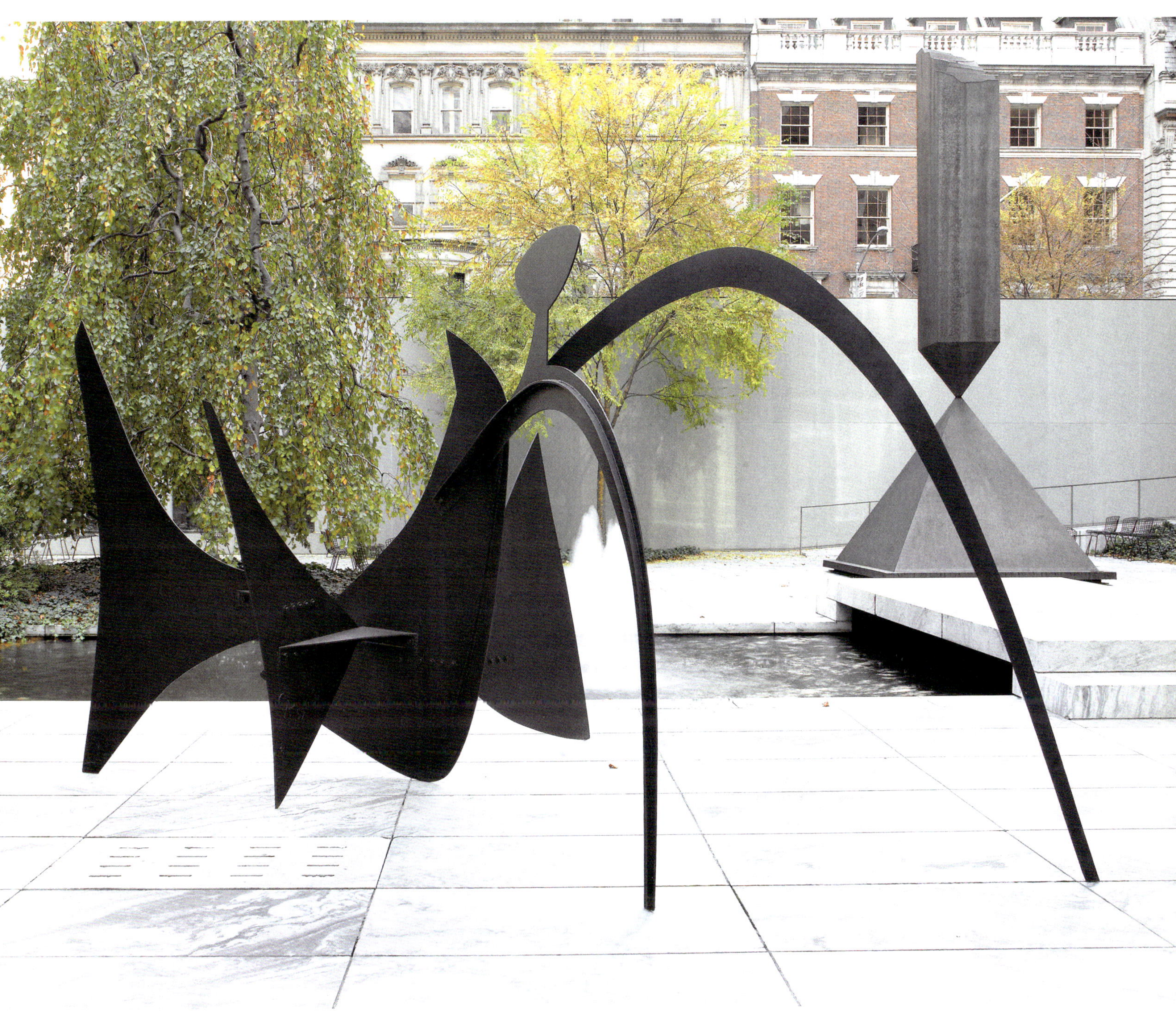

Black Widow. 1959
Sheet steel and paint, 7 ft. 8 in. × 14 ft. 3 in. × 7 ft. 5 in.
(233.7 × 434.3 × 226.1 cm)
The Museum of Modern Art, New York.
Mrs. Simon Guggenheim Fund

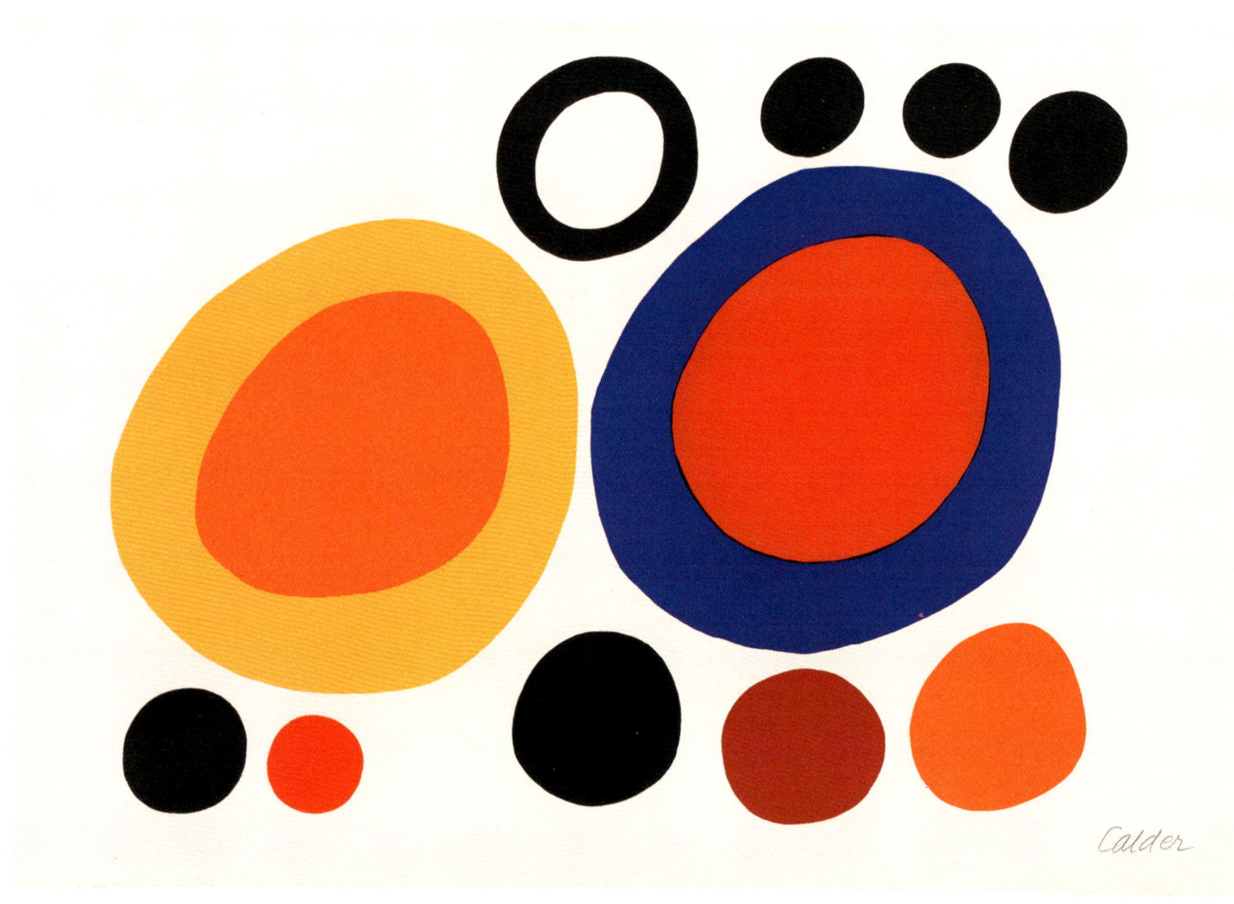

Smoke Rings (**Rondelles de fumée**). 1960
Lithograph, comp. (irreg.): 21 5⁄16 × 24 1⁄4 in. (54.1 × 61.6 cm);
sheet: 29 1⁄4 × 35 5⁄16 in. (74.3 × 89.7 cm)
Publisher: Maeght Éditeur, Paris. Printer: Maeght Imprimerie,
Levallois-Perret, France. Edition: unknown
The Museum of Modern Art, New York. John B. Turner Fund

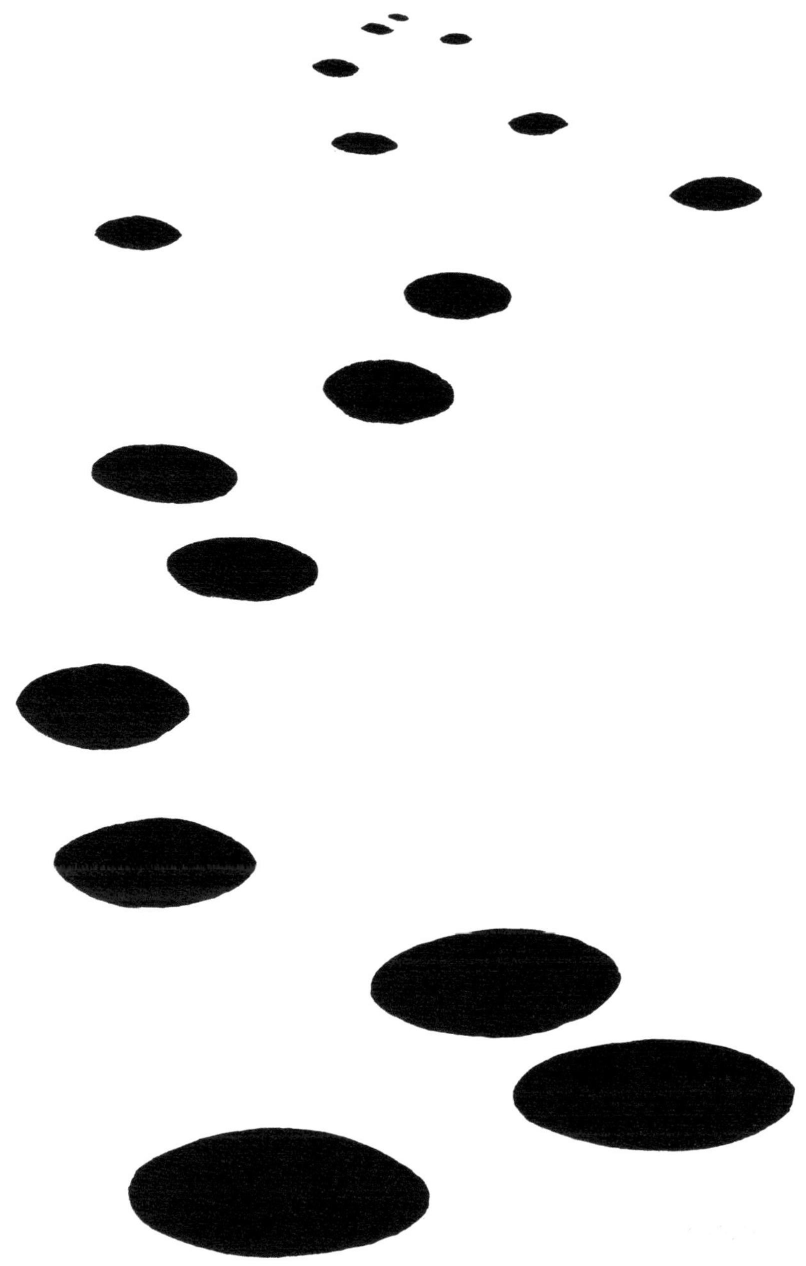

Flying Saucers (**Soucoupes volantes**). 1969
Lithograph, comp. (irreg.): 42 ⅜ × 27 5⁄16 in.
(107.6 × 69.4 cm); sheet: 43 3⁄16 × 29 11⁄16 in. (109.7 × 75.4 cm)
Publisher: Maeght Éditeur, Paris. Printer: Maeght
Imprimerie, Levallois-Perret, France. Edition: 75
The Museum of Modern Art, New York.
Gift of Dr. and Mrs. Barnett Malbin

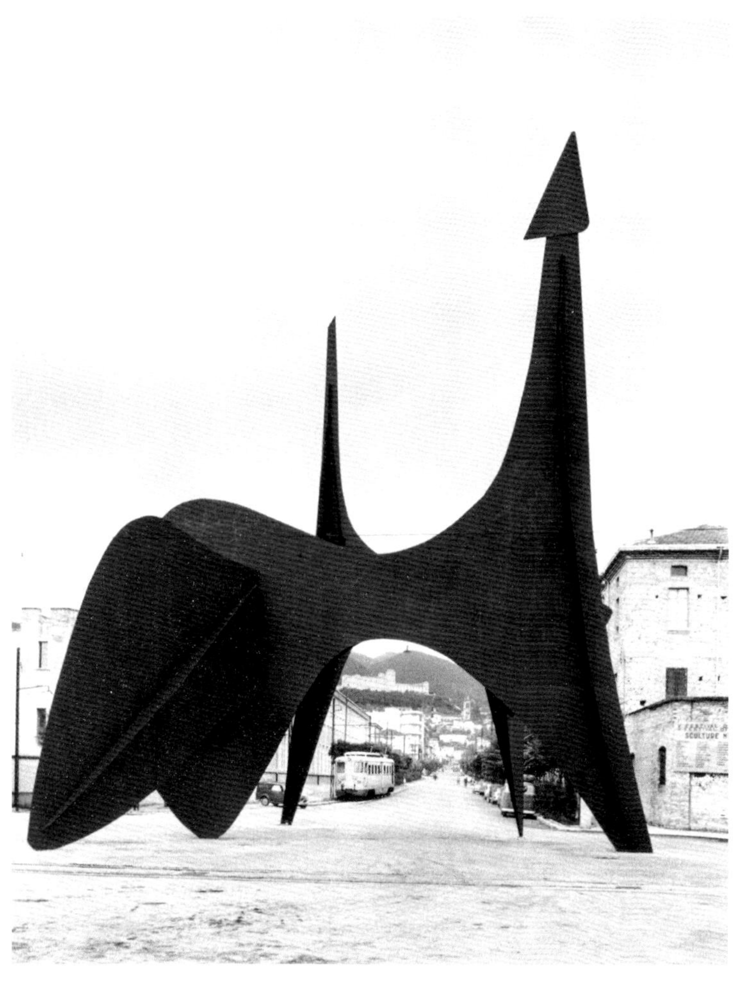

Teodelapio (maquette II). 1962
Sheet aluminum and paint, 23 ¾ × 15 ¼ × 15 ¾ in. (60.3 × 38.7 × 40 cm)
The Museum of Modern Art, New York. Gift of the artist
Above: Installation view of the public sculpture, commissioned by the city of Spoleto, Italy, for which this maquette was made, 1962. Photograph by Ugo Mulas

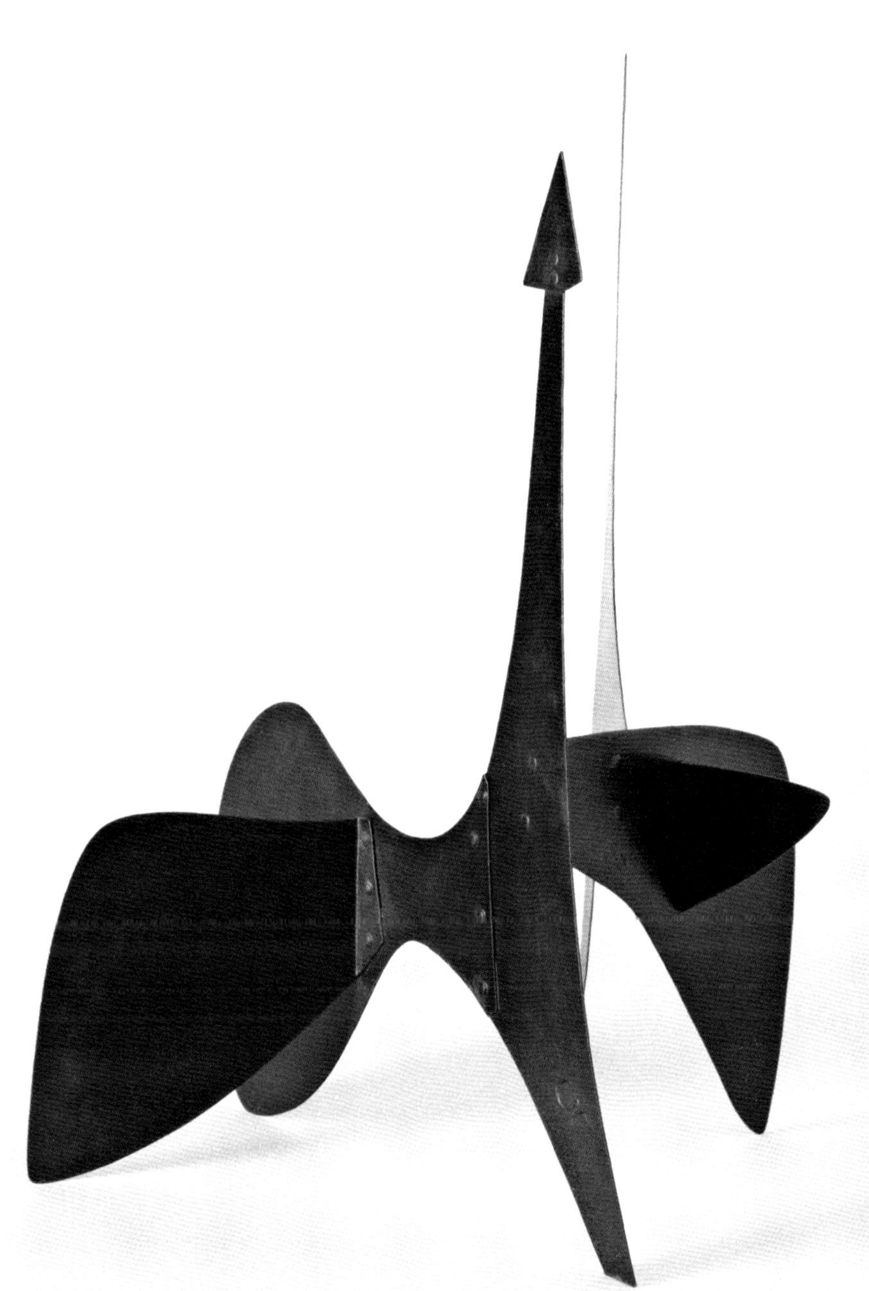

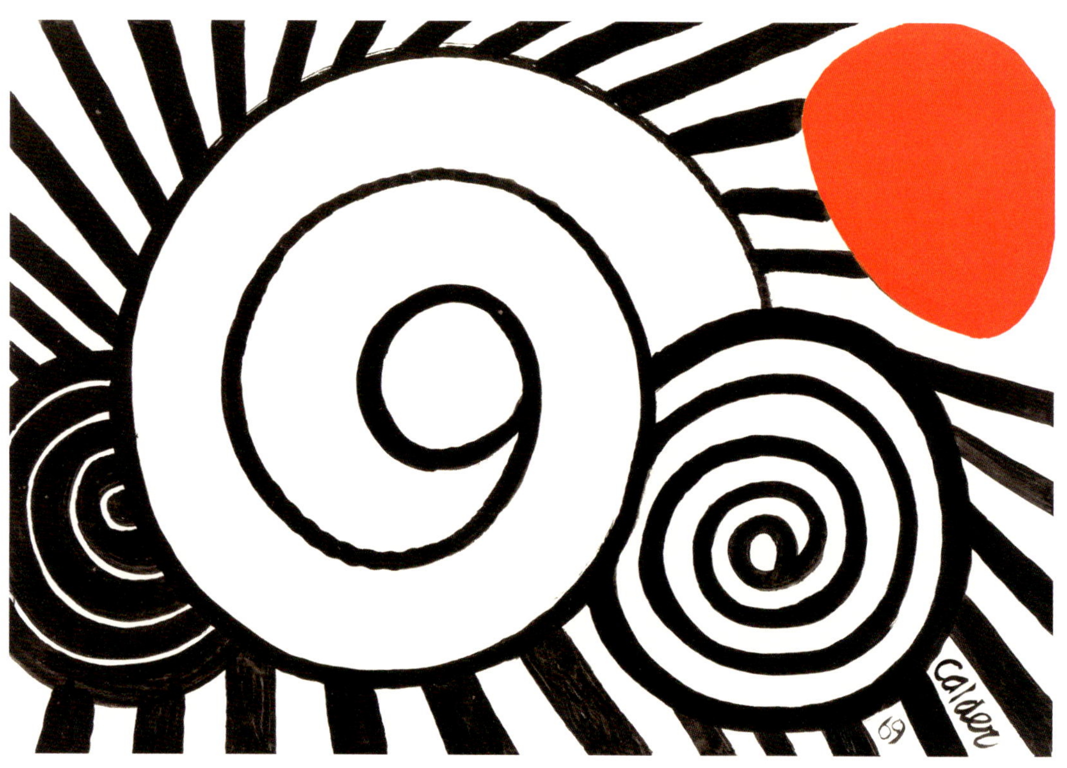

Untitled. 1969
Ink and gouache on paper, 29 ½ × 43 ⅛ in. (74.9 × 109.5 cm)
The Museum of Modern Art, New York. Gift of the artist

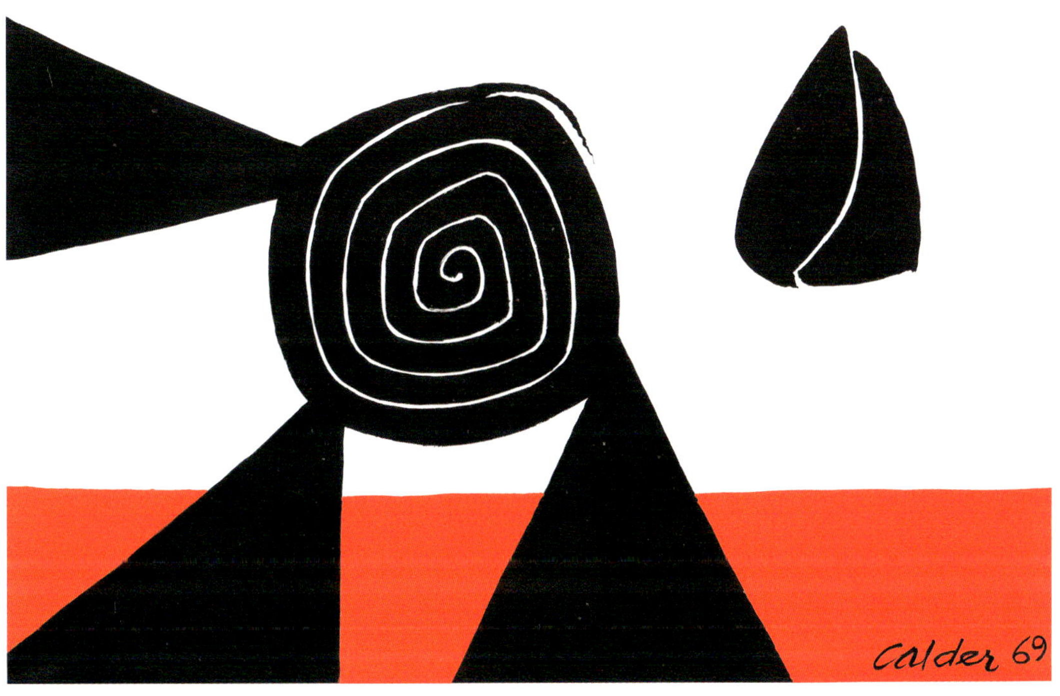

Untitled. 1969
Oil and gouache on paper, 29 ½ × 43 ¼ in. (74.9 × 109.9 cm)
The Museum of Modern Art, New York. Gift of the artist

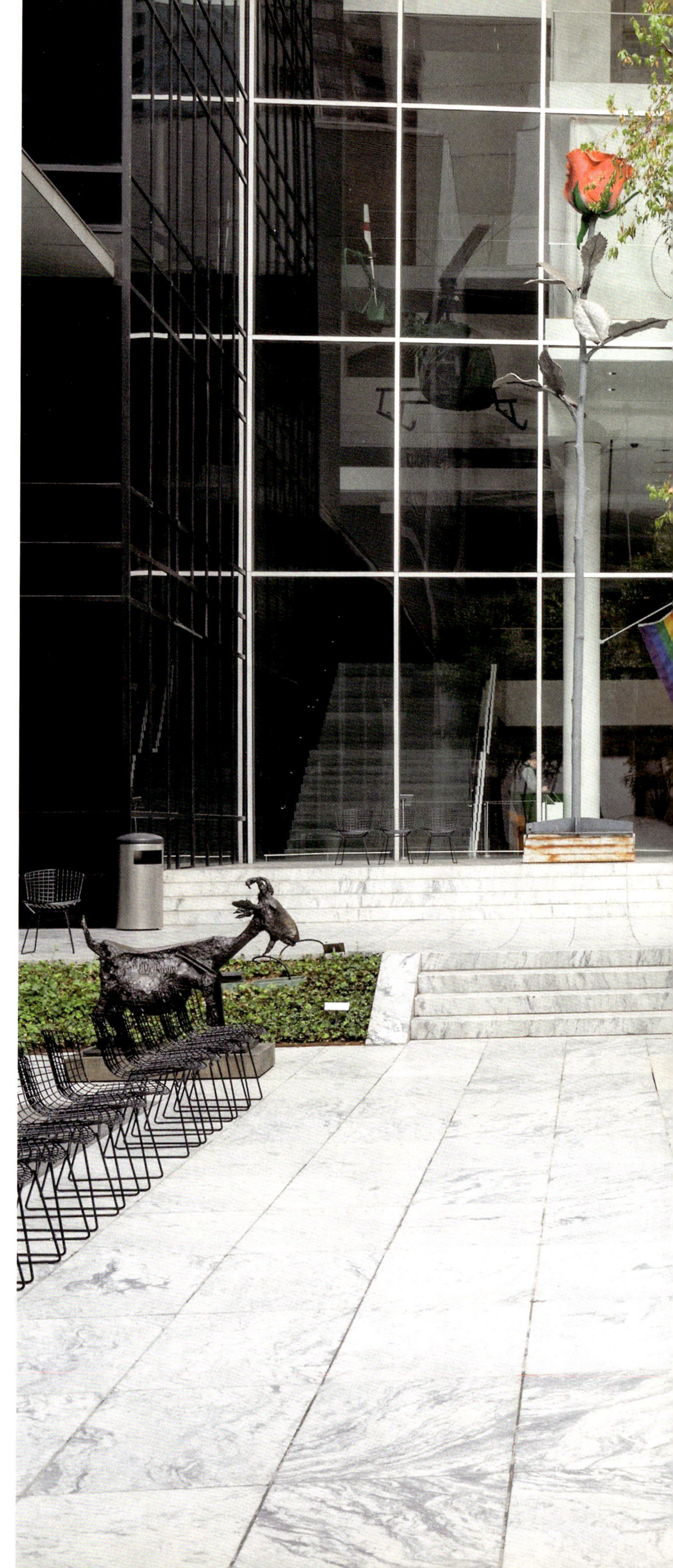

Sandy's Butterfly. 1964
Steel, stainless sheet steel, iron rods, and paint,
12 ft. 8 in. × 9 ft. 2 in. × 8 ft. 7 in. (386.1 × 279.4 × 261.6 cm)
The Museum of Modern Art, New York. Gift of the artist

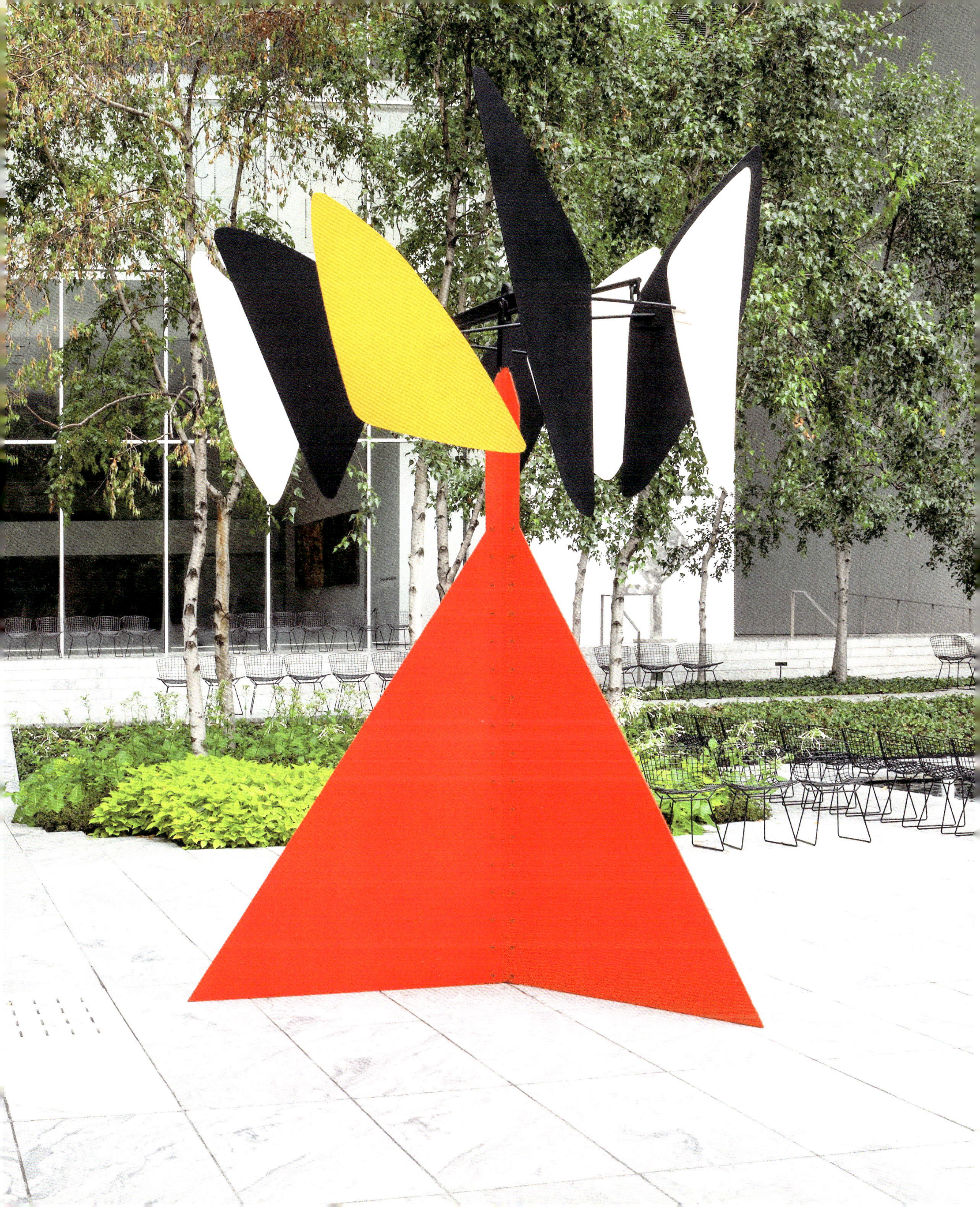

Additional Works by Alexander Calder in the Collection of The Museum of Modern Art

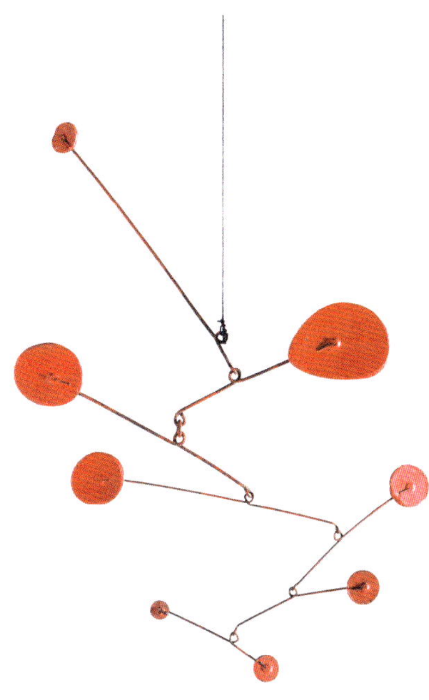

Untitled. 1959
Sheet metal, wire, cotton thread, and paint, 8½ in. (21.6 cm) high × 5 in. (12.7 cm) diam.
The Museum of Modern Art, New York.
Nina and Gordon Bunshaft Bequest

Untitled. n.d.
Pencil on paper, 8 ½ × 11 in. (21.6 × 27.9 cm)
Study Collection. Gift of the Gilbert B. and Lila Silverman Instruction Drawing Collection, Detroit, 2018

Untitled mobile. n.d.
Felt-tip pen on paper, 11 ¾ × 8 ¼ in. (29.9 × 21 cm)
Study Collection. Gift of the Gilbert B. and Lila Silverman Instruction Drawing Collection, Detroit, 2018

Untitled. n.d.
Ink on paper, 6 ¼ × 13 ½ in. (15.9 × 34.3 cm)
Nina and Gordon Bunshaft Bequest, 1995

Untitled. 1932
Ink on paper, 21 ¾ × 29 ¾ in. (55.3 × 75.6 cm)
Nina and Gordon Bunshaft Bequest, 1995

Pattern for **The Big Ear**. 1943
Synthetic polymer paint on cut-and-pasted brown wrapping paper, 7 ft. 3 ½ in. × 37 ¼ in. (222.3 × 94.6 cm)
Study Collection. Gift of Margaret Miller, 2018

Untitled. 1946
Lithograph, comp.: 18 7⁄16 × 14 ¼ in. (46.8 × 36.2 cm); sheet: 19 ¾ × 15 11⁄16 in. (50.2 × 39.8 cm)
Edition: unknown
Gift of the artist, 1969

Untitled. 1946
Lithograph, comp.: 18 ⅜ × 14 7⁄16 in. (46.7 × 36.7 cm); sheet: 19 ¾ × 15 ¾ in. (50.2 × 40 cm)
Edition: unknown
Gift of the artist, 1969

Untitled. 1946
Lithograph, comp.: 10 × 12 in. (25.4 × 30.5 cm); sheet: 19 11⁄16 × 15 ¾ in. (50 × 40 cm)
Gift of the artist, 1969

Sheep. 1955
Pen and ink on paper, 14 ½ × 11 ½ in. (36.8 × 29.2 cm)
Study Collection. Gift of Mr. and Mrs. Walter Bareiss, 1957

Lunar View (Aspect lunaire). 1961
Aquatint, plate: 13 5⁄16 × 18 9⁄16 in. (33.8 × 47.1 cm); sheet: 19 5⁄8 × 25 7⁄8 in. (49.9 × 65.7 cm)
Publisher: Maeght Éditeur, Paris
Printer: Maeght Imprimerie, Levallois-Perret, France
Edition: proof outside an edition of 90
John B. Turner Fund, 1970

The Skull in the Nest (Le Crâne dans le nid). 1961
Aquatint, plate: 11 × 14 15⁄16 in. (27.9 × 37.9 cm); sheet: 19 13⁄16 × 26 1⁄8 in. (50.3 × 66.4 cm)
Publisher: Maeght Éditeur, Paris
Printer Maeght Imprimerie, Levallois-Perret, France
Edition: proof outside an edition of 90
John B. Turner Fund, 1970

The Giant Yellow Ant-Eater (Tamonoir jaune). 1963
Lithograph, comp. (irreg.): 14 7⁄8 × 21 1⁄16 in. (37.8 × 53.5 cm); sheet: 18 7⁄8 × 25 ½ in. (47.9 × 64.8 cm)
Publisher: Maeght Éditeur, Paris
Printer: Maeght Imprimerie, Levallois-Perret, France
Edition: proof outside an edition of unknown number
John B. Turner Fund, 1970

Snow-Plough (Chasse-neige). 1963
Lithograph, comp. (irreg.): 11 ¾ × 16 1⁄16 in. (29.9 × 40.8 cm); sheet: 18 3⁄8 × 22 5⁄16 in. (46.7 × 56.7 cm)
Publisher: Maeght Éditeur, Paris
Printer: Maeght Imprimerie, Levallois-Perret, France
Edition: proof outside an edition of unknown number
John B. Turner Fund, 1970

Alexander Calder—Los Angeles County Museum of Art, April 1, 1965. 1965
Lithograph, 32 × 24 5⁄8 in. (81.3 × 62.5 cm)
Peter Stone Collection of Posters by Artists, 1976

Moonlight in a Gust of Wind (Un Clair de lune dans un coup de vent). (1965–66)
Lithograph, comp. (irreg.): 14 × 22 13⁄16 in. (35.6 × 57.9 cm); sheet: 18 ¾ × 25 5⁄8 in. (47.6 × 65.1 cm)
Publisher: Maeght Éditeur, Paris
Printer: Maeght Imprimerie, Levallois-Perret, France
Edition: 90
John B. Turner Fund, 1970

The Red Sun (Le Soleil rouge). 1965
Lithograph, comp. (irreg.): 20 5⁄16 × 27 5⁄16 in. (51.6 × 69.4 cm); sheet: 21 15⁄16 × 31 7⁄8 in. (55.7 × 81 cm)
Publisher: Maeght Éditeur, Paris
Printer: Maeght Imprimerie, Levallois-Perret, France
Edition: proof outside an edition of 90
John B. Turner Fund, 1970

Calder—Rétrospective Alexandre Calder—Galerie Krugier & Cie, 5, grand-rue, Genève, 9 Juin–30 Juillet 1966. 1966
Poster, 27 ½ × 18 in. (69.9 × 45.7 cm)
Peter Stone Collection of Posters by Artists, 1976

Gouaches Totems, Galerie Maeght, Calder. 1966
Lithograph, 29 ¾ × 21 1⁄8 in. (75.6 × 53.7 cm)
Don Page Fund, 1966

La Proue de la table, by Yves Elléouët. 1967
Illustrated book with seven etchings and journal with letterpress reproductions, overall (closed): 15 3⁄8 × 11 ¾ × ½ in. (39.1 × 29.9 × 1.3 cm)
Publisher: Le Soleil Noir, Paris
Printer: Lacourière, Paris
Edition: 55
Gift of Associated American Artists, 1969

The Bicycle (free reconstruction after **"The motorized mobile that Duchamp liked"**). 1968
Wood, metal, motor, cord, and steel wire, 61 ½ × 59 × 26 1⁄8 in. (156.2 × 149.9 × 66.4 cm)
Gift of the artist, 1969

ORTF à tous. 1968
Lithograph, 40 1⁄16 × 23 1⁄8 in. (101.8 × 58.7 cm)
Peter Stone Collection of Posters by Artists, 1976

Black Man. (1969)
Lithograph, comp. (irreg.): 29 ¼ × 41 ¼ in. (74.3 × 104.8 cm); sheet: 29 7⁄16 × 43 1⁄8 in. (74.8 × 109.5 cm)
Publisher: Maeght Éditeur, Paris
Printer: Maeght Imprimerie, Levallois-Perret, France
Edition: 75
John B. Turner Fund, 1970

Humanité, Fête de l'humanité 6 et 7 Septembre 1969 / Vincennes / Exposition de sculptures. 1969
Lithograph, 31 1⁄16 × 22 11⁄16 in. (79 × 57.6 cm)
Peter Stone Collection of Posters by Artists, 1976

Slanting Red Nose. 1969
Gouache on paper, 29 ½ × 43 ¼ in. (74.9 × 109.9 cm)
Gift of Mr. and Mrs. Klaus G. Perls, 1969

Untitled. 1969
Gouache on paper, 29 ½ × 43 ⅜ in. (74.9 × 110.2 cm)
Gift of the artist, 1969

Untitled, from **Flight**. 1971
Lithograph from a portfolio of eleven lithographs and one screenprint, by various artists, comp. (irreg.): 23 ⅛ × 18 9/16 in. (58.8 7 × 47.2 1 cm); sheet: 25 ⅞ × 19 ⅝ in. (65.8 7 × 49.8 9 cm)
Publisher: International Rescue Committee, New York
Printer: Mourlot, Paris
Edition: artist's proof before an edition of 300
Gift of Jerry I. Speyer and Katherine Farley, 2003

Calder Circus. 1972
Offset lithograph, 36 × 27 ½ in. (91.4 × 69.9 cm)
Gift of Peter Stone, 1983

Calder's Circus, Whitney Museum of American Art, April 20–July 11, 1972. 1972
Lithograph, 36 × 27 ⅜ in. (91.4 × 69.5 cm)
Peter Stone Collection of Posters by Artists, 1976

The Horse. (1976)
Lithograph, comp. (irreg.): 29 ⅛ × 21 5/16 in. (74 × 54.1 cm); sheet: 29 ⅝ × 21 5/16 in. (75.3 × 54.1 cm)
Edition: unknown
Gift of Brewster Gallery, New York, 1978

Checklist of the Exhibition

These are the artworks included in **Alexander Calder: Modern from the Start**, at The Museum of Modern Art, New York, March 7–August 7, 2021. They are arranged chronologically, and alphabetically within each year. The works reproduced in this volume are identified by page number.

Cow. c. 1926
Wire, wood, and string, 5 ¾ × 8 ⅛ × 6 in. (14.6 × 20.6 × 15.2 cm)
The Museum of Modern Art, New York. Gift of Edward M. M. Warburg, 1941
page 50

Josephine Baker III. c. 1927
Steel wire, 39 × 22 ⅜ × 9 ¾ in. (99.1 × 56.8 × 24.8 cm)
The Museum of Modern Art, New York. Gift of the artist, 1966
page 49

Soda Fountain. c. 1927
Steel wire and wood, 12 ½ × 6 ¼ × 3 ½ in. (31.8 × 15.9 × 8.9 cm)
The Museum of Modern Art, New York. Gift of the artist, 1966
page 53

Cat Lamp. 1928
Steel wire and paper, 8 ¾ × 10 ⅛ × 3 ⅛ in. (22.2 × 25.7 × 7.9 cm)
The Museum of Modern Art, New York. Gift of the artist, 1966
page 64

Cow. 1928
Wood, 12 ⅝ × 15 × 8 ⅞ in. (32.1 × 38.1 × 22.5 cm)
Calder Foundation, New York. Purchase, 2017
page 12

Elephant Chair with Lamp (The Elephant Hunter's Chair). 1928
Galvanized steel, steel wire, lead, cloth, paper, and paint, 7 ⅞ × 3 ½ × 4 ⅛ in. (20 × 8.9 × 10.5 cm)
The Museum of Modern Art, New York. Gift of the artist, 1966
page 64

The Horse. 1928
Wood, 15 ½ × 34 ¾ × 8 ⅛ in. (39.4 × 88.3 × 20.6 cm)
The Museum of Modern Art, New York. Acquired through the Lillie P. Bliss Bequest (by exchange), 1943
page 51

The Hostess (Dowager). 1928
Steel wire and wood, 12 × 4 × 12 in. (30.5 × 10.2 × 30.5 cm)
The Museum of Modern Art, New York. Gift of Edward M. M. Warburg, 1941
page 52

Marion Greenwood. 1928
Brass wire, 12 ⅝ × 11 ⅛ × 11 ⅜ in. (32.1 × 28.3 × 28.9 cm)
The Museum of Modern Art, New York. Gift of the artist, 1966
page 54

Portrait of a Man. c. 1928
Brass wire, 12 ⅞ × 8 ¾ × 13 ½ in. (32.7 × 22.2 × 34.3 cm)
The Museum of Modern Art, New York. Gift of the artist, 1966
page 55

Sow. 1928
Steel wire, 7 ½ × 17 × 3 in. (19.1 × 43.2 × 7.6 cm)
The Museum of Modern Art, New York. Gift of the artist, 1944
page 46

Cow (Vache). c. 1929
Steel wire, 6 ½ × 16 × 4 ¼ in. (16.5 × 40.6 × 10.8 cm)
The Museum of Modern Art, New York. Gift of Edward M. M. Warburg, 1941
page 47

Shark Sucker. 1930
Wood, 10 ¾ × 30 ⅞ × 10 ¼ in. (27.3 × 78.4 × 26 cm)
The Museum of Modern Art, New York. Gift of the artist, 1966
page 61

Fables of Aesop. 1931
Illustrated book with fifty-two letterpress prints and one supplementary drawing (ink on paper), page (each, irreg.): 9 13⁄16 × 7 11⁄16 in. (24.9 × 19.5 cm); drawing: 9 13⁄16 × 7 1⁄4 in. (24.9 × 18.4 cm); overall (closed): 10 3⁄16 × 7 7⁄8 × 3⁄4 in. (25.9 × 20 × 2 cm)
Publisher: Harrison of Paris, Paris; Minton Balch and Company, New York
Printer: Aimé Jourde
Edition: 665
The Museum of Modern Art, New York. Gift of Monroe Wheeler, 1966
pages 58, 59

Many. 1931
Ink on paper, 19 5⁄8 × 25 1⁄2 in. (49.9 × 64.8 cm)
The Museum of Modern Art, New York. Gift of Mr. and Mrs. Klaus G. Perls, 1968
page 60

Untitled. 1931
Ink on paper, 30 3⁄4 × 22 3⁄4 in. (78.1 × 57.8 cm)
Calder Foundation, New York. Purchase, 2016

The Catch II. 1932
Ink on paper, 19 1⁄8 × 14 1⁄8 in. (48.6 × 35.9 cm)
The Museum of Modern Art, New York. Gift of Mr. and Mrs. Peter A. Rübel, 1965
page 56

Circus Interior. 1932
Ink on paper, 19 × 14 in. (48.3 × 35.6 cm)
The Museum of Modern Art, New York. Gift of Mr. and Mrs. Peter A. Rübel, 1965
page 57

Cowboy and Rope Ladder. 1932
Ink on paper, 19 × 14 1⁄8 in. (48.3 × 35.9 cm)
The Museum of Modern Art, New York. Gift of Mr. and Mrs. Peter A. Rübel, 1965
page 57

Dancing Torpedo Shape. 1932
Wood, wire, sheet metal, and paint, with motor, 28 3⁄4 × 23 1⁄2 × 11 in. (73 × 59.7 × 27.9 cm)
Calder Foundation, New York. Purchase, 2018

Double Arc and Sphere. 1932
Wood, wire, rod, string, and paint, with motor, 32 1⁄2 × 11 1⁄2 × 11 1⁄4 in. (82.6 × 29.2 × 28.6 cm)
Calder Foundation, New York. Purchase, 2018

Space Tunnel. 1932
Watercolor and ink on paper, 22 3⁄4 × 30 1⁄2 in. (57.8 × 77.5 cm)
Calder Foundation, New York

A Universe. 1934
Iron pipe, steel wire, wood, paint, and thread, with motor, 40 1⁄2 × 30 in. (102.9 × 76.2 cm)
The Museum of Modern Art, New York. Gift of Abby Aldrich Rockefeller (by exchange), 1934
pages 62, 63

Untitled. c. 1934
Wood, wire, sheet metal, paint, and motor, 11 3⁄4 × 8 × 7 in. (29.9 × 20.3 × 17.8 cm)
The Museum of Modern Art, New York. Kay Sage Tanguy Bequest, 1964
page 78

Grandeur–Immense (plate, folio 7), from **23 Gravures**, by Anatole Jakovski. 1935
Drypoint from an illustrated book with twelve etchings (one with aquatint and drypoint), five drypoints, three engravings (one with drypoint), two lithographs, and one woodcut, plate: 10 7⁄16 × 7 3⁄4 in. (26.5 × 19.7 cm); sheet: 12 9⁄16 × 9 3⁄4 in. (31.9 × 24.8 cm)
Publisher: Éditions Orobitz et Cie, Paris
Printer: Tanneur, Paris
Edition: 50
The Museum of Modern Art, New York. Purchase Fund, 1945
page 94

J and *S* cuff links. c. 1935
Brass, 1 3⁄4 × 1 1⁄4 × 1 in. (4.5 × 3.2 × 2.5 cm) and 2 × 1 1⁄4 × 3⁄4 in. (4.9 × 2.8 × 1.9 cm)
The Museum of Modern Art, New York. James Thrall Soby Bequest, 1979
page 86

Ring. c. 1935
Brass and glass, 1 1⁄2 × 1 1⁄2 × 1 1⁄2 in. (3.8 × 3.8 × 3.8 cm)
The Museum of Modern Art, New York. James Thrall Soby Bequest, 1979
page 88

Brooch. c. 1936
Brass and steel, 3 5⁄8 × 4 3⁄4 in. (9.2 × 12.1 cm)
The Museum of Modern Art, New York. Gift of Mrs. Katharine Kuh, 1955
page 89

Cutlery. 1936
Brass, iron, and silver, fork: 9 ¾ × 1 ¾ × 1 ½ in. (24.8 × 4.5 × 3.8 cm); knife: 9 ½ × 1 × ½ in. (24.1 × 2.5 × 1.3 cm); spoon: 7 ¾ × 1 ½ × ½ in. (19.7 × 3.8 × 1.3 cm)
The Museum of Modern Art, New York. James Thrall Soby Bequest, 1979
page 65

Dragonfly brooch. 1936
Brass and steel, 3 ½ × 7 × 1 in. (8.9 × 17.8 × 2.5 cm)
The Museum of Modern Art, New York. James Thrall Soby Bequest, 1979
page 88

Gibraltar. 1936
Lignum vitae, walnut, wood, paint, and steel rods, 51 ⅞ × 24 ¼ × 11 ⅜ in. (131.8 × 61.6 × 28.9 cm)
The Museum of Modern Art, New York. Gift of the artist, 1966
page 73

Swizzle Sticks. 1936
Plywood, paint, steel rod, string, wood, wire, and lead, 56 ⅜ × 45 ⅝ × 48 ½ in. (143.2 × 115.9 × 123.2 cm)
The Museum of Modern Art, New York. James Thrall Soby Bequest, 1979
pages 68, 69

White Panel. 1936
Plywood, sheet metal, tubing, wood, rod, wire, string, and paint, 7 ft. ½ in. × 47 in. × 51 in. (214.6 × 119.4 × 129.5 cm)
Calder Foundation, New York. Mary Calder Rower Bequest, 2011

Devil Fish. 1937
Sheet metal, bolts, and paint, 68 × 64 × 47 in. (172.7 × 162.6 × 119.4 cm)
Calder Foundation, New York
page 74

Apple Monster. 1938
Wood, wire, and paint, 66 × 55 ½ × 32 ½ in. (167.6 × 141 × 82.6 cm)
Calder Foundation, New York. Gift of Alexander S. C. Rower in memory of Mary Calder Rower, 2015

Black Beast (maquette). 1939
Sheet metal and paint, 21 × 28 × 17 in. (53.3 × 71.1 × 43.2 cm)
Calder Foundation, New York

Candelabra. 1939
Rolled-steel tubing and sheet-iron candle holders, ten sections, dimensions variable
The Museum of Modern Art, New York
Commissioned for The Museum of Modern Art's tenth-anniversary dinner, May 8, 1939
pages 83–83

Lobster Trap and Fish Tail. 1939
Sheet aluminum, steel wire, and paint, 8 ft. 6 in. (259.1 cm) high × 9 ft. 6 in. (289.5 cm) diam.
The Museum of Modern Art, New York
Commissioned by the Advisory Committee of The Museum of Modern Art, New York, 1939
page 85

Spider. 1939
Sheet aluminum, steel rod, steel wire, and paint, 6 ft. 8 ½ in. × 7 ft. 4 ½ in. × 36 ½ in. (204.5 × 224.8 × 92.7 cm)
The Museum of Modern Art, New York. Gift of the artist, 1966
page 81

Spiny (maquette). c. 1939
Sheet aluminum and paint, 26 × 30 × 14 ⅜ in. (66 × 76.2 × 36.5 cm)
The Museum of Modern Art, New York. Nelson A. Rockefeller Bequest, 1979
page 79

Untitled. 1939
Sheet aluminum, steel wire, and paint, 14 ⅝ × 9 × 10 ⅞ in. (37.2 × 22.9 × 27.6 cm)
The Museum of Modern Art, New York. Kay Sage Tanguy Bequest, 1964
page 77

Belt buckle. c. 1940
Brass, 5 ⅜ × 4 ⅞ in. (13.7 × 12.4 cm)
The Museum of Modern Art, New York. Gift of the artist, 1967
page 88

Black Beast. 1940
Sheet metal, bolts, and paint, 8 ft. 7 in. × 13 ft. 7 in. × 6 ft. 6 ½ in. (261.6 × 414 × 199.4 cm)
Calder Foundation, New York
page 110

Bracelet. c. 1940
Silver, 4 ¾ × 4 × 2 in. (12.1 × 10.2 × 5.1 cm)
The Museum of Modern Art, New York. Purchase, 1967
page 86

Brooch. c. 1940
Silver and steel, 12 ⅜ × 9 ½ in. (31.4 × 24.1 cm)
The Museum of Modern Art, New York. Gift of the artist, 1967
page 88

Comb. c. 1940
Brass, 6 ½ × 3 ⅞ × ¾ in. (16.5 × 9.8 × 2 cm)
The Museum of Modern Art, New York. Gift of the artist, 1967
page 89

Eucalyptus. 1940
Sheet metal, wire, and paint, 7 ft. 10 ½ in. × 61 in. (240 × 154.9 cm)
Calder Foundation, New York. Gift of Andréa Davidson, Shawn Davidson, Alexander S. C. Rower, and Holton Rower, 2010

Flying-bird brooch. c. 1940
Silver and steel, 12 ¼ × 11 ⅞ in. (31.1 × 30.2 cm)
The Museum of Modern Art, New York. Gift of the artist, 1967
page 86

For 3 Years of Fairly Good Behavior (**Pour 3 ans d'assez bonne conduite**). 1941–43
Plexiglas, wire, and paint, 10 ¼ in. (26 cm) high × 29 in. (73.7 cm) diam.
The Museum of Modern Art, New York. Kay Sage Tanguy Bequest, 1964
page 76

Necklace. 1941
Silver, inner circumference: 26 in. (66 cm); outer circumference: 34 in. (86.4 cm)
The Museum of Modern Art, New York. James Thrall Soby Fund, 1943
page 87

Untitled. 1941
Gouache and ink on paper, 22 ¼ × 30 ⅞ in. (56.5 × 78.4 cm)
The Museum of Modern Art, New York. James Thrall Soby Bequest, 1979
page 103

Score for Ballet 0–100, from **VVV Portfolio**. 1942, published 1943
Etching from a portfolio of five etchings (one with aquatint), three duplicated drawings (two watercolor on paper and one crayon on paper), one collage, one engraving, and one gelatin silver print, plate: 11 5⁄16 × 14 13⁄16 in. (28.7 × 37.6 cm); sheet: 14 × 17 15⁄16 in. (35.6 × 45.6 cm)
Publisher: VVV, New York
Printer: Atelier 17, New York
Edition: 50
The Museum of Modern Art, New York. The Louis E. Stern Collection, 1964
page 95

Untitled. 1942
Etching, plate: 11 3⁄16 × 13 15⁄16 in. (28.4 × 35.4 cm); sheet: 14 15⁄16 × 19 ⅛ in. (37.9 × 48.6 cm)
Edition: unknown
The Museum of Modern Art, New York. Gift of the artist, 1969
page 104

Black Constellation. 1943
Wood and wire, 17 × 41 ½ × 8 in. (43.2 × 105.4 × 20.3 cm)
Calder Foundation, New York. Gift of Sandra Calder Davidson in memory of Jean Davidson, 2014

Morning Star. 1943
Sheet steel, steel wire, wood, and paint, 6 ft. 4 ¾ in. × 48 ⅜ in. × 45 ¾ in. (195 × 122.9 × 116.2 cm)
The Museum of Modern Art, New York. Gift of the artist, 1966
page 91

Tines. 1943
Pitchfork tines, glass, wire, shell, string, and paint, 50 × 58 × 3 ½ in. (127 × 147.3 × 8.9 cm)
Calder Foundation, New York

Untitled. 1943
Wood and paint, 28 ⅞ × 10 × 8 ¾ in. (73.3 × 25.4 × 22.2 cm)
The Museum of Modern Art, New York. Gift of Pierre Matisse in memory of Patricia Kane Matisse, 1982
page 93

Untitled. 1943
Ink on paper, 21 ¾ × 30 ¼ in. (55.3 × 76.8 cm)
Calder Foundation, New York. Anonymous gift, 2004
page 42

Wall Constellation with Red Object. 1943
Wood, steel wire, and paint, 24 ½ × 15 ¼ × 9 ½ in.
(62.2 × 38.7 × 24.1 cm)
The Museum of Modern Art, New York. James Thrall Soby Fund, 1943
page 92

Wall Constellation with Row of Objects. 1943
Wood, wire, and paint, 28 × 36 × 6 in.
(71.1 × 91.4 × 15.2 cm)
Private collection, New York

The Big I. 1944
Etching, plate: 6 ⅞ × 8 ⅞ in. (17.5 × 22.5 cm);
sheet: 11 7⁄16 × 15 15⁄16 in. (29.1 × 40.5 cm)
Publisher: Wittenborn & Co., New York
Printer: Atelier 17, New York
Edition: 30
The Museum of Modern Art, New York. Gift of Wittenborn & Co., 1955
page 104

Portrait of Curt Valentin. 1944
Ink on paper, 11 ⅝ × 10 ⅛ in. (29.5 × 25.7 cm)
The Museum of Modern Art, New York. Gift of Ludwig Charell, 1955
page 101
The signature that appears at the drawing's lower-right corner is likely not Calder's.

Three Young Rats and Other Rhymes, compiled by James Johnson Sweeney. 1944
Illustrated book with eighty-five letterpress prints and one supplementary drawing (ink on paper), page (each, irreg.): 12 3⁄16 × 9 7⁄16 in. (31 × 24 cm); overall (closed): 12 11⁄16 × 9 13⁄16 × 1 1⁄16 in. (32.2 × 24.9 × 2.7 cm)
Publisher: Curt Valentin, New York
Printer: Golden Eagle Press, Mount Vernon, New York
Edition: 700
The Museum of Modern Art, New York. The Louis E. Stern Collection, 1964
pages 98–99

Belt buckle. c. 1945
Brass, 3 ⅛ × 4 7⁄16 × ⅜ in. (7.9 × 11.3 × 1 cm)
The Museum of Modern Art, New York. Gift of the artist, 1967
page 89

Man-Eater with Pennants. 1945
Sheet iron, steel rods, and paint, 14 ft. (426.7 cm) high × approx. 30 ft. (914.4 cm) diam.
The Museum of Modern Art, New York. Purchase, 1945
page 97

Untitled. 1946
Lithograph, comp.: 14 13⁄16 × 11 ¼ in. (37.6 × 28.6 cm);
sheet: 19 5⁄16 × 15 11⁄16 in. (49.1 × 39.8 cm)
Publisher: Buchholz Gallery, New York
Printer: Mourlot, Paris
Edition: 25
The Museum of Modern Art, New York. Gift of the artist, 1969
page 102

Untitled. 1946
Lithograph, comp.: 16 ¼ × 12 in. (41.3 × 30.5 cm);
sheet: 19 ¾ × 15 ¾ in. (50.2 × 40 cm)
Printer: Mourlot, Paris
Edition: 25
The Museum of Modern Art, New York. Gift of the artist, 1969
page 105

Untitled. 1946
Lithograph, comp.: 11 13⁄16 × 15 11⁄16 in. (30 × 39.8 cm);
sheet: 15 11⁄16 × 19 ¾ in. (39.8 × 50.2 cm)
Printer: Mourlot, Paris
Edition: 25
The Museum of Modern Art, New York. Gift of the artist, 1969
page 105

Plate from **Le Surréalisme en 1947**, edited by André Breton. 1947
Lithograph from an illustrated book with eighteen lithographs, four etchings (two with aquatint), two woodcuts, one photogravure, and one ready-made object, comp. (irreg.): 9 ⅛ × 8 in. (23.2 × 20.3 cm);
page: 9 7⁄16 × 8 in. (24 × 20.3 cm)
Publisher: Pierre à Feu (Maeght Éditeur), Paris
Printer: Mourlot, Paris
Edition: 950
The Museum of Modern Art, New York.
Henry Church Fund, 1947
page 100

Snow Flurry I. 1948
Sheet steel, steel wire, and paint, 7 ft. 10 in. (238.8 cm) high × 6 ft. 10 ¼ in. (208.9 cm) diam.
The Museum of Modern Art, New York. Gift of the artist, 1966
page 107

A Bestiary, compiled by Richard Wilbur. 1955
Illustrated book with fifty-six letterpress plates, page (each): 12 ½ × 9 3⁄16 in. (31.8 × 23.3 cm); overall (closed): 12 ¾ × 9 ⅜ × 11⁄16 in. (32.4 × 23.9 × 1.8 cm)
Publisher: Pantheon Books, New York
Printer: Spiral Press, New York
Edition: 825
The Museum of Modern Art, New York. The Louis E. Stern Collection, 1964
pages 108, 109

Black Widow. 1959
Sheet steel and paint, 7 ft. 8 in. × 14 ft. 3 in. × 7 ft. 5 in. (233.7 × 434.3 × 226.1 cm)
The Museum of Modern Art, New York. Mrs. Simon Guggenheim Fund, 1963
page 113

Untitled. 1959
Sheet metal, wire, cotton thread, and paint, 8 ½ in. (21.6 cm) × 5 in. (12.7 cm) diam.
The Museum of Modern Art, New York. Nina and Gordon Bunshaft Bequest, 1994
page 123

Smoke Rings (**Rondelles de fumée**). 1960
Lithograph, comp. (irreg.): 21 5⁄16 × 24 ¼ in. (54.1 × 61.6 cm); sheet: 29 ¼ × 35 5⁄16 in. (74.3 × 89.7 cm)
Publisher: Maeght Éditeur, Paris
Printer: Maeght Imprimerie, Levallois-Perret, France
Edition: unknown
The Museum of Modern Art, New York. John B. Turner Fund, 1970
page 114

Teodelapio (maquette II). 1962
Sheet aluminum and paint, 23 ¾ × 15 ¼ × 15 ¾ in. (60.3 × 38.7 × 40 cm)
The Museum of Modern Art, New York. Gift of the artist, 1966
page 117

Sandy's Butterfly. 1964
Steel, stainless sheet steel, iron rods, and paint, 12 ft. 8 in. × 9 ft. 2 in. × 8 ft. 7 in. (386.1 × 279.4 × 261.6 cm)
The Museum of Modern Art, New York. Gift of the artist, 1966
pages 120–21

Flying Saucers (**Soucoupes volantes**). 1969
Lithograph, comp. (irreg.): 42 ⅜ × 27 5⁄16 in. (107.6 × 69.4 cm); sheet: 43 3⁄16 × 29 11⁄16 in. (109.7 × 75.4 cm)
Publisher: Maeght Éditeur, Paris
Printer: Maeght Imprimerie, Levallois-Perret, France
Edition: 75
The Museum of Modern Art, New York. Gift of Dr. and Mrs. Barnett Malbin, 1976
page 115

Untitled. 1969
Ink and gouache on paper, 29 ½ × 43 ⅛ in. (74.9 × 109.5 cm)
The Museum of Modern Art, New York. Gift of the artist, 1969
page 118

Untitled. 1969
Oil and gouache on paper, 29 ½ × 43 ¼ in. (74.9 × 109.9 cm)
The Museum of Modern Art, New York. Gift of the artist, 1969
page 119

Exhibition History

Exhibitions at The Museum of Modern Art in which Calder's work was shown. They are listed in reverse chronological order.

A Century of Sculpture (Exh. 2431), organized by Ann Temkin and Cara Manes, October 21, 2020–May 1, 2021

Sur moderno: Journeys of Abstraction—The Patricia Phelps de Cisneros Gift (Exh. 2424), organized by Inés Katzenstein, October 21, 2019–September 12, 2020

Artist's Choice: Amy Sillman—The Shape of Shape (Exh. 2422), organized by Amy Sillman with Michelle Kuo, October 21, 2019–October 4, 2020

Dan Graham: Child's Play (Exh. 2382a), organized by Ann Temkin and Cara Manes, July 17, 2017–May 13, 2018

How Should We Live? Propositions for the Modern Interior (Exh. 2364), organized by Juliet Kinchin and Luke Baker, October 1, 2016–April 23, 2017

Sculpture from the Collection, 1960–1969 (Exh. 2359), organized by Ann Temkin and Cara Manes, June 26, 2016–June 26, 2017

Latin America in Construction: Architecture, 1955–1980 (Exh. 2317), organized by Barry Bergdoll, Carlos Eduardo Comas, Jorge Francisco Liernur, and Patricio del Real, March 29–July 19, 2015

Gifted: Collectors and Drawings at MoMA, 1929–1983 (Exh. 2172), organized by Esther Adler, October 19, 2011–February 12, 2012

On Line: Drawing through the Twentieth Century (Exh. 2135), organized by Cornelia H. Butler and Catherine de Zegher, November 21, 2010–February 7, 2011

Sculpture in Color (Exh. 2080), organized by Ann Temkin, Anne Umland, and Leah Dickerman, May 18, 2009–January 11, 2010

Focus: Alexander Calder (Exh. 2016), organized by Anne Umland with Veronica Roberts, September 14, 2007–April 14, 2008

Artist's Choice: Herzog & de Meuron, Perception Restrained (Exh. 1976), organized by Terence Riley and Christian Larsen, June 21–September 25, 2006

Transforming Chronologies: An Atlas of Drawings, Part 2 (Exh. 1972), organized by Luis Pérez-Oramas, May 10–October 2, 2006

The Abby Aldrich Rockefeller Sculpture Garden: Inaugural Installation (Exh. 1934), organized by Kynaston McShine, November 20, 2004–December 31, 2005

Painting and Sculpture: Inaugural Installation (Exh. 1931), organized by John Elderfield, November 20, 2004–December 31, 2005

To Be Looked At: Painting and Sculpture from the Collection (Exh. 1899), organized by Kynaston McShine, June 29, 2002–September 6, 2004

MoMA2000: Making Choices; Paris Salon, organized by Robert Storr, Peter Galassi, and Anne Umland, part 3 (Exh. 1862), April 26–September 26, 2000; part 2 (Exh. 1850), March 15–August 22, 2000

MoMA2000: Making Choices; The Raw and the Cooked (Exh. 1853), organized by Robert Storr, March 30–September 19, 2000

The Museum as Muse: Artists Reflect (Exh. 1828), organized by Kynaston McShine, March 14–June 1, 1999

Giacometti to Judd: Prints by Sculptors (Exh. 1805), organized by Starr Figura, June 9–October 13, 1998

The Maximal Sixties: Pop, Op, and Figuration (Exh. 1757a), organized by Laura Hoptman, January 18–April 29, 1997

Master Prints from the Collection (Exh. 1744), organized by Wendy Weitman, May 18–October 1, 1996

Impressions of Nature (Exh. 1725), organized by Wendy Weitman, September 16, 1995–January 2, 1996

Adding It Up: Print Acquisitions, 1970–1995 (Exh. 1714), organized by Riva Castleman, May 27–September 5, 1995

A Century of Artists Books (Exh. 1697), organized by Riva Castleman, October 19, 1994–January 24, 1995

Three Masters of the Bauhaus: Lyonel Feininger, Vasily Kandinsky, and Paul Klee (Exh. 1672), organized by Wendy Weitman, January 27–May 17, 1994

Joan Miró Prints and Books from New York Lenders (Exh. 1667), organized by Deborah Wye, October 13, 1993–January 11, 1994

Reading Prints (Exh. 1645), organized by Wendy Weitman, March 4–July 6, 1993

Art of the Forties (Exh. 1574), organized by Riva Castleman, February 20–April 30, 1991

Still Life into Object (Exh. 1565), organized by Lindsay Leard, November 22, 1990–March 19, 1991

Drawn in America, 1898–1945 (Exh. 1563), organized by Bernice Rose, November 1, 1990–March 1991

Abstractions (Exh. 1504), organized by Wendy Weitman, November 17, 1988–March 26, 1989

Master Prints from the Collection (Exh. 1469), organized by Wendy Weitman, November 20, 1987–March 8, 1988

Surrealist Prints from the Collection of The Museum of Modern Art (Exh. 1460), organized by Deborah Wye, August 6–December 8, 1987

Naked/Nude (Exh. 1424), organized by Audrey Isselbacher, May 29–September 30, 1986

Sculptors' Drawings (Exh. 1420), organized by Beatrice Kernan, April 26–September 2, 1986

American Prints: 1900–1960; Recent Acquisitions: Illustrated Books (Exh. 1412a), organized by Deborah Wye, December 18, 1985–May 20, 1986

Contemporary Works from the Collection (Exh. 1410), organized by Alicia Legg, November 21, 1985–April 1, 1986

"Primitivism" in 20th Century Art: Affinity of the Tribal and the Modern (Exh. 1382), organized by William S. Rubin and Kirk Varnedoe, September 19, 1984–January 15, 1985

Selections from the Permanent Collection: Painting and Sculpture (Exh. 1372), organized by William S. Rubin and Alicia Legg, May 17, 1984–August 4, 1992

Prints from Blocks: Gauguin to Now (Exh. 1345), organized by Riva Castleman, March 3–May 15, 1983

Movin' (Exh. 1280a), December 6, 1979–February 10, 1980

Art of the Twenties (Exh. 1277), organized by William S. Lieberman, November 14, 1979–January 22, 1980

Thirty Sculptors' Drawings (Exh. 1263), organized by William S. Lieberman, May 18–June 6, 1979

Abstraction-Création, Art Non-Figuratif (Exh. 1185), organized by Howardena Pindell, September 20–December 4, 1977

Posters by Painters (Exh. 1162), organized by J. Stewart Johnson, January 21–March 23, 1977

Prints: Acquisitions, 1973–1976 (Exh. 1157), organized by Riva Castleman, November 23, 1976–February 20, 1977

Alexander Calder, 1898–1976 (Exh. 1153), November 11–December 7, 1976

Between World Wars: Drawing in Europe and America (Exh. 1143), organized by William S. Lieberman, August 20–November 14, 1976

Prints by Sculptors (Exh. 1099b), May 21–September 1, 1975

American Prints, 1913–1963 (Exh. 1082a), organized by Riva Castleman, December 3, 1974–March 3, 1975

Seurat to Matisse: Drawing in France (Exh. 1064), organized by William S. Lieberman, June 13–September 8, 1974

Recent Acquisitions, 1968–1973 (Exh. 1038a), organized by Riva Castleman, June 15–September 25, 1973

American Prints from the International Program (Exh. 982), November 3–8, 1971

A Selection of Drawings and Watercolors from the Museum Collection (Exh. 965), organized by Elaine Johnson, May 11–October 19, 1971

Mrs. Simon Guggenheim, 1877–1970: In Memoriam (Exh. 919), organized by Betsy Jones, February 25–March 17, 1970

A Salute to Alexander Calder (Exh. 916), organized by Bernice Rose, December 18, 1969–February 15, 1970

Twentieth-Century Art from the Nelson Aldrich Rockefeller Collection (Exh. 892), organized by Dorothy C. Miller, May 28–September 1, 1969

The Machine as Seen at the End of the Mechanical Age (Exh. 877), organized by K. G. Pontus Hultén, November 27, 1968–February 9, 1969

Dada, Surrealism and Their Heritage (Exh. 855), organized by William S. Rubin, March 27–June 9, 1968

Five Sculptures from the Museum Collection (Exh. 847), January 8–March 3, 1968

The 1960s: Painting and Sculpture from the Museum Collection (Exh. 834), organized by Dorothy C. Miller, June 28–September 24, 1967

Drawings: Recent Acquisitions (Exh. 830), organized by William S. Lieberman, June 6–November 22, 1967

Calder: 19 Gifts from the Artist (Exh. 819), organized by Dorothy C. Miller, February 1–September 4, 1967

The Taste of a Connoisseur: The Paul J. Sachs Collection (Exh. 815), organized by William S. Lieberman, December 21, 1966–March 5, 1967

Drawings from the Museum Collection (Exh. 811), October 31, 1966–May 8, 1967

Recent Acquisitions: Kay Sage Tanguy Bequest (Exh. 774), September 17–December 14, 1965

44 Drawings: Recent Acquisitions (Exh. 773), organized by William S. Lieberman, September 6, 1965–January 23, 1966

Recent Acquisitions: Painting and Sculpture (Exh. 756), organized by Alfred H. Barr Jr., February 16–April 25, 1965

Art in a Changing World: 1884–1964: Painting and Sculpture from the Museum Collection (Exh. 732), opened May 27, 1964

Painting and Sculpture from the James Thrall Soby Collection (Exh. 679a), February 1–March 4, 1961

Birds and Beasts from The Museum of Modern Art (Exh. 676b), December 3, 1960–January 8, 1961

Art Lending Service Retrospective (Exh. 657), January 27–March 20, 1960

Recent Sculpture U.S.A. (Exh. 644), organized by James Thrall Soby and Dorothy C. Miller, May 13–August 16, 1959

Children's Holiday Carnival (Exh. 625), December 9, 1957–January 12, 1958

Children's Holiday Carnival (Exh. 610), December 10, 1956–January 13, 1957

Selections from the Art Lending Service (Exh. 585), October 5–24, 1955

Sculpture of the XXth Century (Exh. 536), April 28–September 7, 1953

International Sculpture Competition: The Unknown Political Prisoner (Exh. 529), January 27–February 8, 1953

Recent Acquisitions (Exh. 509), May 6–June 8, 1952

Posters by Painters and Sculptors (Exh. 503), March 4–May 11, 1952

Abstract Painting and Sculpture in America (Exh. 466), January 23–March 25, 1951

Modern Art in Your Life (Exh. 423), organized by Robert Goldwater, October 5–December 4, 1949

Painting and Sculpture in Architecture (Exh. 419), August 3–October 2, 1949

The House in the Museum Garden (Exh. 405), April 12–October 30, 1949

Timeless Aspects of Modern Art (Exh. 393), November 16, 1948–January 23, 1949

Children's Holiday Fair of Modern Art (Exh. 338), December 3, 1946–January 5, 1947

Modern Handmade Jewelry (Exh. 330), September 17–November 17, 1946

Children's Holiday Circus of Modern Art (Exh. 303), December 4, 1945–January 6, 1946

The Museum Collection of Painting and Sculpture (Exh. 290), June 20, 1945–February 13, 1946

Recent Acquisitions (Exh. 276), February 15–March 18, 1945

Hayter and Studio 17: New Directions in Gravure (Exh. 259), June 18–October 8, 1944

Art in Progress: 15th Anniversary Exhibitions; Dance and Theatre Design (Exh. 258d), organized by George Amberg, May 24–September 17, 1944; **Painting, Sculpture, Prints** (Exh. 258a), May 24–October 15, 1944

Modern Drawings (Exh. 252), February 16–May 10, 1944

Alexander Calder: Sculptures and Constructions (Exh. 242), organized by James Johnson Sweeney, September 29, 1943–January 16, 1944

The Arts in Therapy (Exh. 216), February 3–March 7, 1943

20th Century Sculpture and Constructions (Exh. 199), October 2–26, 1942

Children's Festival of Modern Art (Exh. 173), March 11–May 10, 1942

Organic Design in Home Furnishings (Exh. 148), September 24–November 9, 1941

Animals in Art: Designing a Stage Setting (Exh. 136), July 1–15, 1941

Painting and Sculpture from the Museum Collection (Exh. 127), opened May 6, 1941

New Acquisitions: American Painting and Sculpture (Exh. 124), March 10–May 3, 1941

We Like Modern Art (Exh. 120), December 27, 1940–January 12, 1941

Painting and Sculpture from the Museum Collection (Exh. 110), October 23, 1940–January 12, 1941

Art in Our Time: 10th Anniversary Exhibition (Exh. 85), May 10–September 30, 1939

Three Centuries of American Art (Exh. 76a), organized by Iris Barry, May 24–July 31, 1938

Fantastic Art, Dada, Surrealism (Exh. 55), organized by Alfred H. Barr Jr., December 9, 1936–January 17, 1937

Modern Painters and Sculptors as Illustrators (Exh. 47), April 27–September 2, 1936

Cubism and Abstract Art (Exh. 46), organized by Alfred H. Barr Jr., March 2–April 19, 1936

Modern Works of Art: 5th Anniversary Exhibition (Exh. 37), November 19, 1934–January 20, 1935

Painting and Sculpture by Living Americans (Exh. 9), organized by Alfred H. Barr Jr., December 3, 1930–January 20, 1931

Further Reading

The Calder Foundation, New York, maintains an extensive list of resources at www.calder.org

Barron, Stephanie, and Lisa Gabrielle Mark, eds. **Calder and Abstraction: From Avant-Garde to Iconic**. Los Angeles: Los Angeles County Museum of Art; Munich: DelMonico Books/Prestel, 2013. Texts by Barron, Ilene Susan Fort, Aleca Le Blanc, Jed Perl, and Harriet Senie.

Calder, Alexander. **Calder: An Autobiography with Pictures**. Edited by Jean Davidson. New York: Pantheon Books, 1966.

Matter, Herbert. **Calder by Matter**. Edited by Alexander S. C. Rower, with texts by Rower, Jed Perl, and John T. Hill. Paris: Cahiers d'art, 2013.

Perl, Jed. **Calder: The Conquest of Time; The Early Years, 1898–1940**. New York: Alfred A. Knopf, 2017.

——. **Calder: The Conquest of Space; The Later Years, 1940–1976**. Alfred A. Knopf, 2020.

Prather, Marla. **Alexander Calder, 1898–1976**. Washington, D.C.: National Gallery of Art; New Haven, Conn.: Yale University Press, 1998. Text by Arnauld Pierre and chronology by Alexander S. C. Rower.

Rose, Bernice. **A Salute to Alexander Calder**. New York: The Museum of Modern Art, 1969.

Rower, Alexander S. C., Claire Garnier, Emilia Philippot, and Bernard Ruiz-Picasso, eds. **Calder–Picasso**. Paris: Musée Picasso/Skira, 2019. Texts by Estrella de Diego, Donatien Grau, Laurent Le Bon, Chus Martinez, Jordana Mendelson, Jed Perl, Ruiz-Picasso, and Rower.

Simon, Joan, and Brigitte Leal, eds. **Alexander Calder: The Paris Years, 1926–1933**. New York: Whitney Museum of American Art; Paris: Centre Pompidou; New Haven, Conn.: Yale University Press, 2008. Texts by Simon, Leal, Henry Petroski, Quentin Bajac, Eleonora Nagy, Carol Mancusi-Ungaro, Pepe Karmel, Annie Cohen-Solal, and Arnauld Pierre; and chronology by Alexander S. C. Rower.

Sweeney, James Johnson. **Alexander Calder**. New York: The Museum of Modern Art, 1943.

Acknowledgments

Working in the Department of Painting and Sculpture at The Museum of Modern Art, I have come to know Alexander Calder's sculptures through installing them in MoMA's galleries and The Abby Aldrich Rockefeller Sculpture Garden, year after year, in various contexts. This book, and the exhibition that occasioned it, however, provided an opportunity to engage with the work in a deep and sustained manner—to delve into the Museum's collecting and exhibition history, and to become familiar with the constellation of characters and events that created an extraordinary relationship between this artist and this institution.

The project could not have been realized without of the support of the Calder Foundation, New York. Alexander S. C. Rower, its president, has been a generous and generative partner, offering wisdom and expertise on his grandfather's work at every turn. It was a pleasure to be able to work with and to learn from him. Working with the Foundation yielded productive collaborations with many patient and vital colleagues: Lily Lyons and Melissa Claus, on the exhibition and related programming; Susan Braeuer Dam, on this publication; Alexis Marotta and John Sapp, on archival research; and Beryl Gilothwest and Kaitlyn Kramer. We also thank Matthew Castle, of Castle Art Services. The Calder Foundation was also a crucial lender to this exhibition, providing a group of works that rounded out the story of Calder and The Museum of Modern Art. I thank them for their generosity and flexibility.

At MoMA, I am grateful to Glenn D. Lowry, The David Rockefeller Director, for his enthusiastic support of this project, and to Ramona Bronkar Bannayan, Senior Deputy Director, Exhibitions, Collections, and Programs, who oversaw the exhibition's organization with great thoughtfulness. It has also depended on the leadership of Peter Reed, former Senior Deputy Director, Curatorial Affairs; Sarah Suzuki, Senior Deputy Director, Curatorial Affairs; James Gara, Chief Operating Officer; and Todd Bishop, Senior Deputy Director, External Affairs.

We extend our deepest thanks to our sponsors: the Kate W. Cassidy Foundation; The International Council of The Museum of Modern Art; the Jon and Mary Shirley Foundation; The Lipman Family Foundation; the Jo Carole Lauder Publications Fund; the Dale S. and Norman Mills Leff Publication Fund; and the generous donors to the Annual Exhibition Fund.

In the Department of Painting and Sculpture, Ann Temkin, The Marie Josée and Henry R. Kravis Chief Curator, gave me wise counsel and guidance at every step. I am most grateful to Zuna Maza and Makayla Bailey, from the Studio Museum in Harlem/MoMA Fellowship Collaboration, both of whom were true partners in this project: Zuna brought superior judgment, hard work, and a lot of heart to the making of this exhibition and catalogue; Makayla dove in toward the end, and she was extraordinarily dexterous in her handling of all things. Other curatorial colleagues provided support of all kinds—thank you, in Painting and Sculpture, to Beverly Adams, Charlotte Barat, Lily Goldberg, Tamar Margalit, Kayla Dalle Molle, Romy Silver-Kohn, Lilian Tone, Anne Umland, and Janet Yoon; in the Department of Drawings and Prints, to Christophe Cherix and Emily Cushman; in the Department of Architecture and Design, to Juliet Kinchin and Paul Galloway; and in the Department of Film, to Ashley Swinnerton and Katie Trainor.

In the Department of Publications, I thank Christopher Hudson, former Publisher; Curtis Scott, Associate Publisher; Don McMahon, Editorial Director; Hannah Kim, Business and Marketing Director; and Naomi Falk, Rights Coordinator. Marc Sapir, Production Director, laid the groundwork for the book and championed it all the way to its printing. Amanda Washburn provided a graceful design for the catalogue, and Emily Hall, a graceful edit. Rebecca Roberts lent her sharp eye. In Exhibition Planning and Administration, I thank Erik Patton and Margaret Aldredge, a true advocate for the project, and in Collection Management and Exhibition

Registration, Stefanii Ruta Atkins, Jessica Nilsen, Kathleen Hill, Lori Mahaney, and Tom Krueger. Lynda Zycherman and Megan Randall, Sculpture Conservators, brought the depth and breadth of their knowledge to the exhibition's preparation. In collaboration with the tremendous sculpture conservators Abigail Mack and Ellen Rand of Monumenta Art Conservation and Finishing, they restored *Man-Eater with Pennants* (1945)—a major project. I am indebted to these terrific colleagues, and to Laura Neufeld, Paper Conservator, and Reinhard Bek, of Bek & Frohnert Contemporary Art Conservation. Lana Hum brilliantly created the exhibition's design with assistance from Matthew Cox, Hiroko Ishikawa, and Benjamin Akhavan. I am particularly grateful to Michelle Elligott, Michelle Harvey, Ana Marie Cox, Christina Eliopoulos, Molly Lieberman, and Elizabeth Thomas in the Library and Archives; Leah Dickerman, Rob Baker, Prudence Peiffer, and Sean Yetter on the Creative Team; Claire Corey, Damien Saatjian, and David Klein in Advertising and Graphic Design; Ava Childers in the General Counsel's office; Amanda Hicks, Olivia Oramas, and Jack Spielsinger in Communications; Kurt Heumiller, Robert Gerhardt, Denis Doorly, Jonathan Muzikar, and Paul Abbey in Imaging and Visual Resources; and our many colleagues in Education, CETech, and Art Handling and Preparation.

To the following people, who have touched this project in myriad ways, I also offer my thanks: Masha Chlenova, Darby English, Peter Fischli, Jarrett Gregory, Jennifer Harris, Melinda Lang, Nora Lawrence, Nancy Walsh Manes, Robert Manes, Laura Phipps, Paulina Pobocha, Veronica Roberts, Jay Sanders, and Sarah Smith. I dedicate this book to my husband, Sean, and to my son, Luca, who was born in the middle of its preparation.

—Cara Manes
Associate Curator
Department of Painting and Sculpture
The Museum of Modern Art

Leadership support for the exhibition is provided by the Kate W. Cassidy Foundation.

Generous funding is provided by The International Council of The Museum of Modern Art and by the Jon and Mary Shirley Foundation.

Additional support is provided by The Lipman Family Foundation, Inc.

Leadership contributions to the Annual Exhibition Fund, in support of the Museum's collection and collection exhibitions, are generously provided by Jerry I. Speyer and Katherine G. Farley, the Sandra and Tony Tamer Exhibition Fund, The Contemporary Arts Council, Eva and Glenn Dubin, Alice and Tom Tisch, Mimi Haas, the Noel and Harriette Levine Endowment, The David Rockefeller Council, the William Randolph Hearst Endowment Fund, the Eyal and Marilyn Ofer Family Foundation, the Marella and Giovanni Agnelli Fund for Exhibitions, Anne Dias, Kathy and Richard S. Fuld, Jr., Kenneth C. Griffin, The International Council of The Museum of Modern Art, Marie-Josée and Henry R. Kravis, and Jo Carole and Ronald S. Lauder.

Major contributions to the Annual Exhibition Fund are provided by The Junior Associates of The Museum of Modern Art, Emily Rauh Pulitzer, Brett and Daniel Sundheim, the Terra Foundation for American Art, and Anna Marie and Robert F. Shapiro.

The publication is made possible by the Jo Carole Lauder Publications Fund of The International Council of The Museum of Modern Art. Additional funding is provided by the Dale S. and Norman Mills Leff Publication Fund.

Photograph Credits

In reproducing the images contained in this publication, The Museum obtained the permissions of the rights holders whenever possible. In those instances where the Museum could not locate the rights holders, notwithstanding good faith efforts, it requests that any information concerning such rights holders be forwarded so that they may be contacted for future editions.

All works by Alexander Calder © 2021 Calder Foundation, New York / Artists Rights Society (ARS), New York.

"Bettmann/Bettmann" via Getty Images: 71

Photograph courtesy Calder Foundation, New York / Art Resource, New York:
photograph by Elizabeth Goodspeed Chapman: 24 [fig. 16]
© The Estate of Pedro Guerrero: 75
© Bibliothèque Kandinsky, Centre Georges Pompidou, Marc Vaux Collection. Rights reserved: 13 [fig. 3], 43 [fig. 1]
© Ugo Mulas Heirs. All rights reserved: 116
photograph by Soichi Sunami: 14 [fig. 4]

Photograph © 2021 Calder Foundation, New York / Artists Rights Society (ARS), New York: 12 [figs. 1, 2], 18 [fig. 9], 20 [fig. 11], 21 [fig. 12], 22 [fig. 13], 23 [fig. 14], 42 [all], 45 [fig. 4], 67, 70, 97, 111
photograph by Herbert Matter: 4, 44 [all]
photograph by James Thrall Soby: 20 [fig. 11], 67

Photograph by Elizabeth Goodspeed Chapman, courtesy Robert Storr: 24 [fig. 15]

The Museum of Modern Art Archives:
photograph by George Amberg: 25 [fig. 18], 74
© Dan Budnik, all rights reserved: 2–3, 35 [fig. 27]
photograph by Eliot Elisofon: 18 [fig. 8]
International Council and International Program Records, I.A.370: 31 [fig. 24]
© Ellsworth Kelly Foundation, courtesy Matthew Marks Gallery: 32 [fig. 25]
photograph by Herbert Matter, © 2021 Calder Foundation, New York / Artists Rights Society (ARS), New York: 4
photograph by Beaumont Newhall: 16 [fig. 6]
Newspictures: back cover, 10, 25 [fig. 17], 26 [fig. 19]
photograph by Soichi Sunami: 6, 17 [fig. 7], 26 [fig. 20], 27 [fig. 21], 28 [fig. 22], 30 [fig. 23], 32 [fig. 25], 110
Photograph by Louis Werner: 19 [fig. 10]

The Museum of Modern Art, Department of Imaging and Visual Resources: 64, 92, 93, 123
Heidi Bohnenkamp: 85, 108 [all], 109 [all]
Peter Butler: 62, 63, 94
Denis Doorly: 96, 107
Robert Gerhardt: 17 [fig. 7], 19 [fig. 10], 58 [all], 59 [all], 86 [top left, bottom left], 87–89 [all], 98–101 [all]
Thomas Griesel: 50, 56, 64 [left], 81, 95, 102, 104 [top left], 113–15, 118
Kate Keller: 46, 103, 117
Paige Knight: 15 [fig. 5], 51, 53, 54, 61, 64 [right), 77
Erik Landsberg: 49, 52
Jonathan Muzikar: 57 [all], 65, 76, 78, 79, 82–83, 86 [top right], 91
Mali Olatunji: 47
John Wronn: 2, 30 [fig. 23], 55, 60, 68, 69, 73, 104 [bottom right), 105 [all], 119, 120–21

Published in conjunction with the exhibition *Alexander Calder: Modern from the Start*, at The Museum of Modern Art, New York, March 7–August 7, 2021

Organized by Cara Manes, Associate Curator, Department of Painting and Sculpture, The Museum of Modern Art, New York, with Zuna Maza and Makayla Bailey, Curatorial Fellows, Department of Painting and Sculpture, The Museum of Modern Art, New York

Leadership support for the exhibition is provided by the Kate W. Cassidy Foundation.

Generous funding is provided by The International Council of The Museum of Modern Art and by the Jon and Mary Shirley Foundation.

Additional support is provided by The Lipman Family Foundation, Inc.

Leadership contributions to the Annual Exhibition Fund, in support of the Museum's collection and collection exhibitions, are generously provided by Jerry I. Speyer and Katherine G. Farley, the Sandra and Tony Tamer Exhibition Fund, The Contemporary Arts Council, Eva and Glenn Dubin, Alice and Tom Tisch, Mimi Haas, the Noel and Harriette Levine Endowment, The David Rockefeller Council, the William Randolph Hearst Endowment Fund, the Eyal and Marilyn Ofer Family Foundation, the Marella and Giovanni Agnelli Fund for Exhibitions, Anne Dias, Kathy and Richard S. Fuld, Jr., Kenneth C. Griffin, The International Council of The Museum of Modern Art, Marie-Josée and Henry R. Kravis, and Jo Carole and Ronald S. Lauder.

Major contributions to the Annual Exhibition Fund are provided by The Junior Associates of The Museum of Modern Art, Emily Rauh Pulitzer, Brett and Daniel Sundheim, the Terra Foundation for American Art, and Anna Marie and Robert F. Shapiro.

The publication is made possible by the Jo Carole Lauder Publications Fund of The International Council of The Museum of Modern Art. Additional funding is provided by the Dale S. and Norman Mills Leff Publication Fund.

Produced by the Department of Publications, The Museum of Modern Art, New York

Hannah Kim, Business and Marketing Director
Don McMahon, Editorial Director
Marc Sapir, Production Director
Curtis R. Scott, Associate Publisher

Edited by Emily Hall
Designed by Amanda Washburn
Production by Marc Sapir
Proofread by Rebecca Roberts
Printed and bound by Veronalibri, Verona, Italy

This book is typeset in Beto.
The paper is 150 gsm Magno Satin.

Published by The Museum of Modern Art
11 West 53 Street
New York, New York 10019-5497
www.moma.org

Library of Congress Control Number: 2020946326
ISBN: 978-1-63345-116-2

Distributed in the United States and Canada by
ARTBOOK | D.A.P
75 Broad Street, Suite 360
New York, New York 10004
www.artbook.com

Distributed outside the United States and Canada by
Thames & Hudson Ltd.
181A High Holborn
London WC1V 7QX
www.thamesandhudson.com

Printed and bound in Italy

Cover: **Spiny** (maquette). c. 1939 (see page 79)
Pages 2–3: Dorothy C. Miller installing **Black Widow** (1959) in The Abby Aldrich Rockefeller Sculpture Garden, c. 1963. MoMA Archives, New York
Page 4: Calder in his studio, c. 1943. Photograph by Herbert Matter
Page 6: **Lobster Trap and Fish Tail** (1939) installed over the stairwell in MoMA's lobby, 1949. MoMA Archives, New York
Page 10 and back cover: Calder installing the exhibition **Alexander Calder: Sculptures and Constructions**, 1943. MoMA Archives, New York

Trustees of The Musem of Modern Art

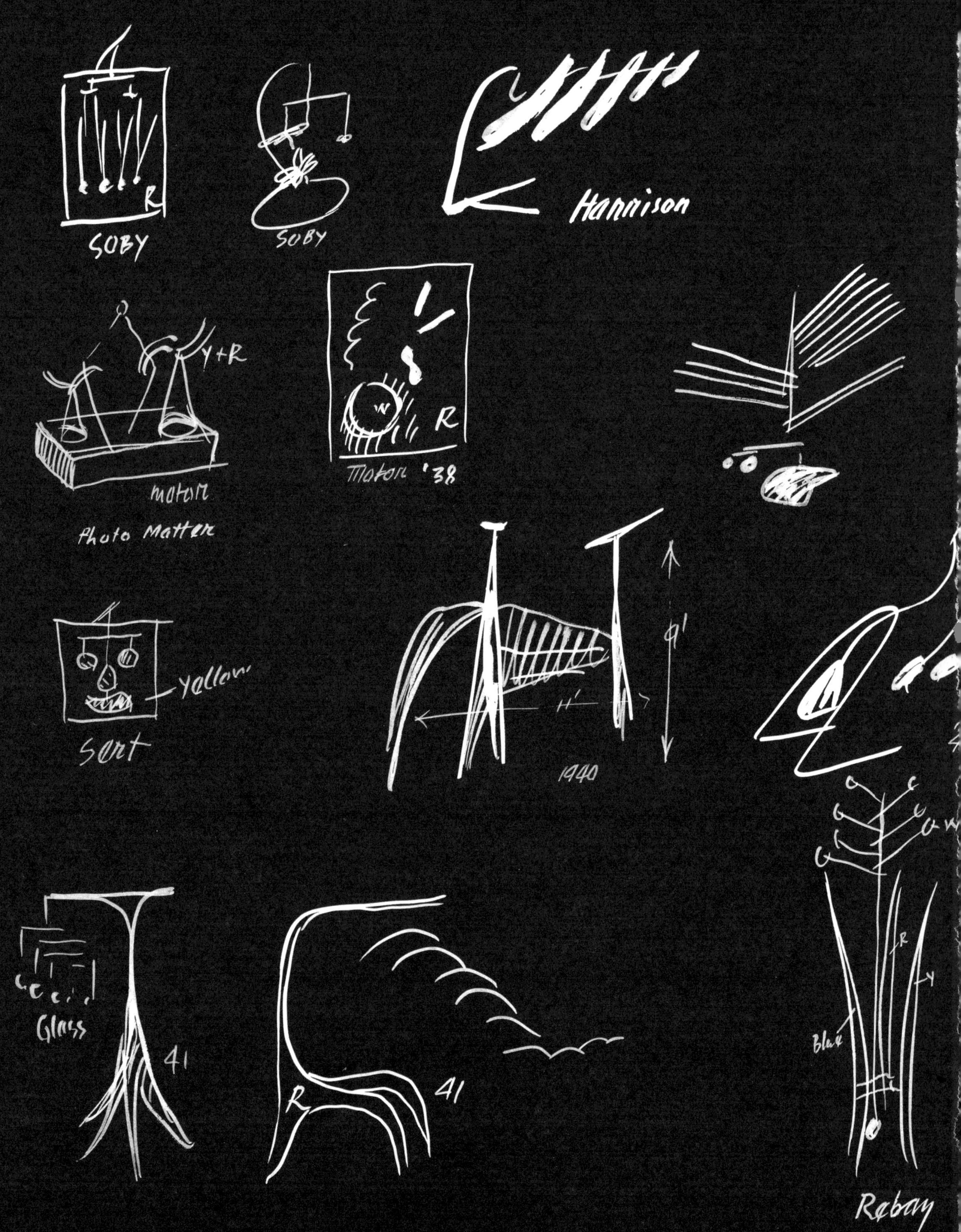
R
SOBY
SOBY
Harrison
Y+R
R
motor
Motor '38
Photo Matter
Yellow
Sert
4'
4'
1940
Glass
41
R
41
R
Y
Blue
Rebay